SIMONE DE BEAUVOIR
A study of her writings

Simone de Beauvoir

SIMONE DE BEAUVOIR
A study of her writings

Terry Keefe

Senior Lecturer, French Department, University of Leicester

BARNES & NOBLE BOOKS
TOTOWA, NEW JERSEY

First published in the USA 1983 *by*
Barnes & Noble Books
81 Adams Drive
Totowa, New Jersey, 07512

Library of Congress Cataloging in Publication Data

Keefe, Terry.
   Simone de Beauvoir.

   Bibliography: p.
   1. Beauvoir, Simone de, 1908–
Criticism and interpretation. I. Title.
PQ2603.E362Z75 1983   848'.91409   83-6024
ISBN 0-389-20365-3

Acknowledgements

Our thanks are due to the following for permission
to reproduce their photographs:
J. Niepce-Rapho, Documentation Française, cover
Keystone, frontispiece
BBC Hulton Picture Library, p.22
John Hillelson Agency Ltd, p.43
Gilles Peress, John Hillelson Agency Ltd, p.114
Gisèle Freund, John Hillelson Agency Ltd, pp. 129 and 211

Photoset by Mastergraphic, Hull
Printed and bound in Great Britain by
Mackays of Chatham Ltd.

CONTENTS

For Sheila

PREFACE

Much of the interest shown in Simone de Beauvoir since the Second
World War has centred on either her feminism or her association with
Jean-Paul Sartre. But fascinating and important as these topics are,
concentration on them has often resulted in a distorted picture of
Beauvoir as a writer, which is what she considers herself to be, first and
foremost. My own objective, therefore, has been to produce a
balanced, if relatively brief, study of all of her books. Even the review
of her life and development in Chapter 1, which is intended to form a
broad framework within which the material on her individual
published works may be placed, is based largely upon her memoirs,
which readers should consult for further information. Anyone
approaching Beauvoir's writings with a reasonably open mind has a
very great deal to gain and I hope that this emerges from the following
pages, even where criticism of her ideas and literary achievements is
severe.

I am grateful to the Research Board at the University of Leicester,
which has twice furnished financial support for trips to Paris in
connection with this book. I owe a special debt to my colleague and
friend John Hemmings, who has given me help and encouragement in
many ways over a number of years, and to my wife, who provided
direct assistance in the last stages of the preparation of the work.
Needless to say, neither bears any degree of responsibility for whatever
errors the text may contain.

University of Leicester, February 1982.   Terry Keefe

TEXTS, ABBREVIATIONS AND REFERENCES

abbreviation used	date of original publication	Beauvoir's Major Works	publisher	edition used here (where different from original)
	1943	L'Invitée (She Came to Stay)	Gallimard	'Folio'
	1944	Pyrrhus et Cinéas	Gallimard	'Idées' (with PMA)
SA	1945	Le Sang des autres (The Blood of Others)	Gallimard	'Folio'
	1945	Les Bouches inutiles	Gallimard	
	1946	Tous les hommes sont mortels (All Men Are Mortal)	Gallimard	'Folio'
PMA	1947	Pour une morale de l'ambiguïté (The Ethics of Ambiguity)	Gallimard	'Idées'
	1948	L'Amérique au jour le jour (America Day by Day)	Morihien	Gallimard, 1954
ESN	1948	L'Existentialisme et la sagesse des nations	Nagel	
	1949	Le Deuxième Sexe (The Second Sex)	Gallimard	'Idées' (2 vols.)
	1954	Les Mandarins (The Mandarins)	Gallimard	'Folio' (2 vols.)
	1955	Privilèges (Must We Burn Sade?)	Gallimard	'Idées' (entitled Faut-il brûler Sade?)
	1957	La Longue Marche (The Long March)	Gallimard	
MJFR	1958	Mémoires d'une jeune fille rangée (Memoirs of a Dutiful Daughter)	Gallimard	'Folio'
FA	1960	La Force de l'âge (The Prime of Life)	Gallimard	'Folio' (2 vols.)
FCh	1963	La Force des choses (Force of Circumstance)	Gallimard	'Folio' (2 vols.)
	1964	Une Mort très douce (A Very Easy Death)	Gallimard	'Folio'
	1966	Les Belles Images	Gallimard	'Folio'
FR	1968	La Femme rompue (The Woman Destroyed)	Gallimard	'Folio'
	1970	La Vieillesse (The Coming of Age)	Gallimard	'Folio' (2 vols.)
TCF	1972	Tout compte fait (All Said and Done)	Gallimard	'Folio'
QPS	1979	Quand prime le spirituel (When Things of the Spirit Come First)	Gallimard	
CA	1981	La Cérémonie des adieux, suivi de Entretiens avec Jean-Paul Sartre	Gallimard	

(The English titles are those of translations published in England or America.)

For a comprehensive list of Beauvoir's publications of all kinds up to 1977, much useful information, and an appendix of 'textes inédits ou retrouvés', see C. Francis and F. Gontier: Les Écrits de Simone de Beauvoir, Gallimard, 1979 (Écrits).

Page references in the body of the book and the notes use the abbreviations set out above where the context does not make it clear which text is involved. In the case of works in two volumes, references to the second bear the Roman numeral 'II', except for La Force de l'âge, whose two volumes in the 'Folio' edition are numbered consecutively.

For full details of all other writings referred to in the notes, see Bibliography. The translations in the Appendix are my own.

PART I
Life and Autobiographical Writings

1 An Outline of Beauvoir's Life and Development

MJFR[1] Simone de Beauvoir was born on 9 January 1908 in Paris. Her father was secretary to a lawyer at the Court of Appeals, but his real passion was literature in general and the theatre in particular. Her mother, who had come from a rich and pious provincial family, was having difficulty in adjusting to life in the capital, though she found her own way of maintaining her strict Catholic principles and worked hard to pass them on to Simone and her younger sister Hélène.

Beauvoir's early childhood was, for the most part, a very secure and happy one. She was prone to somewhat violent bouts of rage and occasionally found reason to suspect that all was not as it seemed in the adult world. Nevertheless, she saw her own position as being a highly privileged one, by virtue of the love of her family and of God, and accepted without demur the beliefs and values offered to her. And if life in Paris failed to excite her greatly, the long summer holidays regularly spent in the country in Limousin gave her a love of nature that was never to diminish.

31   In October 1913 Beauvoir began her formal education at a strict and rather pretentious girls' school (Cours Désir). Her father took more interest in her development at this point but was called up with the outbreak of World War I, leaving Beauvoir to draw closer to her mother as they patriotically helped out in practical ways with the war effort. By now the strong contrast between her mother's piety and her father's extreme scepticism about religion was a significant factor and she came to make a radical distinction between the intellectual and the spiritual,[2] firmly placing God in a realm quite separate from the world of human intercourse and culture. She thus had no difficulty in remaining satisfied with her place in the world, particularly as she had a very close companion in her sister. It was in relation to 'Poupette' that Beauvoir learned the habit of communication and also, because of the age-gap of two and a half years, the joy of acting autonomously to help others.

70   Although Beauvoir's parents censored her reading, books constituted a vitally important source of pleasure and instruction during her

childhood. She soon had the idea of writing stories herself and was amusing her family with these from the age of seven or eight. Early 'decisions' not to have children and to become a teacher sprang from a rather objectionable sense of her own superiority—her slightly older cousin Jacques being the only child to whose judgement she was prepared to defer—but her arrogance was only a thin surface, through which a deep need for self-justification and the approval of those she loved was always ready to break. By the end of the war the foundations of her world were beginning to shake and she was wondering whether her early childhood was a paradise lost forever.

In spite of this, Beauvoir kept her belief in the necessity that 91 governs all things and retained an exceedingly strong sense of duty, even of mission. Her commitment to God and the spiritual was such that she resolved to enter a convent, though without seeing this as a reason for failing to enjoy, in the meantime, all that the real world had to offer![3] Some of the prohibitions enforced by her parents were puzzling her increasingly and, becoming curious about sexual matters, she learned some of the facts of life from her cousin Madeleine. Yet when she and her sister raised the issue with their mother, they were fobbed off with untruths, something that led Beauvoir to lose much of her faith in adults and their judgement.

During the school year 1917-18 Beauvoir struck up a close friend- 125 ship with Elizabeth Mabille that was to last until the latter's premature death in 1929. Her parents encouraged this relationship with a girl who had much the same academic gifts, as well as a range of additional talents, and Beauvoir herself, without initially sharing confidences with 'Zaza', found herself engaging in genuine conversations for the first time in her life. Because of her own conformism, she was soon conquered by Zaza's spontaneity and independence. Eventually she realised how much this developing friendship meant to her and believed that she had discovered someone she could no longer live without.

The onset of puberty in 1920 caused Beauvoir to think seriously Part II, 135 about her future. She was determined to have a career rather than become a housewife, but the authority of her parents still weighed very heavily upon her. Although she adored her father at this stage, relations with her mother were distinctly uneasy and she developed the need to hide certain things from both of them. The reading of prohibited books and other minor acts of disobedience, however, left her feeling disorientated and vulnerable. Her friendship with Zaza was not especially comforting at the time and contact with Jacques and his male comrades only convinced her that academic standards at Cours Désir were not of the highest. Her slight recalcitrance at school, in turn, produced results that made her more despondent than ever about her dependence upon adults.

177   While Beauvoir still had no interest in contesting her parents' belief in the established social and political order, her own spiritual life was of the deepest concern to her. But one summer's day in Limousin in 1922 she understood the true character of her delight in nature and realised that she no longer believed in God, who had ceased to play any real part in her life. Having no inclination to qualify this insight in any way, she was now obliged to face the implications of God's absence, notably her own solitude and the inevitability of death. It was not difficult to keep her conversion to herself, as her conception of duty and morality was entirely unchanged, but her new secret made her feel more cut off from her parents and even from Zaza. Reading *The Mill on the Floss*, she determined to build upon her isolation and took her decision, at the age of fifteen, to become a writer. The project of writing fiction based upon her own experience suddenly seemed an ideal way of reconciling her need for self-justification and her desire to serve others. Books were the finest gift to make to mankind and could also assure her of a kind of immortality that could compensate for the eternal life so recently lost.

198   None of this prevented Beauvoir from having rather fatalistic views on love and a conception of the ideal relationship with a man which combined her own belief in freedom and her family's ideas about the inferiority of women. In fact, in spite of now having a keener sense of her identity and greater confidence in herself, she still deferred to her parents in most respects. Approaching the end of her time at school she wanted to go on to study philosophy, a subject that she and Zaza had just discovered together, but because her parents had doubts she agreed to read literature and classics instead. In the summer following her last year at school, at the age of seventeen and a half, she was allowed to travel alone for the first time, to visit Zaza. With great optimism, they looked forward together to their new life as students.

Part III,   Beauvoir continued living at home when she first became a student
237   in 1925 and the occasion soon arose for her to admit her loss of faith to her mother. She was relieved not to have to pretend any more, even

though lines of communication between them were broken as a result. Her father had encouraged her to pursue her studies and was proud of her academic success, yet as an anti-feminist he could not fail to be uncomfortable at the independent course his daughter's development and career were taking. This left Beauvoir feeling puzzled, vaguely guilty and ill-at-ease at home. She was strongly influenced by her literature teacher Robert Garric, founder of the 'Équipes Sociales', which were striving to spread culture to the working classes, and this indirectly alienated her still more from her parents. The largely unexpressed conflict drove Beauvoir in upon herself. She became absorbed in literature and started to keep an intimate diary recording her extreme loneliness.

Primarily as a result of disagreements with her father, she now   261 detected serious flaws in the bourgeois values that she had been brought up to accept. Anxious not only to escape from the middle-class world in which everything is classified and judged in advance with no room for ambiguity or doubt, but also to help others to live their lives freely through her writings, she wrote the first few pages of a novel in April 1926. In the summer she was to compose a complete story based upon her own inner life and dilemmas. From her reading of modern French authors Beauvoir discovered that her own estrangement from the bourgeoisie was far from unique and since she considered her cousin Jacques to be a refined embodiment of the admirable state of 'inquiétude', she attached more and more importance to the time spent with him. At times she saw marriage to him as a solution to all of her problems, but on other occasions recognised that he had no real desire to escape from the bourgeois order that she now so despised. Her first year as a student had proved disappointing and at this stage her life seemed empty.

She joined the 'Équipes Sociales' in July 1926, but the experience   309 was less satisfying than she had expected. Relations with Zaza and Poupette were good, yet Beauvoir was unhappier than ever at home during the academic year 1926-27. Whenever she felt useful, or loved, life took on a brighter aspect, and her mood tended to alternate between a kind of foolish arrogance and rather self-indulgent depression. Similarly, her attitude to Jacques oscillated from one extreme to the other. For the first time she now had contact with left-wing intellectuals and despite her continuing subordination of social and political questions to metaphysical and moral ones, her hatred of conservatism hardened as she envisaged the possibility of radical changes in society.

340   Beauvoir regained some of her enthusiasm for life as a result of a new friendship with Jean Pradelle,[4] and during the summer of 1927 started writing a long novel, which she was eventually to abandon. She was no clearer about her feelings for Jacques, however, and began to doubt that she would ever have a fully satisfactory relationship with a man. Nevertheless, she was doing a little teaching and enjoying it, and was more dedicated than ever to becoming a writer. In the spring of 1928 she completed her undergraduate course and decided to write a higher-degree thesis (on Leibniz) and prepare for the 'agrégation' at the same time. She began escaping from home in the evenings, frequenting bars and night-spots in the belief that she was finding her freedom at last. Her own ethical principles were still fairly orthodox Christian ones, yet she was coming to realise, thanks largely to the influence of her new Polish friend Stépha, that she and Zaza were extremely naïve in their general assumptions about the values and conduct of other people.

Part IV,   With the prospect of being able to leave home after the 'agrégation'
395 and the sense that she now belonged to a community of genuine scholars and researchers, Beauvoir began the academic year 1928-29 in high spirits. She was irritated to discover Zaza's reluctance to break with her bourgeois background, but was scarcely aware that some of her own deeper problems were relics of her upbringing. She was still in no way a feminist, being content to believe that she was fortunate and unusual in combining the heart of a woman with the brain of a man! She was, however, coming more and more to feel the need to fulfil the sensual side of her nature, which taboos from her past would not yet allow her to express freely. Part of the attraction of André Herbaud, who became a good friend of hers in the spring of 1929, lay in the fact that he treated her as a complete human being and not simply as a mind. By early summer she had finally decided that she could do without Jacques and that all she wanted from life was to have someone special to love, some children, some friends and to be able to write good books.

467   At the beginning of July 1929 Beauvoir was invited to join Herbaud, Paul Nizan and Jean-Paul Sartre, who were preparing for the 'agrégation' oral together. The trio were merciless in their treatment of the whole bourgeois order of things, as well as of any kind of

idealism, and Beauvoir rapidly realised that they were implicitly asking her to do what she had always wanted, to face up to reality without evasion. Herbaud left Paris on learning that he had failed the written exam, however, and she began seeing Sartre regularly on his own. She was immensely impressed by the way in which he was interested in everything and took nothing for granted; by his capacity to see her life in the light of her own values; and, above all, by his absolute confidence in his future as a writer. Unlike Beauvoir, he had already thought out an original philosophy of his own and for the first time in her life she felt intellectually dominated by someone, as Sartre exposed the weaknesses in her cherished views. She now saw that others had pursued the implications of the absence of God more systematically than she, had understood the technical difficulties of writing a novel better, and had a clearer idea of what they wanted to say. The future suddenly seemed much more difficult to her, but also more real. And at least she was no longer alone, for by August she realised she had found in Sartre the companion she had wished for since the age of fifteen and that he would always have a place in her life. Beauvoir was successful in the 'agrégation' (Sartre came out top of the national list and she was second), and after the summer she moved out of the family flat into a room of her own.

She briefly renewed contact with Jacques, but was sure by now that   482
she did not love him, so that news of his forthcoming marriage caused her little distress. The rest of his life was, in fact, a complete disaster: he was to die in a pitiful state at the age of forty-six. It was, however, a personal tragedy taking place at the time that did most to confirm 1929 as the end of the first broad phase of Beauvoir's life. Zaza had fallen in love with Jean Pradelle some months earlier, but her mother was opposed to the relationship and Pradelle himself had reasons for not wanting to marry her immediately. In spite of Beauvoir's help and exhortations, Zaza was unable to cope with the various pressures brought to bear upon her and became ill. She died, possibly of meningitis or encephalitis, after only four days in hospital, leaving Beauvoir deprived of her only real childhood friend and obscurely feeling that she had somehow paid for her own new-found freedom with Zaza's death.

Some part-time teaching and a few private pupils provided   FA Part I,
Beauvoir with a modest income from September 1929 and she devoted   Ch. 1
as much time and energy as possible to her relationship with Sartre. As

she had at last broken the constrictive grip of her family, they could revel together in what they saw as complete freedom and independence. Though largely indifferent to political matters, they in fact shared a certain euphoria of the French Left at this time and believed the world to be at their feet. They soon came to agree, moreover, that whilst their love for each other was a 'necessary' part of their lives, it should be allowed neither to degenerate into constraint or habit nor to prevent them from eventually enjoying 'contingent' love-affairs with others. They concluded a pact never to lie to each other or to conceal anything.

35 Sartre's national service did not prevent Beauvoir from continuing to see him very regularly and she was delighted to make new friends through him. Most of them shared a great hostility towards the bourgeoisie and all of them an inexhaustible interest in the conduct and motives of individuals. While away from Sartre, Beauvoir read voraciously but lost no opportunity to enjoy new experiences of all kinds, with friends or on her own. There was a chaotic aspect to her life for a period and she no longer felt much compulsion to write, though she continued to try to do so, largely on Sartre's insistence. Yet at least from time to time she was overcome by the feeling of having lost her way, of having become over-dependent upon Sartre. She was also rather disturbed by the intensity of her own sexual needs and, temporarily, by Sartre's friendship with the actress Camille.

88 In the spring of 1931 one anxiety was removed when Sartre's plans to go to Japan fell through and he took up a teaching post in Le Havre. Beauvoir's subsequent posting to Marseilles came as a blow, but they decided that it would be wrong to marry specifically in order to be able to live in the same town, reconciling themselves to frequent train journeys during the following year. Beauvoir hoped that the distance between Le Havre and Marseilles would at least help her to overcome the temptation of 'abdicating' in favour of Sartre and thereby be-
Ch.2, 95 traying her own ambitions and even her separate identity. In the summer they undertook the first of the innumerable foreign trips that they were to make together over the years and began to devise, in Spain, their own method of learning about new places. The opposite of a guided tour, it consisted in taking as much account of the present as of the past, seeing the seamy areas as well as the monuments.

103 When Beauvoir took up her teaching post in Marseilles in the autumn, she made it her duty to explore the region and used much of

her free time to carry out extremely long, solitary walks in the surrounding country. This practice, which became a kind of mania with her, was one way of expressing her general optimism about life and did much to restore her confidence in herself. She rather enjoyed encouraging her pupils to respect the truth rather than 'common sense', especially as her duties left her with sufficient leisure to begin writing another novel. She set out to record our temptation to give up our freedom to those we love, but failed to solve the problem of transposing her own personal experience into a story having both credibility and originality. Nevertheless, her attempt excited her greatly and gave her valuable insight into the importance of narrative viewpoint. She was able to look back on the academic year in Marseilles with considerable satisfaction and was deeply at ease with herself when she set off for Spain in the summer of 1932 with Sartre and two friends.

A new teaching post in Rouen took her, in the autumn, to a town of Ch.3, 136 very limited appeal to her. Yet she was near enough to Paris to spend a great deal of time there and able to see Sartre in Le Havre more or less whenever she wished. They were starting to develop their own methods of judging others—in which the concept of 'mauvaise foi' played a major part— but were constantly sensitive to new attempts to understand people better and to defend human freedom. Their sympathy with the struggle of the working classes, however, still did not extend to any direct political involvement on their part and they were content to hope that their views would be diffused through their conversations, teaching and writings. Like most of their contemporaries they failed to perceive the ominous quality of political events in Germany. It was apparent that Sartre's desire to encapsulate life in words was greater than Beauvoir's and this occasionally led to conflict between them. She nevertheless began writing yet another novel, but once more was eventually to abandon it because of her failure to integrate her own experience into the story in a fully satisfactory way.

With Sartre studying in Berlin for a year from September 1933 180 Beauvoir became somewhat caught up in the pettiness and gossip of a provincial French town. She continued to see old Paris friends like Pagniez, made new ones in her colleague Colette Audry and a young Russian girl, Olga Kosakievicz, and regularly met a contemporary of Sartre's, Marco Zuorro. Her views and life-style were unconventional by prevailing standards in Rouen and she was frowned upon by the local townspeople and some of her fellow-teachers. She visited Sartre in Berlin in February 1934 and he came to Paris at Easter, when Sartre explained his enthusiasm for the philosophical method of inquiry of Edmund Husserl. In the summer they made a long tour of Germany and Austria together, trying without great success to convince themselves that the spread of Nazism, of which they had evidence all around them, was a relatively insignificant or temporary phenomenon.

Ch.4, 229   During the following year Beauvoir's increasing awareness of the passage of time caused her to experience brief periods of melancholy, while Sartre was the victim of severe depression. After a walking holiday in the centre and south of France in the summer of 1935, however, he began to shake off the mood and Beauvoir in the meantime had embarked upon another work of fiction, this time a collection of five loosely linked short stories called *La Primauté du spirituel*. Back in Rouen in the autumn she soon came to consider her association with Olga as a special one. In addition to never having known anyone who needed her to the extent that Olga did, Beauvoir found the Russian girl to be an intelligent and sensitive companion to whom she could talk more intimately than to any woman of her own age. Olga blossomed rapidly in the company of Beauvoir, Sartre, Marco and their new young comrade Jacques Bost. Beauvoir and Sartre were so taken with her youth and 'authenticity' that they came to ascribe almost mythical significance to her, resolving to establish a permanent trio to replace the couple that they had previously formed. Yet although Olga greatly enriched their lives by making them see the world through her eyes, the trio never attained equilibrium and harmony. Everything, moreover, was somewhat exaggerated and distorted by the fact that they were not living in Paris, where there would have been much to distract them. Although all three were eventually to emerge undamaged from the experiment, as well as on good terms with one another, Beauvoir was at last forced to recognise and accept the full implications of the existence of others and to acknowledge that her unique rapport with Sartre was something not to be taken for granted but to be worked at and nurtured.

Ch.5, 315   When Beauvoir began teaching in Paris in autumn 1936 the trio was still functioning, though she was finding it a considerable strain and a permanent drain on her energy resources. With Sartre able to visit at least twice a week from his new post in Laon and Marco, Bost and Olga also in the capital, her social life was at its most active. In the

16

spring she fell ill with congestion of the lungs and realised, perhaps for the first time, that she was as vulnerable as anyone else to the accidents and misfortunes of life. Within a matter of months, however, her personal situation was better than ever: she had recovered her health; Olga had effectively put an end to the trio, without acrimony; and Sartre's literary career was well and truly launched by the successful publication of his story 'Le Mur' and Gallimard's decision to take *La Nausée*. Beauvoir's trip to Greece in the summer brought her face to face with poverty and human misery, as had her voyage to Italy during the previous year, but this failed to prevent her from conceiving an intense love of both countries.

Having completed her collection of stories (which was to be turned 360 down by two publishers), in the autumn of 1937 Beauvoir began writing a novel on themes that had been close to her heart for some time. The political situation in Europe necessarily impinged more and more upon her now, yet she continued trying to shut such problems out. By now Sartre was also teaching in Paris and they maintained their keen interest in new books, the theatre and the cinema. When they returned from a trip to Morocco in the summer of 1938 they were faced with a graver political situation than ever, but even the Munich Crisis failed to shake Beauvoir's conviction that war could not possibly happen. The discipline of teaching and contact with her pupils still suited her well enough and she was able to put much of her energy into the writing of *L'Invitée*. Nevertheless, from the spring of 1939 onwards she was no longer able to see herself as a political innocent, beginning to feel shame at the egoism of her attitudes throughout the thirties and to acknowledge both that abstention is never a genuine political option and that war could and should not be avoided. History had finally caught up with her and would never let go: a ten-year period since the attaining of her independence and her first meeting with Sartre in 1929 had come to a close and a new phase of her life was about to begin.

Sartre was mobilised as soon as war broke out, but for a period, like Ch.6, 425 everyone else, Beauvoir had little reason to believe in the reality of the war. She saw Olga, visited her friends Dullin and Camille outside Paris, and passed some time in Brittany and the Loire Valley. Back in Paris in October she continued writing *L'Invitée*, resumed her teaching and in general led a fairly comfortable, if rather fretful existence. At the beginning of November she contrived to go to see

Sartre in Alsace. They were still hoping that the war might end with little bloodshed and Beauvoir's life in Paris became more relaxed, even monotonous. While Sartre was on leave early in February 1940 they reflected together on what would happen after the war, finding that they had changed as a result of the major collective events they were living through and agreeing that a new morality of commitment needed to be constructed. When the 'phoney war' came to an end in June Beauvoir fled from the capital with friends as the German forces swept across France. But once it was clear what the nature of the Occupation would be, she went back to have news of Sartre. She now experienced the effects of war on the personal level, for Sartre had been taken prisoner and continued to be held. Although life in Paris was still relatively unconstrained, if somewhat strange, she had to adjust to the fact of the German Occupation and the possibility of a very long wait.

Ch. 7, 532   The anti-semitism of the German occupiers soon became apparent and Beauvoir found the official line of the Vichy régime equally odious. She was deeply shocked, too, not only by news of the death of Nizan, but also by the manner in which the Communist Party regarded him as a traitor. Although she now recognised that individuals must bear their share of responsibility for the state of society and the world, reading Hegel convinced her that her own commitment was to all that was concrete and individual rather than to the abstract and the universal. Conditions in Paris became more difficult during the winter, but she managed to continue writing and to see a great deal of her friends. When Sartre returned to Paris at the end of March 1941 he convinced Beauvoir of the need for active resistance against the occupiers, but they felt unqualified to engage in sabotage and confined their activities to gathering and diffusing information. By now Beauvoir had ceased to regard adversities as acts of injustice perpetrated against her and was prepared to adjust to the world rather than expecting it to adapt to her wishes.

561   Beauvoir lost her father in July, shortly before she and Sartre set off on a cycling and camping holiday in the unoccupied zone. When they returned to Paris severe German reprisals for acts of violence had become the order of the day, as had furious reactions on the part of collaborators against these acts of resistance. The movement that Sartre had created was already beginning to break up and he and Beauvoir eventually agreed, with reluctance, to abandon it. She

finished *L'Invitée* and immediately began writing another novel, which spoke of the Resistance. At Christmas 1941 and Easter 1942 Beauvoir was able to go off with Sartre as usual and her literary career proper was launched in June, when *L'Invitée* was accepted for publication by Gallimard. By the time they returned from their summer holiday in the Basque country and Provence, hope of an Allied victory had greatly increased, although bad news about people they knew still periodically spread gloom over the gatherings at the Flore café. Beauvoir completed her second novel, *Le Sang des autres,* early in 1943 and was happy to be able to pursue some of the thorny problems it raised in an essay on ethics, *Pyrrhus et Cinéas.* At the end of the school year, having by now been teaching for twelve years, she was dismissed from her post on vague moral grounds.

Two factors in particular helped Beauvoir to live through the last year of the German Occupation. In August 1943 *L'Invitée* was published and for the first time she experienced the pleasure of knowing that her work was making a certain impact upon the lives of others. Secondly, she and Sartre had the good fortune to make a number of new friends at this time, including Michel Leiris, Raymond Queneau and Albert Camus. They were all drawn together by their common situation and a determination to provide an ideology for the post-war period, since the Liberation was now in sight. The level of artistic activity in Paris was extremely high at this time, but hostilities were far from over and Beauvoir and her circle of friends took to organising regular all-night 'fêtes' as a way of combating their anxiety and frustration. In July 1944 she completed her only play, *Les Bouches inutiles,* just a month or so before Paris was finally liberated. After five long, dark years Beauvoir's joy, like that of her friends, knew no bounds as she contemplated, with an enthusiasm tempered by great sadness, the new future that was opening out for her. Ch.8, 637

The state of mind of Beauvoir and Sartre immediately after the Liberation was naturally one of great optimism. They believed that the end of Fascism throughout the whole of Europe was at hand and that the catastrophe that had overtaken France would bring about a radical revision of its social structures. They were now convinced that their own fate was intimately bound up with that of others and were determined to resist all forms of oppression actively, although Beauvoir was content to take her lead from Sartre in the domain of politics. In relation to the French Communist Party they saw them- FCh, Ch.1

selves as critical fellow-travellers, anxious to defend, against Marxist doctrine, the individual, human dimension of existence, but acknowledging that the unity of the Resistance had concealed the reality and importance of the class struggle. *Pyrrhus et Cinéas* was well received as one of the first books to appear after the Liberation, and thanks to Sartre's earnings Beauvoir was able to devote most of her time to writing. In February 1945 she undertook a long trip to Spain and Portugal and on her return to France wrote newspaper articles condemning the régimes of Franco and Salazar. The end of the war in Europe in May was less significant to her than the terrible accounts of the concentration camps brought back by returning deportees and reporters.

Ch.2, 59 The autumn of 1945 was an especially important period for the reputations of Beauvoir and Sartre. In September *Le Sang des autres* was published to great acclaim and within weeks the first two volumes of Sartre's *Les Chemins de la liberté* were also in print. In October they launched a new literary and political journal, *Les Temps modernes*. And in November Beauvoir's play *Les Bouches inutiles* was produced on the Paris stage, although without great success. For some years their 'existentialism'—a label that they eventually accepted—was to be at the very forefront of the intellectual scene in France. Their works were clearly giving expression to views that had great appeal to the French public on some level and their names were regularly on people's lips. While Sartre was irritated by the notoriety, Beauvoir rather enjoyed it at first, but they were both disturbed by the disintegration of the unity that had characterised the Resistance and by the overt hostility shown towards Sartre by the Communists. Editorial work on *Les Temps modernes,* which was, apart from other things, an excellent organ for the presentation of their attitudes on live issues, took up much of Beauvoir's energy and she collaborated closely with Maurice Merleau-Ponty. Back in Paris after her first trip to North Africa, lecturing and exploring in Tunisia and Algeria, she met Boris Vian and continued to see a great deal of Camus. Still preoccupied by ethical questions as much as by history, she began to compose an essay designed to construct a morality upon the foundations of Sartre's *L'Être et le Néant* and wrote three articles on moral topics. During a lecture-tour in June 1946 she and Sartre took special interest in the state of politics in Italy, comparing it with the increasingly complex situation in France. Beauvoir was by now working on an essay on the myths of femininity. Her new novel *Tous les hommes sont mortels* was not at all well received but, though disappointed, she still found no reason to entertain serious doubts about her work and continued to trust in the future.

At the end of January 1947 she crossed the Atlantic for the first time to embark on an extensive lecture-tour of America that lasted until late in May. During the last two weeks of her stay she began an affair with Nelson Algren, a thirty-eight-year-old writer with vast experience of the harder and seamier side of life in America, who was now living in Chicago. Politically, she and Sartre were depressed to see the bourgeoisie strengthening its position in France, while on the global scale the Cold War was beginning. They continued to travel at every possible opportunity and Beauvoir returned to Chicago in September to see Algren, but their time in Paris was dominated by constant political dissensions. They felt greater sympathy towards the Soviet Union than towards America, yet maintained a certain distance from the Communist Party and were attacked as a result. At the same time, they were strongly anti-Gaullist and this brought about the cancellation of a series of radio programmes that they began in October. Even their standing in the public eye deteriorated when existentialism came to be identified with the activities of the young revellers of Saint-Germain-des-Prés. Ch.3, 173

Early in 1948 they threw their weight behind the R.D.R., a party newly formed by David Rousset and designed to unite all the non-communist socialist groups in an attempt to build a Europe independent of the two major power-blocs. From the middle of May Beauvoir spent another two months in America, travelling down the Mississippi with Algren, then exploring Guatemala and Mexico. An account of Beauvoir's earlier two visits, *L'Amérique au jour le jour*, had just come out when she returned to Paris and she turned back to her essay about women. In August she and Sartre went to Algeria, only to find among the indigenous population a threateningly high level of misery and bitterness. In the autumn Beauvoir completed the first volume of *Le Deuxième Sexe* and immediately began work on the second. Seeing the R.D.R. veering to the right, she and Sartre withdrew their support in the spring of 1949. Algren came to Europe in June and after a trip to Italy, Tunisia and Algeria together they were closer to each other than ever. By November both volumes of *Le Deuxième Sexe* had been published and Beauvoir found herself in the middle of a storm. Some 202 Ch.4

critics stoutly defended the work, but she was bitterly and often viciously attacked from many quarters. From the rather hysterical reactions to her open and frank discussion of sexual matters and such issues as motherhood, she concluded that she had touched on some kind of nerve and offended the pride of the French male, but was delighted to discover that her book had been a great help to many women.

The political events of 1949 had shown that while there was no third option between America and Russia, the choice between the two was an impossible one to make. Having felt some four years earlier that they were surrounded by friends, Beauvoir and Sartre now found that everyone regarded them as enemies and they abstained from political activity for a while. In May 1950 they went off on another long trip together, crossing the Sahara from Algeria to French Equatorial Africa and finally spending two weeks in Morocco. They returned shortly before the outbreak of war in Korea and although Beauvoir finally decided to carry out her original plan to spend two months with Algren at his new house on Lake Michigan—a stay that was marred by his claim that he no longer loved her—there was a growing belief in France that the war would eventually spread and that Western Europe would be occupied by Russian forces. She and Sartre never entirely believed in the likelihood of a Russian invasion, but the hypothesis forced them to see more sharply what a paradoxical political position they were in. 268

They now spent much of their time in Beauvoir's new flat, working and listening to music. For in 1950 and 1951 she was writing her longest novel, *Les Mandarins*, which is about their growing disillusionment in the immediate post-war years. She returned to Chicago in October 1951, spending a pleasant enough month with Algren, but he was unable to accept a subordinate role in her life, so that their affair duly came to an end, some four and a half years after it had begun. Beauvoir learned to drive and was able to explore parts of France—often with Olga or Bost—as enthusiastically as she had previously done on foot or by bicycle. Yet such excursions provided only intermittent relief from the deep despondency into which she had now sunk. She felt the future slipping away from her, both in that there was no hope of permanent peace in the world and in that her break with Algren seemed to mark the end of her active sexual life and inevitable physical decline. She probably reached the very bottom of Ch.5, 322 her depression in the spring of 1952, when she believed she might have cancer. Once she discovered that this was not the case, her spirits began to rise a little. Sartre's quarrel with Camus scarcely affected her, since it had long been predictable; and Sartre's rapprochement with the Communist Party held out the hope that he would finally emerge from his political isolation. The first major phase of the post-war era was over.

Ch. 6, (II) 9
Beauvoir experienced a general reawakening from the middle of 1952 onwards. She began a liaison with Claude Lanzmann, a twenty-seven-year-old writer and political commentator, and at the turn of the year they decided to live together. Lanzmann's youth and vitality rid Beauvoir of her anxieties about ageing and revived her interest in the world. Their relationship was to last for six years, during which time the pattern of Beauvoir's life was largely dominated by the numerous journeys of varying length that she undertook, sometimes with Lanzmann, sometimes with Sartre and occasionally with both. Her bond with Sartre was in no way weakened by the association with Lanzmann and the political involvement of the two men was to draw her more and more into the political arena and towards Marxism. With the defeat of the French army at Dien-Bien-Phu she found herself for the first time standing in opposition to the huge majority of the French people, for, having deplored France's role in the war in Indo-China from the beginning, she welcomed the defeat itself. When *Les Mandarins* came out in October 1954 Beauvoir was awarded the prestigious Prix Goncourt. She wrote two substantial political articles during this period and these were published, together with an essay on the Marquis de Sade, in the autumn of 1955 as *Privilèges*. She and Sartre spent September and October in China,

Ch. 7
Beauvoir paying her first visit to Russia on the way back. In 1957 she was to produce a comprehensive study of China, *La Longue Marche*. Politically, of course, these were highly troubled times. She was saddened, though not surprised, by France's role in the Suez crisis, but the suppression of the revolution in Hungary in November 1956 came as a severe blow to them. They both declared their unqualified opposition to the Russian intervention, yet not all of their links with the Communists were broken.

Ch. 8, (II) 20
The most urgent political issue of all at this time, however, was the Algerian War. In the middle of 1956 there was little opposition to the war in metropolitan France, so that Beauvoir and Sartre, with their

24

conviction that Algerian independence was both desirable and inevitable, found themselves to be very much in a minority. Beauvoir came to believe that there was a conspiracy of silence to cover up the hideous torture that the French forces were engaging in and she found it increasingly difficult to tolerate the presence of her fellow-citizens. They still thought it possible to work for independence by legal means, especially by writing articles and acting as character-witnesses at trials, but this did not soothe Beauvoir's conscience and even writing—in the autumn of 1956 she had begun to work on the first volume of her autobiography—failed to do more than distract her attention from time to time. When in May 1958 it became apparent   Ch.9 that De Gaulle would be recalled to power in France, Beauvoir and Sartre were horrified at the prospect. Beauvoir had the impression of living through historic moments when the French people were being duped. She felt guilty that she had not been more actively involved in protests over the previous two years and resolved to do more when she and Sartre returned from what was by now their regular summer holiday in Italy. In September, in fact, they both took part in demonstrations and campaigns against De Gaulle's constitutional proposals, only to be shocked at the size of his majority in the referendum. When Sartre was seriously ill at the end of the year and her affair with Lanzmann drew to its natural close, Beauvoir felt that old age and death were beginning to tighten their grip upon her.

In the early part of 1959 some of her worst fears about the new   Ch.10, Gaullist regime were confirmed as information concerning conditions   (II) 238 and continuing torture in Algeria filtered back into France. Beauvoir and Sartre now had no scruples about performing the occasional service for those engaged in clandestine action. The success of *Mémoires d'une jeune fille rangée* encouraged Beauvoir to work all the harder on the second volume of her autobiography and some of the excitement of her early commitment to literature was revived. She also added a new dimension to her life at this time, when she discovered classical music again and allowed it to enhance more and more of her leisure hours. Preoccupied by the Algerian War, she and Sartre had found their curiosity about the world waning and they decided to accept, in February 1960, an invitation to visit Cuba. They were privileged to be able to scrutinise at close quarters the earliest stages of a socialist revolution and to witness, as they saw it, hopes and happiness born out of violence. Beauvoir in particular felt some of her old zest for life returning. When Algren came to Paris in March for some five months they enjoyed each other's company greatly and made trips to Spain, Turkey and Greece together. At the end of May she became involved in the case of a young Algerian girl, Djamila Boupacha, who had been tortured by the French army[5] and in August, together with Sartre and other intellectuals, she signed the Manifesto of the 121, supporting the right of young Frenchmen to resist conscription. Immediately afterwards she and Sartre set off on a two-month visit to Brazil, keen to explore conditions in an underdeveloped Third-World country which was still half-colonised and where the revolutionary forces were still being held firmly in check. When they returned to Europe, via Cuba, in November resistance to the Algerian War had provoked the Government into taking severe measures in France. Beauvoir and Sartre tried to have themselves charged for signing the manifesto, but, not for the last time, the authorities baulked at taking legal action against them

Ch.11, (II) 398   When, later in the month, *La Force de l'âge* was published, Beauvoir gained satisfaction from the knowledge that many people clearly thought about things as she did, yet politically she was still overwhelmed by her sense of shame regarding the war in Algeria. Returning from Rome at the end of October 1961 she considered France to be more of a police-state than ever. There was now no doubt that Algeria would soon become independent, but this was a particularly violent period in Paris, with the plastic explosives of the O.A.S. threatening any prominent left-wing figure. Since in the final stage of the war the Left had few useful options open to it, Beauvoir willingly took part in a number of important demonstrations, heartened to rediscover a kind of fraternity with so many of her fellow citizens, but galled that they had failed to come around to her point of view sooner. She and Sartre visited Russia together in June 1962, but were back in Paris when Algerian independence was officially proclaimed in July. They could only feel that it had come too late to console the French for the price that it had cost.

TCF, Ch.6 387-445   Beauvoir and Sartre were to visit the Soviet Union on five further occasions during the following four years, when they closely followed the losing struggles of dissident Russian writers against the forces of the state. In August 1963, together with a number of other Western writers they visited Khrushchev on his property in Georgia, only to be harangued as the lackeys of capitalism. In October the third volume of

26

Beauvoir's autobiography, *La Force des choses*, was published, but there was little chance to analyse public reaction to it, for before the end of the month Beauvoir had to rush back from Rome to the bedside of her ailing mother. As previously arranged, she managed to fly out with Sartre to Czechoslovakia, where they both sensed that a new wind of freedom was beginning to blow, but she felt obliged to curtail her visit and return to Paris, where her mother died shortly afterwards. Beauvoir spent the winter writing about her mother's last days and *Une Mort très douce* appeared in book-form the following autumn.

Ch. 6
446-48

She considered that she had written enough about her own life for the time being and throughout much of 1965 was working on a novel on the theme of growing old. But she became so disappointed with the outcome that in the autumn she abandoned it to begin writing *Les Belles Images*. Beauvoir agreed, in the spring of 1966, to write a preface to a book by Jean-François Steiner about the wartime camp at Treblinka and for a while she became embroiled in the acrimonious debate over whether or not he had presented the Jewish prisoners as cowards. In the middle of September she and Sartre undertook a month-long tour of Japan, receiving a particularly warm welcome, delivering a series of lectures and, on occasion, speaking out against American intervention in Vietnam. In November *Les Belles Images* was published and immediately became a best-seller. Beauvoir naturally took a special interest in attitudes to women and women's rights when she and Sartre visited first Egypt and then Israel in the spring of 1967. And since their trip took place only a matter of weeks before the outbreak of the Six-Day War in June, they were more deeply affected by this conflict than by any other political events during this period, with the exception of the war in Vietnam. They had taken part in the first major meeting of the Bertrand Russell International War Crimes Tribunal in Stockholm in May and subsequently attended a preparatory meeting in Brussels in September as well as the final plenary session in Copenhagen in November, when severe censure of the U.S.A. was agreed. In January 1968 Beauvoir's collection of three stories, *La Femme rompue*, appeared and was another considerable success. She had completed the work some six months earlier and was by now working on a long study of old age.

Ch. 2
72 - 169

Ch. 2
181-82

Ch. 5
343-86

Ch. 7
497-555

Ch. 7
462-97

Since 1962, seeing the united Right holding the power and the divided Left making no headway, Beauvoir had taken very little interest in politics in France itself. However, when the events of

Ch. 8
576-89

spring 1968 began she and Sartre found themselves strongly involved on the side of the students. They hoped that the whole Gaullist régime might be shaken or even overthrown and, at the beginning of May, signed a manifesto expressing support for the students and asking for the backing of all workers and intellectuals. Later in the month they were invited to the occupied Sorbonne, where Sartre addressed a huge gathering in the amphitheatre. They remained in close contact with student leaders and were bitterly disappointed to see what they regarded as an opportunity for the restructuring of French society slip

Ch.6
453-59

away as the Right regained the reins. In August the editorial team of *Les Temps modernes* strongly denounced the Soviet invasion of Czechoslovakia and a brief visit to the country at the end of November convinced Beauvoir and Sartre that the people's resistance would never be broken.

Beauvoir's study of old age, *La Vieillesse*, which was published in January 1970, expresses one aspect of the deep and growing dis-

Ch.8
589-97

satisfaction with Western capitalist societies that she manifested in a number of prominent ways during the early seventies. Since the events of 1968 and their discovery of positions further to the left than the Communist Party's, she and Sartre had become very much more radical in their political views. Beauvoir now found herself ever more committed in practical ways to the cause of the working classes and of the oppressed in general. In the spring of 1970 she condemned the arbitrary measures taken against the proletarian-left newspaper *La Cause du peuple* and on two occasions in June she, Sartre and some friends distributed it on the streets, defying the authorities to arrest them. For a few months Beauvoir herself took on the responsibilities of the editorship of another revolutionary paper, *L'Idiot international*. She was also becoming involved in the struggles of the 'Mouvement de libération des femmes', taking part in the autumn in a procession in favour of contraception and abortion, as well as in a demonstration against the harsh treatment of young unmarried mothers. She was, moreover, one of the 343 women who signed a manifesto in the spring of 1971, declaring that they had had illegal abortions. Beauvoir had become even more acutely conscious of the need for a free radical press when she investigated, in February, the

Ch.8
602-06

circumstances of a horrifying factory accident in Méru, and she continued to be involved in clashes with the Government over *La Cause du peuple* and *L'Idiot international* throughout 1971.

The fourth volume of her autobiography, *Tout compte fait*, appeared in September 1972, but during that year she threw much of her weight behind the campaign for free contraception and easier abortion, becoming president of a feminist association called 'Choisir'. She saw the state of French law on abortion as being designed to maintain the oppression of women and 'Choisir' lost no opportunity of bringing particular cases to the attention of the public and denouncing the iniquities of the prevailing system. 1973 brought serious personal problems for Beauvoir. The severe arthritic pains that she suffered were eventually brought under control when she began taking cortisone, but in June Sartre lost virtually all of the sight from his one good eye and was to depend heavily upon Beauvoir and others for his remaining years. Nonetheless, at the end of 1973 she returned to the fray, introducing a new regular feature in *Les Temps modernes*, which was to record examples of sexism or discriminatory statements about women in public speeches or in print. In January 1974 she was named president of the new 'Ligue du droit des femmes', and in April the organisation tried unavailingly to present its own woman candidate in the French presidential elections.

Beauvoir was awarded the Jerusalem Prize in 1975 (the first prize she had agreed to accept since the Prix Goncourt) and explained that she bitterly opposed any solution to the conflicts of the Middle East that might endanger Israel as a nation. She also carried on the struggle for women's rights in 1975 and 1976, taking up individual cases, attacking discriminatory laws and supporting women's organisations and rallies. In 1977 she agreed to the adaptation of *La Femme rompue* for television and wrote the dialogue for Josée Dayan's film. During the following year—that of Beauvoir's seventieth birthday—the same director made a full-length film about the writer's life and times, in which she is seen in conversation with some of her closest friends and collaborators, including her sister, Sartre, Lanzmann and Bost. In 1979 Beauvoir agreed to the publication of her first collection of stories and Gallimard brought out *Quand prime le spirituel*, a text they had rejected more than forty years earlier! In the late seventies, however, much of her time and energy was consumed in helping Sartre, reading to him and collaborating with him in his remaining projects, although she continued to travel and to be actively involved with *Les Temps modernes*. When Sartre died in April 1980, their close association had lasted for fifty-one years. Beauvoir herself was exhausted and ill for a short time, but recovered to resume something like her normal routine of commitments and work. At the end of 1981 she published *La Cérémonie des adieux, suivi de Entretiens avec Jean-Paul Sartre*, which comprises an account of Sartre's last ten years and a long series of interviews recorded with him in 1974.

Notes

1 The material in this chapter is taken very largely from Beauvoir's memoirs and is intended, in part, as an introduction to them. The marginal references, therefore, give broad indications of where Beauvoir's own account of a particular period is to be found in the four volumes. In the case of *Tout compte fait,* the references are out of sequence because the arrangement of that book is not chronological. The memoirs, of course, cover Beauvoir's life only up to 1971.

2 Beauvoir discusses her relations with her mother and father in F. Jeanson: *Simone de Beauvoir ou l'entreprise de vivre*, pp. 253-57. There is also further information about them in *Une Mort très douce*.

3 For an analysis of Beauvoir's Christian background and early faith, see A. M. Henry: *Simone de Beauvoir ou l'échec d'une chrétienté*.

4 This is one of a number of false names used in Beauvoir's memoirs. We have preserved them all in this chapter.

5 Beauvoir acknowledges that she wrote only the preface to the work *Djamila Boupacha* (Gallimard, 1962), which bears her name as co-author because she wanted to share legal responsibility for it (FCh II, pp. 436; 449).

2 Beauvoir's Memoirs

Beauvoir was approaching fifty when she began working on her memoirs. The project of writing about her early years had long been close to her heart, but it was not until October 1956 that she settled to the task of conjuring up 'la petite fille dont l'avenir est devenu mon passé' (FCh II, 129). She wrote *Mémoires d'une jeune fille rangée* in some eighteen months and it was published in October 1958. Its considerable success caused her to dwell upon her childhood for a time, until it became clear that she had worked something out of her system in recreating it (FCh II, 249).

The division of the book into parts marks out four phases of decreasing length in Beauvoir's life up to the age of twenty-one—childhood before her acquaintance with Zaza; the rest of her school years; the period of her undergraduate course; the academic year 1928-29—and takes us to a major watershed:

> l'année 1929, d'où datent à la fois la fin de mes études, mon émancipation économique, mon départ de la maison paternelle, la liquidation de mes anciennes amitiés et ma rencontre avec Sartre, a ouvert évidemment pour moi une ère nouvelle. (FA, 410)

The main axis of the work is the changing relationship with her parents: her conformism up to fourteen or fifteen; the discoveries and decisions through which she begins to find herself and tentatively assert her autonomy; the steady but painful movement away from her parents' values; and the eventual acquisition of real independence. The broad pattern of her development is, of course, an extremely common one, and even as she wrote Beauvoir realised how much her story might help young girls struggling for their freedom, but who 'n'osent pas encore oser' (FCh II, 189).

She describes the petit bourgeois background from which she escaped with little rancour, yet also without strongly acknowledging her own debt to it in terms of education and culture, even personality (her general seriousness and sense of duty undoubtedly spring from her upbringing). For if one of her concerns is to show how repressive such

an environment can be, another more general one is to expose the misguided and reprehensible nature of the system of social and political
values to which her family subscribed. In *Mémoires d'une jeune fille
rangée*, the attack on French bourgeois mentality, which needs to be
seen in the context of Beauvoir's other non-fictional works of the
nineteen-fifties,[1] is all the more pointed for being aimed in the first
instance at very specific features of her parents' attitudes, like their use
of language as an instrument of oppression (266), or her mother's
unwillingness to explain prohibitions or discuss matters that disturbed her daughters. It is rather pointless to speculate about how fair
Beauvoir is to her parents, since the real significance of the book is that
it presents her own view of her childhood in a coherent and powerful
form.

What can be said is that her father and mother are shown as
somewhat shadowy figures, lacking in relief or substance, like the
other people who are important in the book. As events in the normal
sense of the term play a relatively small role, the work usually proceeds
by explanations of Beauvoir's state of mind and patterns of conduct, or
of the latest stage of her relations with her parents, her sister, a close
girl friend (Zaza), or her cousin Jacques. Both Zaza and Jacques, in
their totally different fashions, help Beauvoir on her way, but they also
both fail to find the freedom that she herself gains, so that their general
significance in the book is plain enough. Yet it cannot be said that they
altogether come to life for the reader, and some of the rare tedious
passages come where Beauvoir is describing the minute ups and
downs in her relationship with the patently unworthy Jacques, or
explaining Zaza's background at great length. The ending of the book
(where Beauvoir starkly records the facts of Jacques's downfall and
death with scarcely any expression of pity or loss, and allows Zaza to
speak for herself through her letters) is also revealing in this respect.
The understatement, especially in the case of Zaza, is by no means
ineffective and the stories concerned certainly provide a strong, fateful
conclusion to the volume. Beauvoir's relative detachment, however,
contrasts very strongly with the enthusiasm and involvement of the
preceding sequence on Sartre, so that we are left wondering whether,
at the time of writing, Zaza and Jacques were very much more than
symbols for her.

This raises the matter of tone, or the general nature of Beauvoir's
attitude towards her own past, for a certain kind of detachment or

irony is one of the most distinctive features of the book as a whole. Far from seeking to justify herself as a child, she is severely critical of many of her early postures, although some of her judgements are indirect assaults upon the bourgeois background that produced her. She accuses herself of smugness, arrogance, 'mauvaise foi' of many kinds, and undermines various stances that she adopted: her early conformism (44); her pretentions (86); her love of nature (112); her view of sex (266); her 'love' for Jacques (239, 305); her conception of social action (311); her attitude to academic success (339); and so on. Sometimes she is registering a change of perspective that actually occurred before 1929, but more frequently she is looking at herself with the benefit of hindsight. Similarly, we find her retrospectively reconstructing Jacques's life-story (274-75), or explaining features of her father's attitude that she did not understand at the time (244).

There are no grounds for claiming that such a procedure is illegitimate, any more than the use of philosophical notions that she became familiar with later. Her early analysis of her rages (18-19), like her view of Garric (250-51), the odd reference to the nature of consciousness (158), and the stress on her search for necessity in life, has an existentialist flavour, but since her main goal is to understand and explain, she has the right to use whatever are, in her own view, the best conceptual tools available in 1958. She usually makes it clear, after all, when a comment is based upon later knowledge or opinion, sometimes admitting that she is uncertain whether she made a particular comparison at the time (114), or that she definitely did not (118). This goes at least some of the way towards explaining why one has a strong impression of honesty in reading the work. It is as if the later Beauvoir, like the younger one (who was prepared to re-examine all of her ideas when she encountered Sartre's persuasive arguments; 480-81), is always prepared to reconsider in the light of better evidence or a better methodology.

Many aspects or sections of *Mémoires d'une jeune fille rangée* are of particular interest because of what we know of Beauvoir's subsequent career. Thus it is fascinating to read of her original view of language (26); her discovery of the delights of reading and of modern literature; her inclination to 'save' whatever happens to her by recording it in words (95-96); her earliest attempts to write stories herself. And, like Beauvoir, we are bound to pay special attention to the different views of women's position in society to which she was exposed at a tender age. Again, we may wish to scrutinise her loss of faith and subsequent endeavours to find something or someone to fill the gap. There is reason, too, for not ignoring the regular sequences on her summer holidays in Limousin, which show her love of nature and possibly foreshadow the part that travelling was to play in her life.

Nevertheless, in the end this is the story of a girl growing up and the book succeeds in involving us in that process only because Beauvoir displays an impressive capacity for analysing her own state of mind at each stage of her development in a highly penetrating and consistently readable way. Among so many passages of this kind, one could single out her account of the impact that Zaza made upon her (125-31); many delicate but telling passages where she explores her attitude towards sexuality; the explanation of her puzzlement in the face of her father's apparently contradictory expectations (243-49); and, in a different vein, the examination of her attempts to kick over the traces in Paris night-spots (374-80). The nature of Beauvoir's intense but clear-headed interest in her early years gives a unity and autonomy to *Mémoires d'une jeune fille rangée* that subsequent volumes of her memoirs lack. Its subtlety and density, as well as the care with which it is written, make it very much more than a preparation for what is to come.

In the Prologue to *La Force de l'âge* Beauvoir explains how she came to realise that 'le premier volume de mes souvenirs exigeait à mes propres yeux une suite'. Needing to understand more clearly what use she had made of the freedom she had won in 1929, she believed that her inquiry would have some general significance and also enable her to dispel certain misunderstandings. After some hesitations, she began her serious work on the book in the summer of 1958, gathering material, consulting newspapers, rereading her own books, checking with others, writing rough drafts. She completed *La Force de l'âge* in May 1960 and it was published in October. It covers the period from summer 1929 to the Liberation of Paris in August 1944, the first of its two parts ending just before the outbreak of the Second World War in 1939, a watershed in Beauvoir's life as important as that of 1929 (410).

La Force de l'âge is more than half as long again as the first volume of Beauvoir's memoirs and a very different kind of work. Naturally, the radical change in the pattern of her life after 1929 directly dictates major differences in subject-matter. Having broken away from her family, she barely mentions her mother now, and only one paragraph is devoted to her father's death (561). Zaza and Jacques are replaced by a whole host of fascinating new friends and acquaintances, who come and go in the book. Sartre, of course, bulks enormously large and the work is an invaluable source of information about the development of his views and his published works. During this period, too, Beauvoir's own involvement in the business of writing becomes a major pre-occupation instead of an ambition, so that we can follow all of her early unsuccessful attempts to write fiction and eventually see her reactions as her reputation begins to be established. Again, political circum-stances and events make a strong impact upon her existence for the first time in *La Force de l'âge*, with the result that she gradually develops a whole new dimension of awareness and commitment. Finally, travel now takes up a very considerable proportion of her leisure time. At least ten longish trips abroad, as well as numerous shorter journeys, are recounted here, producing both impressive descriptions of a variety of settings and some eloquent portrayals of human misery.[2]

Beauvoir also employs a fairly wide range of techniques for telling her story in this volume. Because for most of the time concerned her year was structured in a particular way by her work as a schoolteacher and because of the regular references to political events, her narrative is now much more noticeably divided into periods, and it has chapters. Inevitably, the periods vary in length (whole school-years, terms, holidays, weekends with Sartre, and so on) and Beauvoir is certainly not over-inclined to use dates to help her reader. But this does mean that her different ways of moving her narrative along are always set within a broadly recognisable chronological framework. Often she proceeds by summaries of her latest thinking about her life, but equally frequently it is the views that she and Sartre have arrived at together, or even just his own particular positions, that constitute the crucial factors. Such comment on their philosophical and political development is one of the work's main sources of interest. As *La Force de l'âge* progresses, Beauvoir is obliged to resort more to brief reviews of political events, but she keeps this within bounds, often relating illustrative little incidents rather than explaining large-scale happen-ings, and almost always using such sketches to introduce the topic of their own attitudes.

To describe the first ten months of the war Beauvoir reproduces a diary that she kept at the time (or, strictly, she inserts into the text slightly edited versions of three such diaries; 433-525). This proves to be a thoroughly appropriate medium for recording in a rather impressionistic, highly evocative manner mobilisation, the 'phoney war', the flight from and return to Paris; and the state of the capital under the Nazis. Even in other sections, the very substance of *La Force de l'âge* lies in the wealth of detail: about films seen, books read, plays produced, 'faits divers' discussed, gatherings of friends, strange characters and incidents. Few books can have conjured up so vividly the quality of the lives of intellectuals in Paris during the whole of this period (the description of a typical day at the Flore café is an excellent little sketch in itself; 606-12). Beauvoir does not entirely avoid the danger of allowing detail to take over at the expense of the shape of her book, but at the beginning (18-35), in the middle (410-22), and at the end (685-95) there are extremely perspicacious 'bilans', in which she pulls many threads together and greatly helps the reader to assimilate her experiences.

The continuity between *La Force de l'âge* and *Mémoires d'une jeune fille rangée* comes partly from the attitudes and character-traits that go right back to Beauvoir's childhood, and partly from the quality of detached self-analysis recognisable in both books. Outstanding and quite distinctive of Beauvoir here is her half-philosophical, half-psychological scrutiny of the danger of becoming over-dependent upon Sartre and her success in overcoming this in Marseilles; her relationship with Olga and the pressures that brought about the failure of the 'trio'; her reactions to her first severe illness; her eventual acknowledgement of the forces of history; and her complex, changing state of mind during the Occupation. Once she has explained, clearly and frankly, the basis and nature of her association with Sartre, there is relatively little need for detailed examination of relations between them, but she sets out intellectual disagreements and altercations between them as objectively as she can, notes her occasional irritation with Sartre's behaviour, and records the stage at which she resolved to revise her view of their relationship. In short, we are given every reason to suppose that she is as honest about the couple that they form as she is about herself as an individual. And if there is not quite the self-mocking tone here that was so characteristic of *Mémoires d'une jeune fille rangée*, the self-criticism and criticism of their shared views is as uncompromising as one could possibly wish: 'nous nous trompions, à peu près en tout' (19). The retrospective quality of Beauvoir's judgements in this volume is more valuable than ever, since it brings out not only her perspective at the time of writing (apparently much the same as when she wrote the first volume of her memoirs), but also those features of the philosophical views adopted early on that remained as constants throughout the years.

La Force de l'âge does not have the unity or the elegance of *Mémoires d'une jeune fille rangée*. It is written in a more colloquial style, on the whole, and does not seem to have been nearly so carefully composed (the transitions from one topic to another are usually poorer and often non-existent). The abstract level of much of Beauvoir's commentary is inevitable, but a few of her general assertions, even aphorisms, strike a sermonising note that clashes with other, more open qualities of the writing. The book is characterised, however, by formidable energy and an irresistible vitality or love of life. More accurately, it is held together by two opposed perceptions that Beauvoir herself categorises as 'la gaieté d'exister et l'horreur de finir' (239). It may be because so much of her work needs to be seen in relation to one or both of these poles that more of her character and personality appears to have been poured into *La Force de l'âge* than into almost anything else she has written.

After completing it in May 1960 Beauvoir again hesitated before finally deciding to write a further volume of her memoirs, in order to capture 'ce moment où, à l'orée d'un passé encore brûlant, le déclin commence' (FCh, 7). *La Force des choses* was finished in the spring of 1963 and published in October. It is a record of Beauvoir's life from the Liberation to autumn 1962, divided into two parts, but this time on a rather arbitrary basis (373).

Because Beauvoir and Sartre reached the height of their fame and notoriety very soon after the Liberation, interesting light is shed from a variety of angles here on both the vogue for existentialism and some of the consequences that popularity can have for the writer. Since this was also an especially productive period for Beauvoir, *La Force des choses* contains extensive information about the origins and composition of many of her major works. And as she has never travelled more than during this phase of her life, accounts of her trips abroad, varying enormously in both volume and nature, take up more than a quarter of the whole book. The description of Brazil, probably the liveliest and most compelling of all, is so long that Beauvoir is happy to see us skip over it (II,311), and records of her visits to a few countries (particularly Russia; II,463-87) reflect the fact that she and Sartre gradually undertook more official trips. Yet there is a genuine element of adventure in some voyages (like crossing the Sahara; 283-309), and certain descriptive sequences (on Rome in the rain, Istanbul, Spain) are exceptionally good.

Beauvoir was, however, closer in time to the events described in this work and, on the whole, it lacks the kind of detachment and self-criticism that characterises the earlier volumes. She looks highly unfavourably upon some of the essays that she published in the forties, and what she sees as her moral idealism at that time clearly irritates her in a general way. At one or two isolated points in Part I, moreover, she acknowledges that she and Sartre were guilty of misjudgement. But such comments are now the exception and are almost totally absent from Part II. In certain sections of the book—for example, where she examines her attitude towards Algren (224-26), or ageing (349-52), and above all in the Epilogue—Beauvoir's self-analysis is as open-minded and astute as ever. But such passages are also rare, having been replaced by much more predictable accounts of her reactions to political events. As she says in her Preface, there is more about politics in this volume, with the gradual break-up of the unity of the Left being recorded in Part I, and Part II being entirely dominated by the Algerian War.

Her claim that this does not make *La Force des choses* a less personal work is only partly acceptable. Of course, Sartre's deep political involvement was bound to cause politics to impinge heavily upon her own life. Even so, the frequent substantial passages devoted to explanation of his political attitudes can hardly be said to tell us much about Beauvoir herself. And although it is manifestly true that she experienced the Algerian War 'comme un drame personnel' (II,501), her handling of it is obviously much more calculated to make a political point ('j'espérais gêner mes lecteurs'; TCF, 164) than to describe a particular phase of her life. It is true that she was almost pathologically obsessed with the idea of being a party to the atrocities committed on the French side (although this preoccupation is never carefully analysed), and that she occasionally succeeds in combining the personal and historical in a way that brings both to life (for instance, in her accounts of manifestations). Nevertheless, the numerous summaries of political events and the detailed, documented indictments of the French Goverment (II,239-45) involve an impersonal element scarcely seen in the earlier memoirs. At the same time, they are not 'objective' in any useful sense either. Indeed, Beauvoir's reading of events is in such black and white terms—she has admitted to this kind of naïvety in matters of politics[3]—that she risks setting up resistance on the part of her reader. Demonstrators are invariably set upon viciously by the police, without any provocation whatever; there is assumed to be no difference between De Gaulle and the O.A.S.; the *negociated* peace at the end is virtually ignored; and so on.

In any case, a disillusioned, world-weary tone pervades much of *La Force des choses*, in which the fire and enthusiasm that distinguished *La Force de l'âge* is largely missing. If the sequences describing Beauvoir's travels are frequently more spirited than the surrounding material, this is clearly because she was happier outside France than within its borders for much of this period. Another major factor in the book, however, is her growing awareness of ageing and death. Many of those to whom she and Sartre had been close died at this time, and Beauvoir became acutely conscious of Sartre's mortality. As far as ageing is concerned, it is noticeable that, quite apart from the sections dealing explicitly with the topic, the work shows in many little details how it became a serious element in her thinking from a surprisingly early stage. French readers were shocked to see her writing so frankly about approaching old age, but some of the stir caused by the final phrase of *La Force des choses*, 'je mesure avec stupeur à quel point j'ai été flouée', arose from Beauvoir's failure to make it clear that the comment was intended to sum up a number of points made at the end rather than to apply just to the matter of ageing. (She has admitted that her Epilogue is 'mal construit'; TCF, 165.) The mood that the work expresses was undoubtedly due—as the title indicates—to a combination of circumstances rather than to a single cause.

This has to be borne in mind, too, when one considers the form of the book. In her Preface Beauvoir stresses that it is 'déséquilibré' by the arbitrary quality of some of the material included, but claims that she had no intention of creating a work of art (although she was later to deny that it was not meant to be a *literary* work; TCF,162). It is, indeed, difficult to regard the composition and construction of *La Force des choses* as displaying much refinement or polish. Together with a number of inconsequential sections, the uneven travelogues and journalistic material make it a very patchy and untidy work. Furthermore, the two diaries from which Beauvoir takes over one hundred pages here (102-26; II,153-237) are of very much less interest and significance than her war diary. They contain a few entertaining incidents but also innumerable trivialities that add nothing to the book as a whole. Nevertheless, the rough-hewn, scrappy nature of *La Force des choses* should not be thought to mark it off as a complete mistake or failure. Beauvoir's argument that it is not a work of art 'mais la vie dans ses élans, ses détresses, ses soubresauts, ma vie qui essaie de se dire et non de servir de prétexte à des élégances' (8) has a certain force, especially when one comes back to the matter of her mood at the time of writing. In 1962 she evidently had relatively little faith in literature as such (II,457-58) and was anxious above all to bear witness to all that had recently happened in France. However successful or otherwise she is in this, the very stylistic 'faults' of *La Force des choses* may be regarded as some kind of measure of the intensity of her feelings and mood as she wrote it. She was unable to distance herself from events in order to select, filter and shape her material as she might have been expected to do. In *this* sense there is perhaps sincerity and raw emotion in the book of a kind not to be found in earlier volumes. Our knowledge that this mood of Beauvoir's was to pass—her alienation from her country has not entirely proved to be a permanent one, and even on old age she has admitted that she was wrong to see the future in such a gloomy light—does not undermine the value of the work in this respect and may even enhance it.

The fourth volume of Beauvoir's memoirs, *Tout compte fait,* was published in the autumn of 1972. It does not follow the chronological order observed in previous volumes, but is organised around certain broad themes. The first chapter looks at her life as a whole, but the others focus on particular aspects of the ten years since the point at which *La Force des choses* ended: her writings, her contact with the arts, her travels, and her involvement with politics.

Beauvoir's opening review of her life— she seeks to 'examiner mon histoire à travers certains concepts et certaines notions' (13)—is an interesting, though not wholly satisfactory undertaking. Its underlying assumptions about the crucial influence of childhood need further elucidation; its proportions are somewhat strange; and it is noticeable that some of the points now emphasised received considerably less attention in earlier volumes. On the other hand, the use to which Beauvoir puts the contrasting notions of freedom (or choice) and chance circumstances does provide a coherent view of her life, bringing out her belief that she has always made the most of her opportunities. Even hypothesis and speculation, as she says, help to define what she actually is, and she does usefully point out some of the basic continuities as well as discontinuities in her life. The following section of Chapter 1, furthermore, in which she examines the current pattern of her life and reflects upon ageing, is one of the very best in the book. She writes in a more balanced frame of mind than at the end of *La Force des choses* and with an openness that is once more extremely refreshing.

Unfortunately, Chapter 1 is entirely typical of the book as a whole in its unevenness, for having written so judiciously about herself Beauvoir goes on to talk of her friends and acquaintances in a manner that is mostly anecdotal and banal. Although the account of her new friendship with Sylvie Le Bon is touching, she is far more concerned to say what has happened to certain people since 1962 than to analyse her relationships. (Why is there so little here about Sartre, and nothing at all on Olga, Bost or Lanzmann?) And in spite of the fascination of, say, the story of Camille's fate, details of the deaths of some of her friends in no way illuminate Beauvoir's own life. Significantly, she does not wish to write about the one death that moved her deeply (138). The chapter ends with a fairly substantial section on her dreams, which she makes no attempt to interpret and is content to describe. No justification is given for including such material, which will appear redundant to even her most avid readers.

On the other hand, Beauvoir's comments, in Chapter 2, on all that she wrote during this period are, as usual, of the greatest interest, providing unique insights into her intentions and attempting to correct misunderstandings of the works. After a lyrical sequence on the joys of reading at the beginning of the following chapter, Beauvoir explains and illustrates which types of books she is now inclined to read. Some of her remarks on non-fictional works elucidate her own attitudes (for instance, towards childhood), but her main purpose is to summarise the contents of certain books and the section develops into a rather insignificant catalogue. The same is true of her potted comments on films and plays she has seen, although the brief con-cluding analysis of the nature of culture and the need for radical reform in education is certainly controversial and challenging.

The accounts of her travels between 1962 and 1971 are spread over three chapters, with mixed results. Chapter 5, on Japan, mingles rather dull economic history with evocative little descriptions (of Noh drama and puppet theatre, for example) and largely factual sketches of towns (including Hiroshima). In Chapter 6, however, she is able to treat a number of trips to Russia together, in order to trace the course taken by official Soviet policy towards intellectuals. She is also able to note the changes in Rome over the years, as she and Sartre regularly spent part of their summer there. Yet the arbitrary juxtaposition, in Chapter 4, of this sequence on Italy and what is largely guide-book material on areas visited in France itself serves no particular purpose. And only rarely now does the personal, impressionistic ingredient in her reports blend with their dry, informative side to make a lively and co-herent whole. Whereas in earlier volumes we often felt that Beauvoir's basic impulse was to share her enthusiasm and excitement about places with her readers, here—perhaps partly because of the grouping of the material— we are rather left with the impression that her main aim is simply to record where she has been and what she has seen. The theme of revisiting—'revoir m'est un bonheur' (294)—is not sufficiently developed to constitute an interesting new slant to the presentation of her travels.

If Beauvoir's involvement in international politics, described in Chapter 7, is carefully thought out and systematic, she entirely fails to explain herself. For instance, her general anti-American stance, illus-trated by her part in the Russell Tribunal of 1967, is justified only in the vaguest way and greatly weakened by her inclination to believe in prophecies of doom: 'le régime n'est plus viable . . . son économie va s'effondrer' (575). Again, her intense interest in the Six Day War of 1967 seems to have stemmed largely from the coincidence of her visits to Egypt and Israel some months before. And she admits that she writes of other countries only where she has been personally affected for one reason or another (556). The final chapter of the book, de-scribing how Beauvoir's attitude towards politics in France changed with the dramatic events of May 1968 and how she came to throw in her lot with French left-wing extremists like the Maoists, is much less arbitrary and brings out her latest thinking on matters that had long been close to her heart, including feminism. There is dogmatism and over-simplification in some of her claims, but the sincerity of her commitment to the cause of the working classes is conveyed as

strongly and poignantly as anywhere in her writings.

Her decision to present this volume of her memoirs in a different form from previous ones is intimately related to her acknowledgement that her life changed very little between 1962 and 1971 (47). In these circumstances, to set out her material under the kind of headings that she had implicitly been using in her chronological narratives (travel, politics, friendships, writings, etc.) was an obvious course to take. The weakness of *Tout compte fait* lies not in the form that Beauvoir chose but in the indifferent execution of her plan. Since her main topics imposed themselves, she should have been much more success-ful in structuring her observations in relation to them. For in most cases her attempts to find categories that clarify her experience (im-portant recurring features in her past, types of books read, types of journeys undertaken, etc.) produce relatively insignificant results. More than this, Beauvoir's powers of discrimination and selection in general are at their feeblest in this book, where there is no good justification for the inclusion of certain sequences and many others are of only the most limited interest. At a time when her reflections and self-analysis might have been at their richest, she largely contents herself with catalogues of one kind or another and fairly unsophis-ticated descriptions of the world around her. Perhaps the book lacks some of the open qualities of earlier volumes because, as Beauvoir claims (53), she no longer has the sense of progressing towards something better. We do well to remember, nonetheless, that *Tout compte fait* can easily be seen to represent a resurgence on her part after the gloom that dominated the second part of *La Force des choses*. In spite of what she says, there are very strong and encouraging signs in the last chapter that her interest in the future has *not* been entirely extinguished, and she is surely wise on this occasion to leave readers to draw their own conclusions from the work.

Taken as a whole, the four volumes of Beauvoir's memoirs (well over three quarters of a million words) must form one of the longest autobiographies in any language by a woman. And yet rather than executing some grand design, she seems to have been led on from one book to the next by circumstances, a general desire to understand her own life, and the reactions of her readers. Perhaps paradoxically, one finds very little evidence that she somehow gains positive pleasure from putting herself on display. In fact, there is considerable justi-fication for her claim that she is lacking in vanity and tends to see herself objectively (FCh, 9-10).[4] For much of the memoirs one is conscious of a certain detachment on the part of the author and it is intriguing to watch its precise nature change as Beauvoir looks at herself as a young girl, a mature woman and an elderly lady. Only in the second half of *La Force des choses* is this gap consistently closed, producing a lack of perspective or a short-sightedness uncommon in her writings. That work is in part a direct cry of anguish and when, in the Epilogue, Beauvoir does briefly manage to distance herself from her experience, she composes one of the profoundest and most poignant sequences in the whole of the memoirs. Broadly speaking, her interest is in the world rather than herself, or rather in the world, with herself as one object in it. At its best, this attitude yields a captivating mixture of disinterested self-analysis and exuberant comment on people and places.

There is obvious truth, too, in Beauvoir's contention that any individual's sincere account of his or her existence is bound to throw some light on those of others (FA, 10). This is why the memoirs have very considerable value as a document on aspects of the intellectual, artistic, social and political life of her times. Different features come into prominence at different stages, but this in itself is part of the way in which the four volumes reflect the movement of history. Not that the memoirs are, or are meant to be, a neutral historical record. Beauvoir writes from within her particular situation and with her own preoccupations, perspectives and convictions, but at least, as she says, the personal element is undisguised (FCh, 10). For all readers this element will be intrusive at some point or other, and perhaps for most the political analysis provided in conjunction with her journeys abroad will be especially suspect, in that she frequently relies almost exclusively for her information on a very small number of contacts in the country concerned. And not only is her broad outlook a distinctively French one (her anti-Americanism, for instance, leads her simply to ignore any encouraging trends in the U.S.A.),[5] it is also essentially a non-communist left-wing one, and she admits that her version of political events and movements in France itself cannot possibly be seen as impartial.

This has to be accepted as one of the facts that define the limits within which Beauvoir's testimony has value. Recognition of it does not prevent us from noting stages at which her view is singularly blinkered, or stages at which her political position does nothing whatever to undermine the documentary value of what she writes (as with her account of the Occupation). And it actually helps us to see where she is speaking for a significant number of her contemporaries. This is certainly the case in her narration of the pre-war period. At the beginning of *La Force de l'âge* she and Sartre share the euphoria of all on the Left (19-20); like many others they are anti-bourgeois but have little constructive to offer (256); like others they are slow to recognise the German menace (415), but eventually accept the inevitability of war (432-33). Beauvoir recognises that, without knowing it, they were quite frequently acting in a way typical of their peers, even in their leisure activities (like discovering skiing or visiting Greece). She presumably fails to see, however, that her specific political preoccupations in the period covered by *Tout compte fait* hardly reflect those of a similarly high number of her compatriots, for there is something distinctly arbitrary in the fact that she devotes nearly three times as much space to the Russell Tribunal as to the events of May 1968, and more than four times as much to Egypt and Israel. The question is a more complex one in connection with *La Force des choses*, which charts divisions in the French Left that make it difficult to say on whose behalf Beauvoir may be speaking at which points. Nevertheless, here as elsewhere the very fact of her intense involvement in major issues at least enables her to register *one* view of a situation that affected millions.

Yet *La Force des choses* serves to remind us of another limitation imposed upon Beauvoir's autobiography: it is the story of someone from the privileged classes and of an intellectual (not, for example, that of 'un manoeuvre, un paysan, un colonel, un musicien'; FCh, 10). This does not mean that there can be no significant comment on matters of social class in the memoirs. On the contrary, an outstanding feature of *Mémoires d'une jeune fille rangée* is the consistency and sharpness with which it presents a certain way of seeing the French bourgeoisie of a particular period, for Beauvoir's parents are shown as belonging in almost all respects to their epoque and class (and as suffering financially, like many similar families, from the effects of the First World War), and both Zaza and Jacques are victims as well as products of a bourgeois environment. 'Prejudiced' the picture of her background may be, but it is obviously *some* kind of reflection of reality, and those who would say that she saw it in that way 'only' because she rejected its values need to explain why she wished to break away in the first place. Like so many intellectuals, Beauvoir lives in a strange no-man's-land as far as social class is concerned. Totally at variance with the bourgeoisie from which she sprang and to which by certain strict socio-economic criteria still belongs, she has very little in common with the working classes to whose cause she is totally committed. At a number of points in the memoirs, one realises the extent of her distance from 'ordinary' people (FCh II,449; TCF,606), yet even this gives her situation a certain representative quality, for the memoirs trace the quandaries, tribulations and satisfactions of the bourgeois left-wing writer attempting to further the cause of the proletariat.

For it would be foolish to underestimate the importance of Beauvoir's autobiography as a record of the life of a well-known author. In addition to giving us privileged access to the creative process and precious details concerning the genesis of Sartre's books as well as her own, the memoirs show us a writer commenting on and evaluating her own works. Such appreciations are almost invariably helpful as pointers to weaknesses as much as strengths in the books, and only partly because they take up both the criticisms and the praise that the works have attracted. Indeed, another dimension to the memoirs is that in which the relations between an author and her readers are explored. The notoriety that she shared with Sartre is duly noted and discussed, but it is little more than an echo of the enthusiasm and success with which the pair entered into almost the whole range of artistic and journalistic activity in the post-war period. The list of famous writers, artists, producers, actors and politicians with whom they were in close contact and whose names appear regularly on the pages of the memoirs is an extraordinary one and constitutes a further sign of the stature of Beauvoir's chronicle. At the same time, at the other end of the spectrum, the relatively trivial incidents or details, the bizarre characters, the isolated conversations, the uncompleted projects, the forgotten ups and downs—these are the phenomena that give such inexhaustible richness to the memoirs and ensure that the atmosphere of the period is so brilliantly evoked.

Perhaps that is enough to make the question of Beauvoir's honesty or sincerity in relating her personal life a secondary one, but since she herself has laid emphasis upon it, it is a matter that is likely to exercise all readers. She clearly has an excellent memory, but certain private written sources correspond to the newspapers, magazines and published works that she reread in order to write about the more public side of her past. At various stages in the memoirs she quotes from (or includes long extracts from) a number of diaries that she herself kept; her own 'carnets'; notes that she wrote (about journeys, dreams, death); her letters to Sartre and her sister; letters from Zaza, Sartre, Algren, Camille and Lise; letters from Sartre to others; Sartre's note-books or 'notes inédites'; and so on. Without providing any guarantee of the 'truth' of what Beauvoir says, this reminder about her sources throws the emphasis where it rightly belongs, on the issue of her *selection* of material in general. In the Prologue to *La Force de l'âge* she makes the interesting point that whereas she omitted nothing from *Mémoires d'une jeune fille rangée*, she no longer feels the detachment or enjoys the freedom in relation to others that would permit her to tell everything (FA, 10-11). Both here and in the Preface to *La Force des choses* she acknowledges that she has made slips and will doubtless make others, but insists that she has never *lied* (FA, 11; FCh, 10). Since, as she says, many readers are struck by the sincerity of the memoirs, these are claims that deserve the fullest examination.

All that can be suggested here is that while Beauvoir does have a peculiarly 'objective' way of looking at her own life, and while no evidence has yet been produced that she actually lies in her auto-biography, these two points—which already give the memoirs very distinctive qualities—do no more than scratch the surface of an exceedingly complex problem. Two closely related questions among many others concern, firstly, her acknowledged omissions and, secondly, possible indiscretion in the memoirs. By its very nature, the topic of omissions is a difficult one for the reader, but even if we look just at Beauvoir's key relationship with Sartre, there are some fairly simple ways of gauging the importance of the matter. She herself admits that her picture of their relationship in *La Force de l'âge* was inexact, in not recording the difficulties generated by their agreement to leave each other free sexually (FCh, 177). Now, this major ad-mission immediately makes one wonder about possible hidden currents beneath the surface of her story. Whether or not one adds to it scraps of knowledge from quite different sources (for example, about Arlette El Kaïm—nowhere mentioned in the memoirs proper—the young woman whom Sartre met in 1956, possibly came close to marrying, and certainly adopted legally in 1965),[6] it does little to strengthen our confidence in the reliability of Beauvoir's account. By omitting all reference to certain phenomena, it is possible to avoid telling lies, but only at the risk of making a great deal of what one *does* say a distortion of the truth. How many of the depressed moods that Beauvoir records in the memoirs are partly attributable to events or people never mentioned?

Other types of omission are more understandable. The total absence of references to the sexual side of Beauvoir's relationship with Sartre makes an unsatisfactory sequel to the great emphasis on her sexual development in *Mémoires d'une jeune fille rangée*—she has recently said that, rewriting her memoirs, she would include 'un bilan très franc de ma sexualité'[7]—but this is easier to accept than the apparently arbitrary nature of Beauvoir's 'discretion'. She is as good as her word in not actually gossiping about her friends and their lives and uses pseudonyms to protect some, yet we have no way of knowing how many were aggrieved by the quantity of personal detail about them that she does include. (Perhaps by 1963 Algren had given permission for Beauvoir to quote from his letters, but her graphic description of their affair in *Les Mandarins*, only some three years after it ended, is known to have offended him.) In any case, even if she exercises some caution in her treatment of her friends in the memoirs, she certainly does not spare her ex-friends or those for whom she never had respect. There is definite malevolence (particularly in *La Force des choses*) in her comments on some of the lesser-known people she meets, and not even the famous (like Rousset, Camus and Koestler) escape her acrimony. Indiscretion here shades into malice and brings us back to the question of honesty and accuracy. Beauvoir doubtless describes relationships as she sees them, but common sense prevents us from believing, for instance, that she and Sartre should have been quite so consistently let down by others, without ever wronging them in any way whatever: 'Ma manière de penser, de sentir, d'agir, va de soi, à mes yeux. J'ai du mal à admettre que c'est à mes yeux seulement' (TCF, 57-58). At the conscious level there is considerable—though not complete—honesty and frankness in the memoirs, but there are also indications that this, in both the literal and figurative senses, is not the whole story: 'peut-être mon image projetée dans un monde autre—celui des psychanalystes par exemple—pourrait-elle me déconcerter ou me gêner. Mais si c'est moi qui me peins, rien ne m'effraie' (FCh, 10).

It would be quite wrong, however, to end a review of the memoirs on a carping note of any kind. They may irritate or even infuriate, but they rarely fail to inform and challenge us, and this on a whole variety of levels. Taken together, the four volumes do not have the harmony, the shape, or even the quality of writing that would make them a major artistic achievement. There are magnificent passages, but also utterly undistinguished, tedious ones; in some cases Beauvoir's mastery of her material is admirable and highly individual, but in others her control is minimal. Yet the very unevenness of the books is part of their fascination as a human document, as is their inconclusiveness. As the carefully chosen titles suggest, Beauvoir traces the pattern of her life in its principal stages—the struggle for independence, then optimism giving way to disillusionment and, later, sober commitment. Yet the structures that she detects elucidate that life by raising questions rather than by supplying neat answers. She doubtless understands her life and times better as a result of writing about them, as we certainly do from reading her account, but the memoirs equally register, in various ways, the elusive quality of human existence, and this is by no means the least of their many virtues:

> Plus je vais, plus le monde entre dans ma vie jusqu'à la faire éclater. Pour la raconter, il me faudrait douze portées; et une pédale pour *tenir* les sentiments—mélancholie, joie, dégoût—qui en ont coloré des périodes entières, à travers les intermittences du cœur. Dans chaque moment se reflètent mon passé, mon corps, mes relations à autrui, mes entreprises, la société, toute la terre; liées entre elles, et indépendantes, ces réalités parfois se renforcent et s'harmonisent, parfois interfèrent, se contrarient ou se neutralisent. Si la totalité ne demeure pas toujours présente, je ne dis rien d'exact. Même si je surmonte cette difficulté, j'achoppe à d'autres: une vie, c'est un drôle d'objet, d'instant en instant translucide et tout entier opaque, que je fabrique moi-même et qui m'est imposé, dont le monde me fournit la substance et qu'il me vole, pulvérisé par les événements, dispersé, brisé, hachuré et qui pourtant garde son unité. (FCh, 376-77)

Notes

1   In particular, *Privilèges* of 1955. See Chapter 6.

2   Claire Cayron has calculated that Beauvoir made 56 journeys in the period covered by *La Force de l'âge* (87 during the period of *La Force des choses*): *La Nature chez Simone de Beauvoir,* pp. 36-37.

3   F. Jeanson: *Simone de Beauvoir ou l'entreprise de vivre,* p.276.

4   On this and other aspects of what we learn about Beauvoir herself from the first three volumes of memoirs, see F. Jeanson, op.cit.

5   English-speaking readers may notice, for instance, that she scarcely registers the existence of John Kennedy, but another measure of her general 'Frenchness' lies in her acknowledgement that *Mémoires d'une jeune fille rangée* has been less popular in America 'parce qu'il s'agit de moeurs qui sont étrangères aux Américains' ('Entretien avec Madeleine Chapsal' in M. Chapsal: *Les Écrivains en personne*; reprinted in *Écrits*, p.388).

6   For a racy, but not necessarily reliable, account of this relationship, see Axel Madsen: *Hearts and Minds*, pp. 194, 206, 240.

7   ' "Ce que je dirais maintenant si je devais récrire mes mémoires". Interview par Alice Schwarzer', *Marie Claire*, Jan. 1978, p.74.

3 Other Autobiographical Writings

In addition to her memoirs proper Beauvoir has written three other works that fall broadly into the autobiographical category: one based upon her travels in America (*L'Amérique au jour le jour*), and each of the other two arising out of the death of someone dear to her (*Une Mort très douce* and *La Cérémonie des adieux*).

L'Amérique au jour le jour, which was published in 1948, is a record of her first two visits to the United States in the previous year: a long lecture-tour and sight-seeing trip stretching from the end of January to late in May and a stay in Chicago during the last two weeks of September. The enormous gap between her previous idea of the country and the reality itself made her want to share her discoveries, but also, on returning to France after the first trip, she experienced a period of depression and found herself trying in some sense to prolong her stay by writing an account of it. With the aid of lists of appointments, some notes, letters written to Sartre, and memories that were still fresh, she reconstructed her journey in detail, then gave the text its final form after her trip to Chicago.

She sometimes calls the work a 'reportage', though it is essentially a personal one, since her aim is to 'raconter au jour le jour comment l'Amérique s'est dévoilée à une conscience: la mienne' (9). This is why the book is cast in the form of a diary, and Beauvoir claims that it is 'scrupuleusement exact'. Yet we are bound to be sceptical about this claim on learning from the memoirs that she felt much more than she registers here when, for instance, she first met Algren (FCh, 177-78), or when she joined Lise and her husband in California (TCF, 108-09). There is also the question of her separate visit to Chicago in September, which was when she saw the features of the city described near the end of the text. In principle, the idea of adding the impressions gained on this occasion to those from her first trip is a good one and there is something to be said, on artistic grounds, for patching her knowledge of Chicago into the main body of her account. But this *is*, after all, a distortion, involving the suppression of certain facts, the invention of little links, and the insertion of false datelines. In allowing what are broadly aesthetic considerations to override the absolute accuracy that she explicitly claims, Beauvoir risks undermining our confidence in her veracity.

Nevertheless, for the most part the book is undoubtedly a faithful enough record of her travels, experiences and reactions in America. In between two fairly lengthy periods in New York, she went up to the Canadian border at Niagara, briefly visited major cities like Washington, Chicago and Boston, and undertook a round-trip of about six weeks taking her first to California, then through Texas and the Deep South and finally back up through Carolina and Virginia. She lectured at some two dozen universities and colleges, engaged in numerous discussions of the arts and politics, met many people she had known before going to America, and made a considerable number of new friends and acquaintances. One of Beauvoir's principal aims in *L'Amérique au jour le jour* is to conjure up America for her readers, perhaps especially those who have never been there, and on this relatively modest level the book is an obvious success. Her text is very informative, about both America in 1947 and the historical processes that made it what it is, but above all she has gifts of observation and powers of expression that bring vividly to life for us a very great deal of what she sees. She dwells rather less than one might expect on the great natural splendours of the country, probably because she finds that Americans are too anxious to 'tame' natural phenomena (177). On the other hand, the basic narrative composed of short, simple, present-tense sentences, as appropriate in a diary, is studded with descriptions of towns and cities. Sometimes she clearly spent too little time in a place to have a distinctive impression to convey (Rochester, Buffalo), but more frequently she rapidly and skilfully sketches pictures that are both sharp and evocative (Reno, San Antonio, Santa Fe), or portrays the particular quarters and activities of a city in striking detail (the Bowery in New York; the gardens of Charleston, South Carolina; the film world of Los Angeles). Since she is adept at characterising atmospheres as well as settings, there are also accounts of particular episodes or moments during her trip (a drunken party in Santa Fe; a Sunday service in Harlem; the circus in Madison Gardens) that impress themselves upon the reader with great force. If she seems less interested in individuals than is the case in her memoirs, this actually serves to tighten the work somewhat, eliminating what might have appeared as digression and giving the book a definite unity.

Part of its fascination is that it describes a broad pattern of initial reactions to the United States that one feels is an extremely common one, although Beauvoir periodically suffers a characteristic kind of anguish associated with her search for a personal project that will enable her to possess America in its plenitude: 'Il faudrait que quelque chose m'arrive, quelque chose de vrai, et tout le reste me serait donné par sucroît' (75). While different preoccupations and rhythms are discernible in different parts of the work, her inquiring attitude pulls the whole together well as she makes her comments arise naturally out of her experiences. And, as she suggests in her Preface, we are able to see her opinions develop during her visit. She was immediately struck by the scale and abundance of everything in America, but soon came to believe that the real choices open to Americans are considerably less extensive than they appear: 'Voici mille possibilités ouvertes: mais c'est la même. Mille choix permis: mais tous équivalents' (27). More and more as her acquaintance with the country grew she found illusions or 'mystifications' in the American way of life and saw the Puritan tradition and a genuine faith in the richness of the world and its resources as conspiring to make Americans singularly unwilling to call anything important into question. As an intellectual, she considered it particularly galling that a version of this 'passivity' should be afflicting even the country's students, teachers, journalists and writers, in whom she detected 'une tradition de défaitisme intellectuel' (300). By the last stages of her visit, however, recognising that America is 'une trop vaste machine aux rouages trop compliqués' (300), Beauvoir was inclined to see all Americans who fail to do what they might in order to question, provoke, probe and reject as caught up in a vicious circle, whereby their initial sense of powerlessness and resignation actually helps to perpetuate the situation they resent: 'Personne ne peut rien parce que tous pensent ne rien pouvoir; et la fatalité triomphe dès qu'on croit en elle' (301). Hence women in general and even the bulk of the male population are, like intellectuals as a group, prisoners of the American system.

Beauvoir could be expected to deplore the right-wing politics of America in general and its obsessive anti-communism, but her views carry more weight when she exposes anti-semitism (312-14); criticises the treatment of Indians (185-86); regularly attacks racism; or deplores the exploitation of cotton-workers (207-09). All of these injustices she ascribes ultimately to the capitalist system, whereby power and profit are concentrated in the hands of a privileged few. However, she is extremely vague, even inconsistent, in her comments about the composition of this favoured group. Whether the Americans she met (who are said sometimes to be almost exclusively intellectuals and sometimes to be perfectly representative of the great mass of Americans) should be regarded—like the masses—as victims of the political system, as its props, or merely as its unwitting accomplices is left unclear. Such ambiguity is not necessarily inappropriate, but it does set a limit to the acuity of Beauvoir's analysis of America in 1947, perhaps bearing out what she says in her Preface: 'souvent, d'ailleurs, je n'aboutis à aucun point de vue arrêté'. Certainly, her view of the United States and its citizens is by no means a wholly unfavourable one. She is always at pains to point out that its ideals are not hollow, or even completely unrealised, ones, and she acknowledges that Europeans have their own ways of going astray. Some of the disillusionment that she experienced about the country was clearly a function of the excessively high expectations and hopes that she had of it on arrival.

It is not difficult to spot misjudgements and distorted emphases in *L'Amérique au jour le jour*: too much space is devoted to descriptions of night-clubs; Beauvoir's claim that the self-made man no longer has his chance is dubious (303); and her assertions that real friendship between women is almost unknown (321) and deep, sustained relationships rare (373) seem quite arbitrary. On the other hand, many of her penetrating remarks about the American way of life, which had originality at the time, have become commonplace (she was later to suggest, for instance, that her discussion of American conformism had anticipated talk of the 'organisation man' by sociologists). There are obvious limits to Beauvoir's acquaintance with, and picture of, the United States. Hers is no systematic survey of a country, for, as she admits, she visited no factories, examined no technological achievements, met no workers or members of the American 'Establishment'. The time she spent in Chicago is so important to the reader—and to Beauvoir herself—precisely because it enabled her to see a very different side of American life from that observed on the rest of her travels, but even here she is conscious that her view was a restricted one (368). Perhaps, for the European, America is simply too big and too diversified to permit one single, comprehensive judgement, and if Beauvoir was ambivalent about the country (265), this was inevitable after her first visit. Convinced at the time that it was one of the places in the world where man's future was being decided, she had changed her mind by 1960: 'c'était encore le pays le plus prospère de la terre, mais non plus celui qui forgeait l'avenir' (FCh II,287). In fact, little since 1947 has revived her enthusiasm for America and much, in her eyes, has confirmed her criticisms. The book owes much of its value to the fact that it records her excitement and disappointments at a historical moment when many Europeans knew little about America and were eager to expose themselves to its impact, for better or worse.

If *L'Amérique au jour le jour* can be seen as one especially long account of a trip abroad, of a type very common in Beauvoir's memoirs, *Une Mort très douce,* published in 1964, is obviously to be linked with those equally familiar sequences where she describes the illnesses or deaths of people she knows well. This relatively short book is divided into eight sections and covers a period of roughly one month. Beauvoir relates in the first section how her mother, who had been taken into hospital in October 1963 after a fall at home, was discovered to have cancer of the intestine, and how it became apparent after an operation that she had only a short time to live. In the second section she reviews her mother's life and analyses her personality. We see the illness taking its inevitable course in the third, while the fourth, with Beauvoir back in Paris after a pre-arranged trip to Czechoslovakia, describes her mother's final days and death. In the last four sections, each very brief, Beauvoir examines and speculates about various aspects of these events, as well as recounting the two days following the death and her mother's funeral. Her decision to write the book apparently came suddenly (together with the title, epigraph and dedication) just a few days after the funeral, and she spent the winter of 1963-64 working on it (TCF,168). Beauvoir is undoubtedly right to claim that part of the success of *Une Mort très douce* is attributable to the ease with which readers can find a relationship between the main sequence of events and their own experience. For even those who have not yet lost a parent or a loved one know that one day they almost certainly will, and nearly all have at least enough acquaintance with hospitals to recognise some of the situations that Beauvoir describes. As a result, some may draw from the book 'les consolations de la fraternité' that many of her correspondants did: 'Mes correspondants me disaient que, malgré sa tristesse, mon livre les avait aidés à supporter, au présent ou à travers leurs souvenirs, l'agonie d'un être cher' (TCF, 169).

Yet the 'universal' quality of the experience related is not developed in quite the way that one might have expected. It is common in the memoirs, after all, for Beauvoir to use her personal tribulations—or joys—as the starting-point for reflections on issues of the utmost philosophical or moral importance. Yet this is not exactly what happens in this text, in spite of the fact that opportunities are by no means lacking. Once her mother is discovered to have terminal cancer, for instance, the problem immediately arises of whether or not to tell her the truth. Beauvoir and her sister appear to have spent very little time considering the matter (42), and they are eventually obliged to go beyond the particular lie they choose to tell by talking and acting generally as if their mother will recover and return to her normal way of life. It is not for others to judge their conduct, but what is interesting is that whether it is morally right to lie to someone in these circumstances is not even one of the many questions that Beauvoir raises in the book after her mother's death. The view that she had no alternative (94) is not one that is easy to reconcile with her assertions in other works to the effect that we have no right to decide what is good for others, and the absence of any theoretical examination of her position is rather striking. Two other topics on which Beauvoir refuses an obvious opportunity for philosophical reflection in the book are euthanasia and death. From early on she wonders what is the point of keeping her mother alive for just a little while longer, and she even accuses one of the doctors of tormenting her unnecessarily. She also refers frequently to an uncle who died in agony, crying out for days: 'Achevez-moi. Donnez-moi mon revolver' (81). Yet the *general* question of mercy-killing, or of not striving officiously to keep some-one alive, is never discussed. And even on the broad theme of death—a vitally important one in so many of her works—Beauvoir's general-isations are very limited. She does note that it is useless to try to 'intégrer la mort à la vie' (141) and makes a few familiar points about death (143, 152). But remarks of this kind constitute a natural way of completing the account and betray no particular inclination to generalise her experience. The fact that Beauvoir is uncharacter-istically restrained on the moral and philsophical levels may be precisely one of the reasons why *Une Mort très douce* is such a suggestive work. The subject is such that readers are bound to compare their own reactions and feelings with hers, but for once they are not told what they ought to think about the underlying issues.

In fact, in some respects this is an intensely personal, almost private work. For one thing, it constitutes a detailed portrait of a particular woman, Beauvoir's mother. Not only do her comments, obsessions, memories and nightmares form a substantial and essential part of the narrative, there are also a number of retrospective sequences early on, including one whole section of the book, specifically designed to familiarise us with the life and personality of the principal participant in the drama. For the most part, the picture is a highly critical one. Beauvoir considers that her mother's life was built on a series of contradictions, seeing her as a typical product of the bourgeois classes, who was actively encouraged to deceive herself (51) and led to accept received opinion (59). What makes this so intensely personal a matter is that here as in *Mémoires d'une jeune fille rangée* Beauvoir makes it very clear that she feels she suffered badly during her own childhood and adolescence as a direct result of her mother's character: 'Possessive, dominatrice, elle aurait voulu nous tenir tout entières dans le creux de sa main' (54). Some parts of the book at least suggest that she has never forgiven her mother for her illiberal attitudes in the home, and in the last analysis it is the fascinating question of Beauvoir's relationship with her mother that lies at the very heart of the work as a whole. It is understandable that readers should be a little disturbed by her attitude in the early part of *Une Mort très douce*, for the tone is certainly a cold one at the beginning, with Beauvoir relating events very flatly and showing an apparent lack of concern: 'somme toute, elle avait l'âge de mourir' (16). She is appalled at her mother's snobbish attitude towards different clinics as well as her scornful comments on 'les femmes du peuple', and she draws a harsh distinction between her physical suffering and her views (26). Even before the discovery of the tumour, however, Beauvoir is already affected by her mother's state and retracts some of her earlier words: 'Quand je me disais: elle a l'âge de mourir, c'étaient des mots vides' (27). Her increasing involvement is soon apparent and produces some touching moments which bear out her own point (TCF, 169) that readers would hardly have found her account so moving, had she been no more than 'un observateur indifférent'. In fact, at an early stage Beauvoir is temporarily overcome by her mother's plight: 'Cette fois, mon désespoir échappait à mon contrôle' (43).

The key to a more important change that comes over her lies in the effect that suffering has on her mother's mentality. Firstly, the latter becomes too preoccupied with survival to express the prejudiced views that formerly offended her daughter and loses the resentment that used to characterise her attitudes. Then when Beauvoir has to spend a number of nights sleeping next to her mother, the bond between them is strengthened considerably: 'Ma vraie vie se déroulait auprès d'elle et n'avait qu'un but: la protéger' (103). Significantly, Beauvoir sees the extreme circumstances as having brought out in her mother the 'femme de sang et de feu' who had remained suppressed and hidden for so many years. The conventional framework of her mother's thought has been shattered, her true feelings have finally risen to the surface, and she has at last achieved a harmony between self-respect and concern for others (149). The moving result of this change is that Beauvoir draws closer to her mother than she has ever been since childhood: 'l'ancienne tendresse que j'avais crue tout à fait éteinte ressuscitait' (109). In this respect, therefore, *Une Mort très douce* is as much about Beauvoir herself as about her mother, and the book has a deeply personal core.

Once these essential aspects of the work are acknowledged, it becomes clearer why three of the four brief final sections should be devoted to analysis of the events and why this analysis should strike a personal rather than a philosophical note. Beauvoir attempts, for one thing, to interpret her mother's failure to send for a priest during her last weeks, concluding that she was not bold enough to rebel against orthodox Christianity but had too strong a love of life to be able to say prayers implying an acceptance of death, and therefore chose silence. This is of particular significance, since, as Beauvoir suggests by her epigraph ('Do not go gentle into that good night . . . '), she too refuses to accept death: 'Maman aimait la vie comme je l'aime et elle éprouvait devant la mort la même révolte que moi' (132). There is, of course, no way of knowing whether this interpretation of her mother's action is accurate and it says much for Beauvoir that in *Une Mort très douce* she keeps description and interpretation sufficiently distinct to leave the way open for other tentative readings. What we can say, however, is that the thought that her mother shared some of the same basic attitudes to life would be bound to be a more important one than ever after the renewal of their intimacy recounted in the book.

Nevertheless, all of this still leaves certain unanswered questions about Beauvoir's relations with her mother. Why, when she speculates that her mother might have died at once, even before the operation, does she not mention their resumed 'dialogue' as one of the benefits that accrued from the extra thirty days of life? And why, in the light of the fact that she seems at last to have forgiven her mother for her strictness and autocracy (blaming this upon her mother's own upbringing; 148), does she not express explicit regret that their dialogue could not be continued? It is somewhat odd that Beauvoir should still be rather puzzled about—and need to analyse—the fact that her mother's passing affected her so deeply! In the final section of the book, moreover, she can only suggest—albeit powerfully and poetically—that it was because it brought her face to face with the reality of Death:

> c'est à son chevet que j'ai vu la Mort des danses macabres, grimaçante et narquoise, la Mort des contes de veillée qui frappe à la porte, une faux à la main, la Mort qui vient d'ailleurs, étrangère, inhumaine: elle avait le visage même de maman découvrant sa mâchoire dans un grand sourire d'ignorance. (151)

Again, readers are not well placed here to doubt the validity of this analysis, but they may well wonder about the significance of Beauvoir's failure to record any serious sense of loss at this point. Does this mean that she has returned to the kind of detached position that she was in before the events of the book, and if so, what importance is one now to attach to the expressions of tenderness in the middle of the text? Or, alternatively, is the deep source of Beauvoir's regularly expressed unease over the inescapable need to lie to her mother on her deathbed some kind of displaced recognition that only the desperate circumstances prevented an open development of their relationship on a new basis, however brief?

> malgré les apparences, même lorsque je tenais la main de maman, je n'étais pas avec elle: je lui mentais. Parce qu'elle avait toujours été mystifiée, cette suprême mystification m'était odieuse. Je me rendais complice du destin qui lui faisait violence. (150)

It is possible that the tragedy and poignancy of this situation is so great that Beauvoir cannot bring herself to voice it directly.

What needs to be recognised is that unresolved questions and ambiguities of this sort form an integral part of *Une Mort très douce* and make an important contribution to the effect that the work has upon us. They bring out the point that the intense relationship, begun when Beauvoir was brought into the world, did not come to an abrupt end with her mother's death. That she felt the need to write a book about it already provides evidence of this, but many of her other writings, fictional as well as autobiographical, suggest that this primary relationship is both a vital permanent thread in the texture of Beauvoir's mental life and too complex or fundamental to be tidily encapsulated in rigid formulas. The distinctive achievement of the book lies in the fact that Beauvoir succeeds in selecting aspects of this highly individual and enduring bond and writing about them in such a way that readers are drawn into her own particular experience without losing sight of its general significance and its similarity to features of their own lives.

La Cérémonie des adieux—the first part of a volume published at the end of 1981: *La Cérémonie des adieux, suivi de Entretiens avec Jean-Paul Sartre*—has obvious affinities with *Une Mort très douce,* in that it recounts the illness and death of someone very important to Beauvoir, in this case Sartre. Covering the period 1970-80, however, it is also a review of his political and literary activity at that time, as well as an account of the last years of their close association. Yet although there is no more than a slight chronological overlap with *Tout compte fait,* this is not a continuation of the memoirs, for much that happened to Beauvoir during these years (in relation, for instance, to her health, her travels, her writings) is either not registered at all, or referred to in only the most perfunctory way. Based upon a diary that Beauvoir kept and upon consultations with others involved, *La Cérémonie des adieux* is her only work centring exclusively on Sartre and the first written without him: 'Voici le premier de mes livres—le seul sans doute—que vous n'aurez pas lu avant qu'il ne soit imprimé. Il vous est tout entier consacré et ne vous concerne pas' (13). It is dedicated to 'ceux qui ont aimé Sartre, l'aiment, l'aimeront' and addressed to those who wish to know more about his final years.

Beauvoir's text is set out in eleven sections, each corresponding to a calendar year. Her account begins in 1970, when Sartre began to put into practice his new theory on the role of the intellectual ('le nouvel intellectuel cherche à se fondre dans la masse pour faire triompher la véritable universalité'; 15-16) by becoming editor of the newspaper *La Cause du peuple* and helping to found an organisation designed to

61

fight against the repression of the working classes. There is a fixed structure to each of the years described (except 1980), for Sartre and Beauvoir invariably made a point of going away for a long period in the summer (usually to Italy), and often for a while in the spring too. Even the time spent in Paris, dominated though it is by Sartre's political involvement and their journalistic and literary pursuits, is to some extent shaped by routines. Not only are there regular commitments throughout the period, like meetings of the editorial board of *Les Temps modernes,* at any given stage there is also a weekly routine whereby, for instance, Sartre spends two nights a week at Arlette's flat and five at Beauvoir's. Although Sartre's health problems begin in the autumn of 1970 (which is another reason why Beauvoir's narrative begins with that year), it is only from 1973 onwards, and particularly when Sartre becomes virtually blind, that different routines are required and that his physical state comes to be the central topic.

The way in which Beauvoir describes the gradual deterioration of Sartre's health will surprise no one who has read her other works with any care. Proceeding as she did in *Une Mort très douce,* she records with clinical precision the physical effects that a series of strokes have upon him and the side-effects of the medicaments that he takes. The 'objectivity' with which she talks, for example, of his incontinence or his messy eating is perfectly typical of the manner in which she deals with matters of the body in other writings, and can only be disapproved of by those who believe that certain topics should never be written about in any circumstances. She often draws touching conclusions from such symptoms (52) and far from diminishing Sartre in our eyes, this gives us a precise measure of the physical indignities he had to suffer and increases our admiration for his spirit. Furthermore, to speak of Beauvoir's 'detachment' in this connection would again be more misleading than helpful. Her suggestion in the Preface that she has not recorded her own emotional reactions (' "Ça ne peut pas se dire, ça ne peut pas s'écrire, ça ne peut pas se penser; ça se vit, c'est tout" '; 13) is inaccurate both because the work as a whole unmistakably expresses the profound anxiety and distress that she felt over Sartre's condition, and because there are a number of points at which she directly notes her anguish. Early on she says she has never experienced 'un tel sentiment d'absurdité et de déréliction' (35); she sometimes mentions that she cried throughout the night (87); she tells us at what point her anxiety gave way to despair (131); she describes a stage at which her own control came close to breaking down (134); and, of course, the final pages do nothing to disguise the devastating effect that Sartre's death had upon her.

Rather less easy to grasp is the nature or significance of Beauvoir's account of Sartre's political stance and activities during this period (his literary work as such was virtually confined to the completion of *L'Idiot de la famille,* about which she says nothing on her own behalf). *La Cérémonie des adieux* certainly constitutes a useful record of the militant campaigns pursued by the extreme Left in France between 1970 and 1980, and one is happy to accept her point that the diverse issues taken up by Sartre were clearly linked in his own mind (47). This aspect of the text, however, remains particularly unsatisfactory. Many a substantial paragraph giving the background details to some political affair or incident in which Sartre chose to involve himself is left simply hanging in the air, and for the last year or two Beauvoir resorts to providing brief lists of the appeals and letters that he signed. The very surprising point about *La Cérémonie des adieux* on the political level is that virtually everything that it tells us about Sartre's attitudes and activities was already registered in print in one form or another and therefore available as public knowledge. Beauvoir summarises views that he expressed in published lectures and reported press conferences; refers to letters to the press and prefaces that he wrote; quotes at length from interviews that he gave and from *On a raison de se révolter;* and so on.[1] Whereas in earlier works she drew on her intimate acquaintance with Sartre to furnish both new insights into his political thinking and fresh details concerning the personal side of his commitment, here she says astonishingly little that could not have been said by anyone assiduous enough to read all of the relevant items.

There seem to be a number of reasons for this feature of the book and they eventually raise the whole matter of the state of the relationship between Beauvoir and Sartre at this time. Part of the problem is that, as Sartre himself commented, Beauvoir was never inclined to throw herself into the business of day-to-day politics as he did ('elle ne veut pas participer à la cuisine politique').[2] It is perhaps inevitable, therefore, that many of her reports here should have a second-hand quality (very frequently she was simply not present at the meetings concerned) and even suggest a certain lack of interest on her part. It is also clear that Sartre's general political perspective changed very little during these years, once he had developed the concept of the 'new intellectual', so that there is less for Beauvoir to dwell upon than in previous periods. Nevertheless, even according to her own account, it seems that Sartre may have been somewhat modifying his views, or at least his emphasis, in the last year or two of his life, under the influence of young political thinkers like Philippe Gavi and, in particular, Pierre Victor (whose real name is Benny Lévy). And it is in this last connection that one begins to feel that perhaps not everything in the book can be taken at face value.

Beauvoir is open enough about the fact that relations between herself and Victor were broken off early in 1978 (140), and acknowledges that this introduced a new element into her relations with Sartre: 'Jusqu'alors, les vrais amis de Sartre avaient toujours été aussi les miens. Victor fut la seule exception . . . je regrettais qu'une partie de la vie de Sartre me fût désormais fermée' (140-41). It also has to be admitted that her explanation of why Sartre needed someone like Victor in the last stages of his life is a very plausible one (151). Yet once we are apprised of the situation that existed around Sartre, we are no longer likely to give automatic credence to all of Beauvoir's comments. When she suggests that he was rushed into signing a particular article by Victor (139-40), expresses harsh judgements on the latter (140), or fears that Sartre, under pressure, may be making too many concessions in discussions with him (148), we may now wish to keep an open mind on these matters. The conflict between Beauvoir and Victor came to a head over his interview with Sartre published in *Le Nouvel Observateur* only a week or two before Sartre's death.[3] Beauvoir took great exception to both the tone and the content of the interview, but again we may be inclined to treat her firm conviction that it does not express Sartre's real views at the time with some caution when we learn of his reaction to the news that she and the editorial team of *Les Temps modernes* were opposed to its publication: 'il n'en a mis que plus d'entêtement à faire paraître immédiatement l'entretien' (150)!

As Beauvoir suggests, her aversion to Victor (and that not until late on) is quite untypical of her reaction towards Sartre's close friends, most of whom during this period were women. If she experienced any feeling of jealousy towards Arlette, Liliane, Wanda or Mélina, she leaves no direct sign of this in the book. Not only does she discreetly stay away from Sartre on occasions when he wishes to see women-friends, there are also indications that the arrangements whereby he is regularly looked after by others too suit Beauvoir quite well. The case of Michèle Vian, however, is rather different and perhaps just enough, once more, to make us wonder whether all is exactly as it seems. Early on she notes that Michèle encourages Sartre to drink too much (although she herself appears to make only spasmodic efforts to have him obey doctor's orders), but there is a revealing incident in 1977, when Sartre becomes drunk on whisky supplied by Michèle. Beauvoir not only records her decision not to allow Michèle to look after him on Saturday evenings any more (!), but also asserts—without any reference to Sartre's own reactions or comments—that Michèle is wholly wrong in her belief that he wishes to 'mourir dans la gaieté' (128). Relatively trivial though this matter may be, seen in the context of Beauvoir's admissions that she cannot understand why Sartre wishes to drink to excess (50, 149), it gives us grounds for asking whether there may not be more possessiveness in her attitude, a rather more rigid determination to hang on to her own particular image of Sartre, than we might otherwise have supposed. There is something of a general difficulty about the accuracy of the snatches of dialogue recorded in La Cérémonie des adieux, in that Beauvoir can hardly be presumed to have written them down in her diary. But even allowing her some licence in this respect, it still seems that *some* of the comments by Sartre that she registers—' "Le reste, ça m'est égal. Mais ici, ça me plaît d'y être" ' (51); ' "Vous êtes une bonne *épouse*" ' (86); ' "Voilà mes vraies vacances qui vont commencer" ' (91)—are included largely in order to establish that she has a unique claim upon him, or conceivably to reassure herself that this is so.

Yet this is never a prominent feature of the book and a degree of possessiveness is not only excusable on Beauvoir's part, but also, perhaps, an inevitable concomitant of the love that leads her to produce such a moving account of Sartre's decline. For however odd an outsider may find certain aspects of their relationship, and in spite of a few discordant notes struck near the end, La Cérémonie des adieux is a monument to the strength of the bond between them. Beauvoir was clearly anxious to provide an accurate account of Sartre's activities and relationships during his final years, and while sometimes her attempts are convincing (as when she explains his exchange of letters with Giscard d'Estaing, or dismisses the alleged reconciliation with Aron), on other occasions they actually read like less than the whole truth (as in her treatment of Victor or Olivier Todd). But this is in any case the least significant part of the homage that the book pays to Sartre. Nowhere in her writings does Beauvoir make us *feel* more for him than here, and she achieves this very largely by selecting and simply recording facts that reflect his plight in various ways (his 'reading' of the same book on Greece over and over again; his very rare outbursts of frustration). Sartre's mental confusions and lapses of memory at one point (59-62) are described in a manner that strongly draws us to him, and the pathos of some of the circumstances evoked is overwhelming: 'Il tenait à la main un sac de plastique dans lequel j'avais rangé ses affaires de toilette. Il nous a regardées partir à travers un rideau de pluie et ses brumes à lui' (96). On the whole, however, it is the contrast between the state of his body and that of his spirit which Beauvoir renders so well and which leaves us feeling what a remarkable man he was. In his own distinctive way Sartre is irrepressible ('il a chantonné: "Je ne veux faire à mon Castor nulle peine même légère"'; 33), yet in showing this she manages at the same time to convey his extreme vulnerability, as well as her own consciousness of both sides of the coin.

The occasions when Beauvoir actually endeavours to interpret the course of events produce mixed results. She may well be justified in her belief that Sartre was deceiving himself about his eyesight, but her apparent surprise at this and the insistence with which she returns to the topic seem disproportionate. On the other hand, her general speculation about the last phase of his life— 'Sartre a eu le déclin et la mort qu'appelait sa vie. Et c'est pourquoi, peut-être, il les a si calmement acceptés' (133)—is cogent and thought-provoking. It would be quite wrong to imply that this aspect of the book is insignificant, for such analysis is a part of the whole and contributes something to the tone of the work. Nevertheless, it cannot be emphasised too strongly that *La Cérémonie des adieux*—like *Une Mort très douce*—makes its greatest impact where Beauvoir allows certain moments to convey without commentary the poignancy of the decline of someone she loved, or the depths of her own feelings. The book is scrappy and the writing, for the most part, wholly undistinguished. Yet some images of Sartre and many brief dialogues between them are so heart-rending, particularly with the weight of their fifty-year relationship behind them, that they eclipse all else. Beauvoir effaces herself just enough in *La Cérémonie des adieux* to permit the personality and stature of Sartre to emerge from the work with great force. But the book is a tribute that could only have been paid by someone as close to him as she was and, when all is said and done, we are as moved by her devotion and the dignity of their association as by anything that happened to Sartre himself: 'Sa mort nous sépare. Ma mort ne nous réunira pas. C'est ainsi; il est déjà beau que nos vies aient pu si longtemps s'accorder' (159).

Published with *La Cérémonie des adieux*, and taking up nearly three quarters of the 559-page volume, is the transcript of a series of interviews that Beauvoir conducted with Sartre in 1974: *Entretiens avec Jean-Paul Sartre*. When she suggested, in June of that year, that they should tape-record Sartre talking about his life and works, he agreed ('"Ça remédiera à ça", m'a-t-il dit en désignant son œil d'un geste bouleversant'; CA,95), conceiving the project as the only kind of continuation of his autobiographical *Les Mots* that his near-blindness would permit. The interviews began during their summer holiday in Rome, with Sartre taking part enthusiastically, except on certain days when he was tired or when the dialogue was uninspired. Back in Paris, they continued the process in late September and a secretary began transcribing the results at the end of the year (CA,97;101-02).

Beauvoir has not published all of the interviews ('j'ai supprimé les conversations qui m'ont paru sans intérêt'; 163) and has to some extent regrouped the selected ones according to subject-matter. From internal evidence, however, it seems that she has departed relatively little from the chronological order of the sessions, possibly extracting shorter sequences from rejected interviews and inserting them at the appropriate thematic point. There is a broad shape to the content of the discussions, which naturally begin by treating Sartre's schooldays and earliest literary attempts; his move from La Rochelle to Paris; and his early major works and fame. For some time the main thread is provided by the succession of literary and philosophical works produced by Sartre, but the conversations pass on to other topics, like travelling; his relations with men and with women; and his attitude towards his body. Inevitably (though perhaps with some reluctance), Beauvoir takes Sartre on from the concept of freedom to the subject of his involvement in politics. The interviews end, appositely, with sections where Sartre reflects on time, looks at his life as a whole, and talks of death as the end of everything.

The very length of these conversations is important, in that they cover a very wide range of aspects of Sartre's life and works. Moreover, being under no particular time constraint, Beauvoir is able to pursue topics or lines of questioning for as long as is necessary. Nevertheless, many of Sartre's major published works are scarcely touched upon here and virtually every subject raised is one that he has discussed elsewhere. In this sense Beauvoir is right to suggest that her interviews contain no unexpected revelations about him. In examining freedom, for instance, they go over ground already well charted in Beauvoir's memoirs and various other writings. Although we learn a little more about the growth of his socio-political awareness during the war, no new *philosophical* light is cast upon these or, indeed, any other issues, even if Sartre sometimes finds a fresh way of looking at matters or a slightly different way of formulating a point. There is no doubt, on the other hand, that the interviews add many a detail to what was previously known about his private life and personality. (Who but Beauvoir could have asked him directly when he first slept with a woman, or have known that he was so restive physically that his elbows wore holes in chairs?) Yet even on the personal level Sartre divulged a very great deal about himself in some of the dozens of other interviews that he gave over the years (including a number after 1974), apparently believing that 'chacun devrait pouvoir dire, devant un interviewer, le plus profond de soi'.[4] In short, Beauvoir's interviews are less exceptional in some respects than one might expect. The nature of their contents, in fact, varies very considerably from mundane information-swapping (for instance, about their travels) to personal avowals and highly abstract philosophising. And since she has made them readable without attempting to give them literary form, there are disjointed as well as sluggish sequences, repetitions, and even contradictions (163).

The unique interest of the conversations for students of Beauvoir, however, is that they show her in the guise of interviewer and, because the subject is Sartre, offer a slant on the key relationship of her life not provided by any of her other works. Occasionally, her interventions tell us something directly about her own ideas or development (her change of views on travelling; her reaction to Marx when she was eighteen; her views on socialism or old age), but she ensures that the main focus is always on Sartre, even to the extent of stopping him from talking about her specifically (390). Her inexperience as an interviewer shows in certain unnatural formulas that she adopts to keep the conversations moving ('Continuez à me parler de . . . '; 'Rêvez un peu sur tout ça'), yet her incomparable knowledge of Sartre also permits her to ask the most pertinent questions (she sometimes reminds him of points he has forgotten about his past), and not infrequently she finds a better or clearer way of expressing or summarising a point than Sartre's own. She structures the discussions quite firmly, but is extremely sensitive to his comments, and there is a remarkable freshness about her reactions to much of what he says, which has been noticed by those who have seen them together.

Sartre himself seems less sharp intellectually than in his interview with Michel Contat some six months later, but often here he gives the impression of 'trying out' certain ideas about his past, and this gives us an invaluable glimpse of the way in which his discussions with Beauvoir regularly proceeded throughout his career: 'Je lui ai exposé toutes mes idées quand elles étaient en voie de formation'.[5] Beauvoir for her part is never reluctant to register surprise, doubt or disagreement in connection with his assertions, but always one has a strong feeling that she is hoping for, and expecting, complete agreement, once the matter has been discussed further. This is doubtless why she is so persistent in following up or returning to certain points, even where Sartre displays resistance. In some measure she may be seen as trying to persuade Sartre to confirm or accept an image of himself that is her own (he is a writer-philosopher rather than a man of politics; he took as much account of philosophy as of literature from the first; and so on), but this is not especially intrusive in interviews that Sartre was happy to see as a joint enterprise ('Mais non, on parle ensemble, c'est une période qu'on a vécue ensemble'; 300) and which he regarded as recording a genuine exchange of views: 'On discutait . . . ça se rapprochait d'un dialogue où chacun avait sa personnalité'.[6] To the extent that his assessment of the interviews is accurate, readers are able for once to come as close as print will permit to observing for themselves the nature and tone of the intellectual interaction that took place between Beauvoir and Sartre over more than fifty years.

In *La Cérémonie des adieux* the implication is that the interviews were broken off because Sartre (like Beauvoir) became heavily involved in preparations for his projected television series, although elsewhere Beauvoir has suggested that it was because he was far more interested in his work with Pierre Victor.[7] In any case, the reason why no attempt was made to publish them during Sartre's lifetime seems to be that Beauvoir at least believed that they were unsuccessful because she and Sartre knew each other too well, whereas interviewers need to have detachment from their subject. Her reasons for wishing to see the conversations published in 1981 are clearly connected with Sartre's death and some of the incidents of his final years. When Sartre's near-blindness came to prevent him from writing, interviews with him clearly assumed great importance. As we have seen, Beauvoir was particularly unhappy about the interview with Victor published just before Sartre died. Her purpose here, therefore, as in *La Cérémonie des adieux*, is largely to put the record straight, to show the *genuine* Sartre near the end of his life. There is much justification for her claim that her interviews, without forcing or distorting his views, enable us to 'suivre les méandres de sa pensée et . . . entendre sa voix vivante' (163). At the same time, both scrutiny of certain facts recorded in *La Cérémonie des adieux* and comparison of these interviews with others that Sartre gave in the seventies show that he had *other* ways of thinking and speaking too. It is a little sad, though entirely under-standable, that Beauvoir should apparently have been unwilling to recognise that the face that Sartre presented to her was, however well she may have known it, only one of the many faces of one of the most creative thinkers and colourful characters of her generation. But fortunately this does little to detract from her achievement in pro-viding a memorable record of the Sartre she knew.

Notes

1   In fact, there are remarkable similarities of wording between Beauvoir's work and the text of 'Les écrits de Sartre (1973-78)' by Michel Contat and Michel Rybalka (in *Obliques*). It is conceivable, though unlikely, that the authors worked from Beauvoir's notes (they had no need to do so, and do not mention doing so). What is more probable is that Beauvoir used this article as the single most convenient source of details about Sartre's publications and political activities, only to find herself transcribing phrases and quotations on a significant scale.

2   '"Sartre talks of Beauvoir", interview by Madeleine Gobeil', *Vogue*, 1965 (reprinted in French in S. Julienne-Caffié: *Simone de Beauvoir*, p.41).

3   'L'Espoir, maintenant', *Le Nouvel Observateur*, 1980.

4   ' "Autoportrait à soixante-dix ans". Entretien avec Michel Contat',
    Le Nouvel Observateur, 1975 (reprinted in Sartre's *Situations X*,
    p. 141).

5   ibid., p. 190.

6   'Entretien avec Simone de Beauvoir et Jean-Paul Sartre' by Michel
    Sicard, *Obliques*, p. 329.

7   ibid.

PART II
Essays

4 Moral Essays

Beauvoir records in *La Force de l'âge* that when war broke out in 1939 and the world became chaotic, she began to seek reasons for undergoing the experience that was in fact imposed upon her from outside. She duly found such justifications in the ideas of fellowship, responsibility and dying for a cause, but had to *force* herself to think in terms of abstract formulas of this type:

> Ainsi entrai-je dans ce que je pourrais appeler la 'période morale' de ma vie littéraire qui se prolongea pendant quelques années. Je ne prenais plus ma spontanéité pour règle; je fus donc amenée à m'interroger sur mes principes et mes buts; et, après quelques hésitations, j'allai jusqu'à composer un essai sur la question. (FA,626)

In fact, in the period 1944-48 Beauvoir published two novels and a play (all with a heavy moral orientation), two separate essays on ethics, and a collection of four articles tracing the implications of existentialism in specific areas.

When she was invited, early in 1943, to write a philosophical piece, she at first refused, seeing nothing to add to Sartre's *L'Être et le Néant*. Having just completed *Le Sang des autres*, however, she recognised that she still had something to say on some of the questions raised in it, particularly on the relationship between the individual's experience and reality in general, and she agreed to write on this theme. She took three months over *Pyrrhus et Cinéas,* completing it in July. When Gallimard brought it out in September 1944, immediately after the Liberation of Paris, it was Beauvoir's first essay and, following *L'Invitée*, only her second published work of any kind.

She uses the figures of Pyrrhus and Cinéas to represent, respectively, the spontaneous, adventurous, active, and the wise, restrained, passive attitudes to life, asking in her introduction what limits it is appropriate for human beings to assign to their actions: 'Quelle est donc la mesure d'un homme? Quels buts peut-il se proposer, et quels espoirs lui sont permis?' (237). The body of the essay is divided into two parts and in the first she finds fault with a number of philosophical attempts to define the goal and range of people's actions and responsibilities. She argues that nothing is decided in advance, that we *choose* our own way of relating to the external world, as well as our relations with others. Because of our very nature, however, it is not possible for us to settle for the present moment, for immobility or abstention: we are forever on the move, forever transcending the present through projects that we have freely chosen to adopt. But neither is it possible for us to identify with everything and to be everywhere, to lose ourselves in the universal or the eternal, since as individuals we cannot deny our own particular existence or escape completely from the world that our presence reveals. This situation creates a dilemma on both the theoretical and the practical levels:

> on retrouve dans l'ordre de l'action la même antinomie que dans l'ordre de la spéculation: tout arrêt est impossible puisque la transcendance est un perpétuel dépassement; mais un projet indéfini est absurde puisqu'il n'aboutit à rien. (267)

Recourse to God is of no avail, according to Beauvoir, for it is always we as individuals who have to interpret God's will and this leaves us not only in the same dilemma as before, but also with Kierkegaard's 'anguish of Abraham': 'Dieu s'il existait serait donc impuissant à guider la transcendance humaine' (276). Is Humanity itself, then, not an absolute, an end towards which our transcendence could and should be directed? The difficulty here is that it is not possible to act on behalf of all people at the same time, for to serve some is to obstruct others: 'Si je sers le prolétariat, je combats le capitalisme; le soldat ne défend son pays qu'en tuant ses adversaires' (282-83). Because human beings are free, furthermore, their future attitude towards anything that we may do in their name is entirely unpredictable and cannot provide a reliable guide for our actions: 'Nobel croyait travailler pour la science: il travaillait pour la guerre' (286). In short, whatever individuals choose to take as their aim or objective will, if achieved, become no more than the starting-point for some other human project. It is not death that is at the source of human anguish, 'c'est, au cœur de ma vie, la négativité qui me permet de transcender sans cesse toute transcendance' (299). If a person were alone in the world, he or she might well be paralysed by the ultimate futility of all projects, but no one lives in complete isolation.

Beauvoir begins the second part of her essay by considering whether as individuals we should not devote our lives to someone else. But even assuming that we are not simply attempting to impose our own wishes upon the other person concerned, we still have to exercise our own judgement in order to interpret what that person really wants, and this involves uncertainty and risk. We can only ever act on the external conditions of other people's lives: we can never actually fulfil their projects *for* them, any more than we can stop them having those specific projects. Yet we each exist as part of the world of others and since we cannot avoid intervening in their lives, we have to choose particular ways of relating to them. There are no ready-made values to which we can refer, so that what we do is good only in so far as others freely recognise it as good, although this is not exactly to say that we do it *for* either others or ourselves:

> Ainsi ce n'est pas *pour* autrui que chacun se transcende; on écrit des livres, on invente des machines qui n'étaient réclamées nulle part; ce n'est pas non plus *pour* soi, car 'soi' n'existe que par le projet même qui le jette dans le monde; le fait de la transcendance précède toute fin, toute justification. (339)

We do need others, however, in order to escape from the contingency or gratuitousness of our existence. It is essential to us that our projects be confirmed and prolonged by the free choice of some of our peers.

Since I cannot *force* others to ratify my own choices, I can only *appeal* to them to do so (358). Nevertheless, I must be able to make such appeals and I should be prepared to use violence, if necessary, in order to preserve this possibility. Similarly, I must do everything in my power to ensure that others are themselves free and able to respond to my appeals: 'Je demande pour les hommes la santé, le savoir, le bien-être, le loisir, afin que leur liberté ne se consume pas à combattre la maladie, l'ignorance, la misère' (361). Using violence to achieve any of these ends is a mark of irremediable failure, but we have no option but to act and accept failure as one of the concomitants of all action: 'C'est dans l'incertitude et le risque qu'il faut assumer nos actes' (365). Cinéas's cynical attitude frees us from the illusion of false objectivity, reminding us that 'il n'y a d'autre fin au monde que mes fins, d'autre place que celle que je me creuse' (366). But Pyrrhus is right to believe that this does not invalidate all human projects: the point of view of eternity, from which such a general judgement would have to be made, is of no relevance to human beings, who are *situated* in the world and choose their own ends accordingly.

For the most part, *Pyrrhus et Cinéas* is an extremely lively and very readable essay, which proceeds at a brisk pace and clearly displays the energy and range of knowledge of its author. The philosophical argument that it develops is, in itself, a highly general and abstract one, yet the text contains numerous references to the works of philosophers and illustrations or examples taken from literature, personal experience, even sometimes the world of science. There are a few turgid passages, but Beauvoir's question-and-answer presentation and certain stylistic devices—Part II begins on a dramatic and intriguing note—retain our interest throughout. To some extent, the essay can be regarded as a popularisation of existentialism, for this was just the moment at which atheistic French existentialism was about to come into the public eye and needed to be explained. Beauvoir relies quite heavily, making no attempt to disguise the fact, upon views she considers to have been established in Sartre's *L'Être et le Néant,* and her general view of humanity visibly owes everything to him. Yet relatively few technical philosophical points are made in *Pyrrhus et Cinéas*: Beauvoir takes Sartre's metaphysical framework for granted and dwells upon the moral implications that may be drawn from it. The reception accorded to the essay and the popularity of existentialism in the post-war years suggest that, in emphasising our freedom to choose or create our own values, she was saying just what many French people wished to hear immediately after the Liberation.

Nevertheless, the essay needs to be judged by philosophical standards and the rigour of Beauvoir's argument, as well as the quality of some of her conclusions, leaves a great deal to be desired. One central flaw attaches to her handling of the concept of transcendence. If it is of the very essence of human beings, metaphysically, that they are engaged in projects, forever reaching beyond themselves ('l'homme est transcendance'; 257), then they will be transcending themselves however 'active' *or* 'passive' their way of life may be. As Beauvoir herself acknowledges at one or two points, reflection itself is transcendence (256), so that this latter concept, in fact, provides no criterion for making a sharp distinction between the attitudes of Pyrrhus and Cinéas. In short, the striking, 'literary' presentation of her argument and the fundamental ambiguity of 'transcendance'—is it an intrinsic feature of all human life or merely a rough measure of the extent to which different human beings circulate in the world and make a positive attempt to manipulate it?—only thinly disguise the fact that Beauvoir is simply making particular judgements about conduct and recommending certain attitudes towards other people.

There are grave weaknesses, too, in these judgements and attitudes themselves. Why, in an attempt in Part II to find a positive basis for morality, Beauvoir should dwell at length on the concept of devotion, only to condemn it, remains unclear. In any case, the conclusion that she draws at this point—that there is ultimately nothing we can do either for or against other people, though how we treat them matters *to us* (325-28)—is a dubious one by any standard. In 1960 she acknowledged this by admitting that in her essay 'la coexistence apparaît comme une espèce d'accident que devrait surmonter chaque existant' (FA,628-29). But the real objection to her view in *Pyrrhus et Cinéas* is not, as she suggests, its failure to recognise that society envelops us from birth. It is that the recommendation that we should promote the development, health and well-being of others only be-cause we *need* them to be free to validate our own choices— 'Le respect de la liberté d'autrui n'est pas une règle abstraite: il est la condition première du succès de mon effort' (358)—has nothing at all to do with ethics, but is a matter of prudence or self-interest. The moral bank-ruptcy of such a position comes out strongly when we remember that Beauvoir is in some measure defending violence in this text ('J'avais compris aussi qu'au sein d'un monde en lutte tout projet est une option et qu'il faut—comme Blomart dans *Le Sang des autres*— consentir à la violence'; FA,627), for she can only urge restraint in its use because such restraint is in our own interests: 'l'homme que je violente n'est pas mon pair, et j'ai besoin que les hommes soient mes pairs' (362). There is clearly something wrong with this stance and she was eventually to undergo a fundamental change of view on the matter.

All of this raises some quite basic questions about Beauvoir's definition of morality and the criteria that she is in a position to adopt in order to distinguish good from bad, right from wrong. Like Sartre, she is sometimes obliged to admit that ultimately she has no grounds for preferring one project to another (300). But this is not a satis-factory point from which to set out to write an essay on ethics. In spite of Beauvoir's disclaimer at the end of Part I, to the effect that she is not concerned with the *content* of human projects but only with the general and formal conditions of their existence, we are left with the impression that there is an odd disproportion between the accuracy and weight of her attacks on certain attitudes—in 1960 she still found this part of her essay 'très sommaire, mais juste' (FA,628)—and the flimsiness of her positive moral prescriptions. In any case, she herself makes particular moral judgements in the text—effectively saying, for example, that an active life is better than a passive one—without making it clear how they are to be justified. The richness of her material and the vigour of her writing should not blind us to this, and perhaps in the end they only point up the fact that in *Pyrrhus et Cinéas* Beauvoir has not yet come close to solving the problem of the basis of a non-believer's morality.

She was soon to tackle this question rather more directly and systematically in *Pour une morale de l'ambiguïté*. After giving a lecture in February 1945 she found herself claiming that 'on pouvait fonder une morale sur *L'Être et le Néant* si l'on convertissait le vain désir d'être en une assomption de l'existence', and a year later she took up the challenge to do so (FCh,98). She spent some six months over her second major essay, which is nearly twice as long as *Pyrrhus et Cinéas* and appeared first in instalments in *Les Temps modernes*, then as a book in November 1947.

In the first section Beauvoir starts from the familiar Sartrean point that the human condition is ambiguous, in that we are both body and consciousness: through our inner experiences we enjoy an obvious independence, yet we are also objects among other objects and can be seriously affected, even crushed, by the external world. What matters is that we should not blind ourselves to this dual situation but face up to it: 'Essayons d'assumer notre fondamentale ambiguïté' (13). There is no justification for human life either beyond or prior to existence, but we can and do give ourselves reasons for living. Beauvoir espouses Sartre's view that we cannot *be*, in the manner of God, but she argues that the very attempt enables us to *exist* as human beings. The question of whether there is any point to life is a senseless one: people have simply to decide whether they wish to go on living and on what conditions. She goes on to counter a number of objections to this general view, claiming that existentialism implies neither subjectivism nor solipsism, but recognises that cooperation between people is feasible and desirable. She also shows how, in spite of their commitment to dialectical materialism, Marxists too are obliged to accept that people make free choices.

Belief in human freedom, in fact, far from leading to moral anarchy or despair, is said to produce a principle that has universal validity. Freedom is the source of all meaning, of all values, and a necessary condition of any justification of human existence:

> l'homme qui cherche à justifier sa vie doit vouloir avant tout et absolument la liberté elle-même: en même temps qu'elle exige la réalisation de fins concrètes, de projets singuliers, elle s'exige universellement. (33)

We cannot deny or refuse our freedom without thereby proving its reality, and it is the patience, courage and consistency with which we pursue our projects that confirm their value and the authenticity of our choices. This being so, we are committed to rejecting and overcoming any constraints that would limit our freedom to persist in our aims over a period of time (44). Hence freedom is not a given, static state but one that we must constantly work to maintain; it is a permanent process of liberation. For Beauvoir, however, 'evil' is a reality too, because of the phenomenon of 'mauvaise foi', whereby some people, unable to face their freedom, deceive themselves about their true condition.

In Part II Beauvoir discusses the situation of children, arguing that there is an arbitrary side to the original attitude that adolescents adopt towards their freedom, since their choices are made on the basis of the contingent circumstances of their upbringing and only later find justification, in the context of their adult lives. Nonetheless, she considers it possible to talk of different *categories* of original choice and to establish a kind of hierarchy among them. Accordingly, she undertakes a series of cautionary descriptions or 'portraits' of significant types, who display the different forms of 'mauvaise foi' set out at the end of the first section. At the very bottom of the ladder, for instance, is 'le sous-homme', who fails to project himself into the world with any enthusiasm or firmness at all: 'Cette apathie manifeste une peur fondamentale devant l'existence, devant les risques et la tension qu'elle implique' (62). This attitude is no more than a short stage away from that of 'l'homme sérieux', who tries to cast off the burden of freedom by claiming that there are absolute values over which we exercise no power of choice whatever. Yet he really knows that this is not so and the truth frequently catches up with him: 'Alors éclate l'absurdité d'une vie qui a cherché en dehors d'elle les justifications qu'elle seule pouvait se donner' (75). This in turn can produce one of the outlooks characteristic of nihilists, who 'souhaitent se délivrer de l'inquiétude de leur liberté en niant le monde et eux-mêmes' (76), and in certain circumstances go on to embrace doctrines like Dadaism, surrealism and Nazism.

Adventurers, on the other hand, see the importance of freedom and throw themselves with great vitality into some enterprise or other for its own sake. They are lucid about the world and theirs is very close to an authentically moral attitude. They do not respect the freedom of others, however, but use them as instruments in affirming their own individuality. Consequently, they are unable to see their projects prolonged and confirmed by the recognition and admiration of other people: their mistake lies in believing that 'on peut quelque chose pour soi sans les autres et même contre eux' (91). In some respects passionate people share this fault, for, living in their own world, they constitute an obstacle to those seeking 'une communion des libertés'. Again, some thinkers, artists and writers react to the difficulties of carrying out projects by trying to withdraw into some kind of eternal sphere, where they can overcome the ambiguity of the human condition. But there is no escape from the real world. As in *Pyrrhus et Cinéas* Beauvoir argues that we all *need* others: 'l'homme ne peut trouver que dans l'existence des autres hommes une justification de sa propre existence' (103-04). And since we need the people around us to be free, existentialist morality, far from being an empty or merely formal doctrine, gives us concrete tasks of liberation to perform.

Beauvoir devotes the long third section of her work to the real difficulties posed by human relations. She quickly dismisses the 'aesthetic' attitude, which consists in looking down on the world with lofty detachment and arguing that, as human beings are free in any circumstances whatever, we need not concern ourselves with the present condition of other people. In fact, we are all firmly situated in the world and must seek freedom for ourselves and others in specific circumstances. But since material obstacles to our projects are simply part of the nature of the world, only human beings can be the real enemies of other human beings. (At this point, of course, Beauvoir's view looks rather different from that propounded in *Pyrrhus et Cinéas*.) Oppression is a reality and produces a whole category of people who are condemned to 'piétiner sans espoir, pour entretenir seulement la collectivité' (120); their life is mere repetition of mechanical gestures and they have only sufficient leisure to recover their strength.

Beauvoir accepts the Marxist position that the attitude of the proletariat has first to be defined negatively: it wishes to abolish itself as a class. And liberations of this kind are in the interests of all, being carried out 'pour que des possibilités neuves s'ouvrent à l'esclave libéré et à travers lui à tous les hommes' (125). Naturally, liberation is a matter of greater urgency for some than for others, but people cannot fulfil themselves morally without working against oppression, and we should each do so in whatever way our own particular situation renders most appropriate. We must not be swayed by oppressors' arguments to the effect that they are conserving the achievements of the past, any more than we should accept that they are working for future generations. It is true that if oppressors need to be overcome in some way, then to that extent it is impossible to respect *everyone's* freedom at the same time, but oppression must at all costs be rejected. Nevertheless, Beauvoir acknowledges that the implications of treating some human beings as objects need to be pondered. For one thing, circumstances will often dictate action, perhaps violent action, not only against oppressors themselves, but also against those who serve them, whether they do so from choice, out of ignorance, or under constraint. Even worse is the fact that we may need to sacrifice ourselves and our friends in the course of the struggle. There is no way of escaping the paradox that 'aucune action ne peut se faire pour l'homme sans se faire aussitôt contre des hommes' (143), but we must strongly resist any temptation to believe that an individual human life is worth little. To urge the subordination of the individual to the collectivity is self-defeating: 'si l'individu n'est rien, la société ne saurait être quelque chose' (152). It is precisely because individuals have a 'valeur singulière et irréductible' that any sacrifice they may make is so weighty, any violence perpetrated upon them such a serious matter. Yet freedom is always the overriding aim, since individuals deprived of their transcendence are nothing (166). In this sense, the difficult choices that we have to make essentially involve reference to the future, which is 'le sens et la substance même de l'action' (166).

However, the idea of a future state of harmony in which human beings will no longer have opposed views, no longer be in dispute, is at the very best a vague and uncertain dream, which provides no kind of justification for our present acts. The future that must constitute an indispensable feature of our terms of reference is a human finite future. Just as society cannot be important if the individual is insignificant, so we lose the present altogether if we engage in an indefinite pursuit of the future. On the moral level, this implies that the end may justify the means, but only if the end is never lost sight of, and if the means do not contradict it while they are being adopted. Not all of our goals have to be short-term or even medium-term ones, but in every case they must be absolute, and not ones that we claim will be justified only by events in the still more distant future: 'Les tâches que nous nous proposons . . . doivent trouver leur sens en elles-mêmes et non dans une fin mythique de l'Histoire' (185).

The different moments of our actions, then, mutually confirm and justify one another, provided we ensure that they are not in contradiction. There are situations in which we can maintain the coherence of our actions only by making them negative (as with the Resistance in occupied France), but when the time comes for reconstruction, the antinomies and problems of action reappear. All that we can do is to remain fully aware of them and keep our positions under constant review:

> En posant ses fins, la liberté doit les mettre entre parenthèses, les confronter à chaque moment avec cette fin absolue qu'elle constitue elle-même et contester en son propre nom les moyens dont elle use pour se conquérir. (193)

The individual as such is one of the central concerns of existentialist morality in general, yet even this can create difficulties, for while we are reluctant to watch people visibly harming themselves in some way, all human beings have the right to make their own judgements about their lives and even their own mistakes. The guiding principle is that we should allow others to seek and maintain freedom in their own way, but no detailed moral code exists and we have to find a new solution in each particular case, accepting the uncertainty involved. Inevitably, there are similar ambiguities when we are obliged to choose between one collectivity and another, between the freedom of one group and that of another. We can only weigh everything in the balance, decide, and accept responsibility for the risks entailed. We should never make such decisions lightly or precipitately, and should try to ensure that we are preventing more harm than we are inflicting. There is no legitimate way of escaping 'la fatigante tension exigée par l'existentialisme' (220), for constant vigilance and self-questioning are indispensable.

Pour une morale de l'ambiguïté is a more specialised and considerably less lively work than Pyrrhus et Cinéas. Beauvoir makes little obvious effort to popularise her views and includes fairly detailed sequences on, for instance, Marxist theory and Hegelian dialectics, which have the effect of slowing down her central argument. Equally, relatively little care appears to have been taken over the presentation of the material as such: one is conscious of repetition, and some sections—even the essay as a whole—are badly lacking in the tightness and shape that characterise a strong philosophical argument. Again, while certain parts of the work contain numerous illustrations of her points, drawn from personal life, politics or literature, others are extremely abstract and dry. A particular disappointment is the series of 'portraits' that dominates Part II. Beauvoir was right to acknowledge later that 'mes portraits ne se situent à aucun niveau de la réalité' and to consider them more arbitrary and more abstract than those of Hegel (FCh,99), for she fails either to bring these types to life or to convince us that there are good philosophical reasons for analysing them. This, together with her obvious tendency to over-schematise, makes Part II by far the least satisfactory section of the essay.

Since, inevitably, the first part is largely introductory—setting out the problems, giving a particular gloss to L'Être et le Néant, establishing certain general principles—and since Beauvoir seriously loses her way in the second, much hinges on the quality of the substantial third part of the work, which is in fact very uneven. As one might expect, she writes especially persuasively about the value of the individual human life (144-48)—a theme or an emphasis that has never ceased to appeal, to young people in particular, since the advent of existentialism. Unfortunately, this plea is set in the context of a general discussion of oppression that is much less convincing, if only because she makes no attempt to distinguish between different kinds of oppression and therefore necessarily weakens her case. One of the valuable features of the essay, as she herself was to note, is that it avoids naïve appeals to 'human solidarity' in general and recognises quite clearly that struggling against one oppression may involve neglecting, and thereby in a sense supporting, another. Nevertheless, Beauvoir does not explain clearly how this can be consistent with the idea that in defending freedom we are somehow working for all people, and in any case the text gives us precious little help on the question of which oppressions to resist, when we have to choose. In a singularly unsuccessful section, 'Le présent et l'avenir' (166-85), she manifestly fails to establish the basis of a distinction crucial to her argument: that between the Utopian future on which it is foolish to rely and the 'finite' future which is the very sense and substance of action. (The point that we *need* to have our projects prolonged and confirmed by others in the future is no more substantiated in this text than it was in *Pyrrhus et Cinéas*.)

The uneven quality of Part III stems directly from the general nature of *Pour une morale de l'ambiguïté* as a whole. In her determination to counter the objection commonly levelled at existentialism from the very first, that it can provide no positive, concrete content for morality, Beauvoir presses her attempt to formulate its precepts too far, with the paradoxical result that some of her key assertions in the constructive parts of her essay are intolerably vague and general, if not meaningless.[1] In some cases, though by no means all, this is bound up with her failure to distinguish between different senses of 'freedom' (for example, between the 'metaphysical' freedom that is the opposite of determinism, and political freedom from oppression), and her consequent need to emphasise the concept of liberation, which does not apply to all of those senses. The result hardly produces an existentialist ethic that is specific: 'il n'y a de libération de l'homme que si, en se visant, la liberté s'accomplit absolument dans le fait même de se viser' (189)! More generally, the notion of facing up to and 'assuming' our condition is a highly nebulous one and throughout the essay its converse, 'mauvaise foi', is badly conflated with simple error, self-contradiction and other faults, in a way that seriously undermines its use as the critical criterion for picking out those moral attitudes that are to be condemned.[2] It will be clear to most readers that Beauvoir is considerably better at raising moral questions than at answering them. The frequency with which she returns, from slightly different angles, to certain crucial problems (Exactly *whom* should we help? *When* does the end justify the means?) makes it apparent that she has no firm, useful solutions to offer. And when she does list virtues or flaws (36, 38, 199), or hint that a particular quality is especially important (like 'chaleur vivante'; 61), no logical justification is provided for her preferences. She herself came to see at least some of these weaknesses, for she was to acknowledge the hollowness of her results in 1963 and suggest that her approach was wrong:

> dans l'ensemble j'ai pris beaucoup de peine pour poser de travers une question à laquelle j'ai donné une réponse aussi creuse que les maximes kantiennes . . . Il était aberrant de prétendre définir une morale en dehors d'un contexte social. (FCh, 99)

She is probably right to believe that, given her premisses, any general account of morality would have somehow to start from society rather than from the individual (although there seems no reason to suppose, as she does, that this necessarily entails a philosophy of history). To this extent, as the only substantial published attempt to deduce ethical principles and definite practical consequences from the metaphysical foundations of French atheist existentialism—Sartre himself having failed to complete the treatise on morality promised in *L'Être et le Néant*—*Pour une morale de l'ambiguïté* may be regarded as a failure. Yet this would be an unduly harsh judgement on a work that can be looked at in other ways and seen as having rather different merits. Perhaps instead of deploring its failure to offer detailed moral precepts, we should acknowledge its success in establishing the impossibility of doing so. For in various ways Beauvoir makes out an excellent case for her view that 'la morale, pas plus que la science et l'art, ne fournissent des recettes. On peut proposer seulement des méthodes' (194). Part I, of course, stresses how individuals have to make their own moral judgements without recourse to pre-existing standards, and it is undoubtedly a virtue of Part III that in 'Les antinomies de l'action' and 'L'ambiguïté' Beauvoir reminds us in the most forceful manner of the unique difficulties associated with moral problems or dilemmas. When she exercises her capacity for illustrating these difficulties by reference to particular cases and for making fine discriminations between one situation and another, her comments constitute outstandingly strong grounds for avoiding ethical generalisations wherever possible and going as far as we can towards treating each case on its merits. The pity is only that she allows herself to ignore these grounds elsewhere in her text.

At its best, then, *Pour une morale de l'ambiguïté* sheds light on the nature of morality as such, on the experience of being a moral agent, even if it rarely tells us exactly what to do. And in this connection, here as in her other writings and those of Sartre, although the concept of 'mauvaise foi' may be incapable of doing all that is asked of it, and although there are occasions on which it is badly abused in a variety of ways (Beauvoir does not always avoid the blatant offence of claiming that those who do not agree with her own views are 'de mauvaise foi'; 22-23, 212), the merciless probing of conduct and motives and the ferreting out of all forms of self-deception can scarcely be other than salutary. They help us to guard against imposture in others, as well as moral complacency in ourselves, and encourage the belief that ethical positions need to be kept under constant review—a view very much more in tune with the times than any assumption that there is a detailed moral code having universal validity.

The four essays collected in *L'Existentialisme et la sagesse des nations,* published in 1948, were first printed in *Les Temps modernes* and actually pre-date *Pour une morale de l'ambiguïté.* They are, however, best examined after the longer text, since in the process of treating rather more specific topics, they presuppose the general view of human beings and morality that it sets out, without systematically formulating that view in any detail ('Ils ne cherchent pas à définir une fois de plus l'existentialisme . . .'; 11). In a brief preface to the collection Beauvoir claims that most attacks on existentialism are mounted on the grounds that philosophy in general is too abstract. Yet life and philosophy are one, for human freedom necessarily implies questioning and choice, so that no one can escape responsibility for the justification of beliefs held.

In the first essay, 'L'Existentialisme et la sagesse des nations', she takes up the suggestion that existentialism is a particularly gloomy philosophy which fails to recognise 'la grandeur de l'homme'. Drawing on proverbs, common sayings, poems, the lyrics of popular songs, and even the mottoes that one finds at the bottom of certain dishes, as well as on the writings of great Christian and secular thinkers, she first shows how these sources yield a deeply pessimistic view of humanity. There is also, however, a very different view implicit in sentimental songs, heroic films and novels, epitaphs, funeral orations, inscriptions and the sort of texts and anecdotes used to instruct children. Human beings here are seen to be noble, patient, courageous, disinterested, spirited, and so on. These two conceptions of human nature, Beauvoir argues, are irreconcilable, yet people are happy to live with these contradictions. Indeed, their first objection to existentialism is that it is a coherent and organised system (34). Existentialism is in fact an optimistic philosophy, which claims that 'l'homme est seul et souverain maître de son destin si seulement il veut l'être' (38). And this is exactly why it disturbs people, for determinism is a comforting doctrine, in that it takes the burden of responsibility from their shoulders. Yet the truth is the truth and it is wasteful for people to go on trying to hide it from themselves. It is liberating for them to become clearly aware of their real situation in the world.

Although the essay needs to be seen against the background of some strong opposition to existentialism in France at the time, it is a badly flawed piece that does little to help the case of Sartre and Beauvoir. For one thing, it is far from clear exactly whom, or what views Beauvoir herself is attacking. The opening suggests that it could be either philosophical commentators or 'leurs lecteurs', or both. But it soon becomes apparent that her target is 'les hommes' or 'les gens' in general, with their adherence to the dismal tenets of conventional wisdom. Yet one is not inclined to accept that some of the attitudes that she discusses—for instance, on Hitler (19), or on love (22)—are adopted by a significant number of people. Doubtless, one could find someone to subscribe to each of the gloomy or cynical beliefs that she lists, but only rarely do they come together in one individual. In a curious change of direction in the middle of the essay Beauvoir seems to recognise this, for having strongly implied that there *are* such people, she now argues that they also believe in the nobility of human beings, so that it is self-contradiction that characterises their general stance. There seems to be no sound reason, however, for accusing those who believe that people are sometimes bad and sometimes good of self-contradiction. And even if there were, this would not constitute grounds for charging them with 'mauvaise foi', which becomes Beauvoir's central accusation towards the end of the essay. Here as elsewhere there is a need to resist her tendency to claim that those whose views differ from her own are not simply in error or self-contradiction, but are actually deluding themselves in order to escape their freedom. This will undoubtedly be so in *some* cases and, indeed, the best of the essay may well lie in the way in which it exposes the inauthenticity of *one* type of attitude towards freedom. Yet to suggest, as Beauvoir does, that this attitude is very widespread is, precisely, to adopt a view of people in general that is quite as pessimistic as those that she is hoping to refute!

In 'Idéalisme moral et réalisme politique' Beauvoir attempts to describe the current form of the conflict between moral idealists, who believe in eternal principles, and political realists, who are prepared to use any means necessary to defend the interests of the community. Faced with increasingly complex issues, people are afraid of their freedom and take refuge in one of these two opposed attitudes, attacking those who try to reconcile ethics and politics. Yet traditional morality, with its reliance on abstract ideals like Justice, Rights, Truth, is rapidly being discredited. It is so rarefied that one is bound to wonder whether efficacity does not override all of its vague demands. There is no doubt an element of idealism in the position of political realists, since they want to bring into being something as yet unrealised, but they believe their ends to be achievable and not utopian. The problem lies, Beauvoir argues, in knowing what is and is not utopian. Political realists will tend to underestimate and conceal the power and scope of their own freedom, claiming to adopt a wholly objective stance, while in fact making their own decisions about what it is right to seek to do (80). Morality is a free commitment that requires constant renewal or reappraisal and this accounts for 'le profond malaise dont souffre la conscience des hommes d'aujourd'hui' (83). But authentic morality is realistic, since it enables people to realise themselves in achieving the ends they have chosen. Indeed, morality and politics are inextricably linked: people must abandon the pure subjectivity of the traditional moralist as well as the alleged objectivity of the political realist, accepting that living in the real world involves 'la souillure, l'échec, l'horreur' (86), but nevertheless 'assuming' their freedom.

In spite of the fact that within the broadly dialectical structure of the argument much more space is devoted to the political realist than to the moral idealist, the essay says nothing specific at all about politics in the narrow sense. It could certainly be argued that we have no right to expect guidance on particular political issues from the essay, yet this does leave Beauvoir open to the charge that her own assertions afford no more help in practical situations than she sees traditional morality as providing. Some of her own observations are so abstract that they beg all of the important questions. And once more her inclination to see every attitude she disapproves of as a refusal to accept freedom—as well as her serious failure to distinguish between lies and self-deception (71)—leads her to group together cases that should be kept apart. Her approach apparently precludes the possibility of lucid and sincere realism, which is an absurd conclusion and one that causes us to ask to what extent the attitudes she describes correspond to positions held by recognisable people and therefore how useful or pointed her attack is. Beauvoir, of course, does not wish to divorce politics from morality and the best sections of the essay are those in which she is dealing with moral dilemmas. She again makes some important points about ends and means, although as elsewhere one feels that the value of her procedure lies more in her view of the nature of morality than in any definite prescriptions that she might wish to offer: 'La morale n'est pas un ensemble de valeurs et de principes constitués, elle est le mouvement constituant par lequel valeurs et principes ont été posés' (81).

'Littérature et métaphysique' is one of Beauvoir's few separate theoretical statements on the nature of literature. Drawing a sharp contrast between the philosophical essay on the one hand and the novel or play on the other, she argues that the meaning of a work of fiction cannot be fully expressed in abstract concepts. It essentially requires the participation of readers, encouraging them to question themselves, entertain doubts, make judgements, and although the skill of writers consists in concealing their own presence in the work, the good novel is marked off by the fact that it constitutes a process of discovery for its author too. That is, in the course of writing authors themselves must have discovered truths they had not suspected and problems to which they have no solution. Rigid, static, completed philosophical theories, therefore, cannot be introduced into fiction without restricting its free development. Metaphysics, however, is not a system but an attitude: 'l'attitude métaphysique . . . consiste à se poser dans sa totalité en face de la totalité du monde' (99). And since existentialist metaphysics is characterised by its attempt to take account of the singular, subjective, dramatic quality of experience, its expression in the form of fiction is particularly appropriate. Provided that the work is seen to be a product of the author's freedom, and provided that readers respond to the appeal to their own freedom, the metaphysical novel provides 'un dévoilement de l'existence dont aucun autre mode d'expression ne saurait fournir l'équivalent' (106).

The essay is perhaps better seen as an article of faith than as a developed argument on the nature of fiction, for it is much less convincing as an exploration of the relationship between metaphysics and literature in general than as an illustration of the close link between Beauvoir's own substantive philosophical views—on freedom in particular—and her approach to the novel (plays drop out of the picture early on in the text). There are, it is true, strong reasons for accepting her claim that a good novel can never be wholly reduced to abstract precepts or formulas, but her assertion that the novelist reproduces raw experience is open to many objections and she herself appears rather confused on this point. Her underestimation of the importance of the novelist's selection and shaping of the events portrayed is just one weakness in a treatment of the artistic as opposed to the philosophical dimension of fiction that is unsatisfactory in almost all respects. It is demonstrably false, for instance, that 'l'envoûtement romanesque' breaks down if the author's presence is revealed in the novel. Beauvoir makes points that are very useful for our understanding of her view of fiction and provides us with one yardstick by which to begin judging her own novels, but 'Littérature et métaphysique' is extremely unsophisticated and highly limited as a contribution to literary theory.

In the final essay, 'Œil pour œil', Beauvoir discusses the concepts of revenge and punishment, with particular reference to the situation in France following the Liberation. She describes how the hatred of particular people that she had come to feel for the very first time during the Occupation did not turn to joy as expected when her enemies were punished, explaining this fact by arguing that the desire for revenge is in no sense a practical, functional one, but one that reflects deep metaphysical needs. All people demand to be treated as subjects, not objects, and the reciprocity that this implies constitutes the metaphysical basis of the idea of justice. Yet any attempt to avenge ourselves by *forcing* someone to respect our freedom is a contradiction in terms, since the other person, too, is free. To see the aggressors suffer is not enough: we have to know that they 'understand' at last, that they somehow acknowledge the point of their suffering. Unfortunately, there is no guarantee that this will happen, and even if it does, the moment and the state of mind can probably not be perpetuated. Private vengeance is a concrete personal phenomenon that is perfectly understandable, but it is likely to engender still further violence and therefore cannot be tolerated by society. Because social justice does not recognise the principle of 'an eye for an eye', however, its use of punishment takes on a symbolic air and the calmer and more ceremonious the proceedings, the more scandalous the legal bloodletting comes to appear. Society repudiates vengeance, but thereby breaks the concrete link between crime and punishment. There is much to be said for the Christian view that we should seek to be charitable rather than vengeful, but some acts are irredeemable, some evil is absolute. If crimes against society can be forgiven, attempts to degrade people into objects must be punished. To understand is not to excuse: people are free and have to be held responsible for the evil as well as the good they do, if their lives are to have any meaning.

In 'Œil pour œil' Beauvoir draws heavily upon her experience during and immediately after the war for her illustrations, and parts of the essay have a deeply personal ring that is often conspicuous by its absence in the collection as a whole. Moreover, her analysis and defence of private vengeance in existentialist terms carry a great deal more conviction than one might expect in much less extreme historical circumstances. In so far as the essay can be taken as a kind of occasional piece arising out of the Occupation and the consequent 'épuration', then, it makes a strong impact. Yet once more Beauvoir's endeavours to broaden her topic and to generalise are considerably less satisfactory. Some of her comments on aspects of the legal processes and the evolution of one's attitude towards the criminal are entirely apposite, but her belief that all crimes in which individuals assert themselves against society are excusable and that these can be clearly distinguished from crimes against humanity is dubious in the extreme. And the essay gives no adequate answer at all to questions about the proper role of the Law and the social implications of acts of vengeance. Curiously, however, Beauvoir's later view on the topic of the essay (FCh, 101) seems a much shallower and more impatient one than her evidently sincere, if unsuccessful, attempt here to wrestle with what was a horrifying real and complex, perhaps even insoluble, dilemma.

Looking at Beauvoir's 'moral' essays as a whole, one soon sees the force of her remark that she had to *make* herself think in terms of abstract formulas and principles. The general precepts that one culls from her writings on ethics—and all such precepts revolve around the concept of freedom—are mostly unexceptionable but extremely indefinite ones, while the strongest, most distinctive impression left by the essays is that of the singularity and irreducible complexity of moral problems. Beauvoir is at her very best in this area when she is analysing particular dilemmas, exposing the dangers of specific situations, the self-deception or self-contradiction inherent in certain attitudes, and showing in which direction solutions do *not* lie. She is so skilled and discriminating in this that her attempts to point the way *out* of moral dilemmas seem, by contrast, highly vague and abstract. With obvious justification, she sees this discrepancy as an inevitable consequence of a doctrine stressing our freedom as individuals to invent our own values. It is arguable, moreover, that at this stage in her development she needed to see how far it was possible to go towards formulating positive moral principles or guidelines, and that if her efforts produce results that are less than satisfactory ('moralisme', as she calls it), the failure could have been a salutary one.

Whether one thinks that it turned out to be such depends largely upon one's judgement on Beauvoir's later perspectives. She came to believe that while the attempt to reinvent rules and reasons after a war that had called everything into question was one that she was bound to make, she had failed to shed her early idealism:

> J'étais—comme Sartre—insuffisamment affranchie des idéologies de ma classe; au moment même où je les repoussais, je me servais encore de leur langage. Il m'est devenu odieux car, je le sais maintenant, chercher les raisons pour lesquelles il ne faut pas marcher sur la figure d'un homme, c'est accepter qu'on lui marche sur la figure. (FCh, 101)

The evident humanism of this last comment will be seen by many as counterbalanced by a potentially dangerous rejection of reasoning and justification in moral matters. It is, in any case, a fact that since publishing the essays discussed here Beauvoir has not written about morality in general terms at all, although she has of course applied the broad views that they express to a variety of particular issues and also embodied them in works of fiction.

Notes

[1] For some specific philosophical criticisms of *Pour une morale de l'ambiguïté*, see, for instance, R. Jolivet: 'La "Morale de l'ambiguïté" de Simone de Beauvoir', *Revue Thomiste*, 1949.

[2] See my 'Simone de Beauvoir and Sartre on *mauvaise foi*', *French Studies*, 1980.

5 Le Deuxième Sexe

In her memoirs Beauvoir explains how long it took her personally to realise that women's position in society is inferior to that enjoyed by men. As a child she had little occasion to notice differences in the upbringing of the two sexes, since she had no brother: 'je ressentis vivement mon enfance, jamais ma féminité' (MJFR, 77). Then at university and after, because of the liberal views of her companions and doubtless because of her own intellectual gifts, she was never forced to regard herself as anything other than the equal of the men around her: 'Je ne niais pas ma féminité, je ne l'assumais pas non plus: je n'y pensais pas' (FA, 419). She claims that before the war she was not aware that such a thing as 'la condition féminine' existed. Even when, towards the end of the Occupation, she began meeting women who had clearly lived their lives as 'êtres relatifs', she still failed to attach much importance to this matter, which affected her only indirectly (FA, 655).

It was in the autumn of 1946, while taking notes for an auto-biographical work, that Beauvoir had to acknowledge the importance of the preliminary question of what being a woman had signified for her. On Sartre's suggestion she began considering the general issue of upbringing and suddenly had a revelation:

> ce monde était un monde masculin, mon enfance avait été nourrie de mythes forgés par les hommes et je n'y avais pas du tout réagi de la même manière que si j'avais été un garçon. (FCh, 136)

She decided to write about women's condition rather than herself and began studying the myths of femininity. She soon recognised that myths themselves cannot be dissociated from their historical or physiological backgrounds and began to extend the scope of her inquiry. Later she also saw the need for a systematic account of how society creates and maintains differences between women and men from childhood to old age, and of the severe limitations that this imposes upon women's opportunities. She dealt efficiently with the vast amount of written material relevant to her research and completed the two volumes of *Le Deuxième Sexe* over a period of less than three years. The first, 'Les Faits et les mythes', was published in June 1949 and the second, 'L'Expérience vécue' in November of the same year.

Le Deuxième Sexe is a massive work—just over one thousand pages in its abridged paperback edition—which draws impressively upon material from a wide range of disciplines, including anthropology, biology, psychology, sociology, literature and history. The first volume is by far the more academic of the two, manifestly having its origins in the extensive research that Beauvoir carried out in the Bibliothèque Nationale (she claims to have consulted almost everything written on the topic at that time in English and French). Its first section, 'Destin', deals with the biological, psychoanalytical and Marxist views of women; 'Histoire' gives an account of women's position in society over the centuries; and 'Mythes' analyses not only archetypal representations of women, but also their portrayal in the works of five famous male writers. The second, and much longer volume depends more heavily upon less formal sources, like Beauvoir's own impressions, encounters and memories. Analysing women's condition in 1949, she examines upbringing and development ('Formation'); the characteristic situations that women face in society ('Situation'); and certain broad types of reaction to the oppression involved ('Justifications'). In a final section, 'Vers la libération', Beauvoir gives her ideas on the pitfalls and possibilities that await the independent woman trying to find a way forward.

In her Introduction, Beauvoir directly attacks the concept of 'l'éternel féminin' that constitutes her underlying target throughout the book. She also gives us some provocative glimpses of the theses to be pursued in later sections. But above all she tries to lay the metaphysical foundations for her work, arguing that Otherness is a basic category of all human thought and that men have always relegated women to it:

> Elle se détermine et se différencie par rapport à l'homme et non celui-ci par rapport à elle; elle est l'inessentiel en face de l'essentiel. Il est le Sujet, il est l'Absolu: elle est l'Autre. (16)

At this point, however, Beauvoir qualifies her central assertion in two important ways. Firstly, she recognises that men have been able to maintain their dominant position only because women have submitted to it rather than rising in revolt against it. She claims not only that women do not have the 'moyens concrets' to conduct such a revolt, but also—and there is a suspicion of circularity and some obscurity in her reasoning here—that although their Otherness is located 'au cœur d'une totalité dont les deux termes sont nécessaires l'un à l'autre' (21), women are heavily handicapped by the oppression that has always prevailed. Furthermore, a woman is unwilling to give up the advantages of an alliance with the sex that has actually made itself superior and to this extent she may be accused of 'mauvaise foi', of giving in to 'la tentation de fuir sa liberté et de se constituer en chose' (23). The second major qualification that Beauvoir makes to her initial postulate is her admission that the majority of men do not explicitly claim that women are inferior. They are unable to measure the importance of the privileges they enjoy and frequently adopt confused or self-contradictory positions:

> beaucoup d'hommes affirment avec une quasi bonne foi que les femmes *sont* les égales de l'homme et qu'elles n'ont rien à revendiquer, et *en même temps*: que les femmes ne pourront jamais être les égales de l'homme et que leurs revendications sont vaines. (30)

She goes on to urge that vague notions of superiority and equality should be abandoned, so that social institutions can be judged in relation to the concrete opportunities that they offer to individuals (33). We have no reliable way of measuring the happiness of others and must therefore adopt the perspective of existentialist morality. Building upon positions she considers established in her moral essays, Beauvoir points out that the opportunities open to the individual need to be defined in terms of freedom and transcendence. The vital fact about woman's situation is that the world of men, in which she is 'l'Autre', is designed to *curtail* her transcendence: 'Le drame de la femme, c'est ce conflit entre la revendication fondamentale de tout sujet qui se pose toujours comme l'essentiel et les exigences d'une situation qui la constitue comme inessentielle' (34-35). It is entirely pointless to deplore, as some critics have, the fact that Beauvoir proposes to look at women's condition through an existentialist lens. But one can fairly note at this stage that she has not yet explained how men gained dominance over women in the first place. Nor are the moral implications of her position clear so far, for her point that women have in some measure *consented* to their oppression would appear to make them blameworthy: 'Chaque fois que la transcendance retombe en immanence il y a dégradation de l'existence en "en soi", de la liberté en facticité; cette chute est une faute morale si elle est consentie par le sujet' (34).

Be that as it may, the existentialist perspective would have no relevance at all if a physiological, psychological or economic destiny governed women's fate, and in Part I of her essay, 'Destin', Beauvoir is concerned to deny that women's position is determined by factors in these categories. There is no argument as such, however, in 'Les données de la biologie', where, after a substantial review of reproductive processes in the animal kingdom, she catalogues the ways in which, largely because their physiology is geared to the survival of the species, women are much more shackled by their bodies than men. Acknowledging that these facts are of great importance and form an essential element of any woman's situation, she asserts that they do not constitute 'un destin figé', are not enough to create a hierarchy of the sexes, and do not explain why woman is the Other (51).

It is at the beginning of the next section, 'Le point de vue psychanalytique', that Beauvoir summarises her views on biological facts most clearly:

> Ce n'est pas le corps-objet décrit par les savants qui existe concrètement, mais le corps vécu par le sujet . . . Ce n'est pas la nature qui définit la femme: c'est celle-ci qui se définit en reprenant la nature à son compte dans son affectivité.[2]

She admires psychoanalysis for recognising this, but has some general criticisms of it, as well as particular objections to Freud's view of feminine psychology, which she considers he elaborated on the basis of a masculine model. For Beauvoir, sexuality is not an irreducible fact, but at one and the same time a manifestation of a 'recherche de l'être' that is more fundamental and a reflection of social and historical circumstances. A woman is not the victim of contradictory impulses but a human agent having to choose between 'le rôle d'*objet*, d'*Autre* qui lui est proposé, et la revendication de sa liberté'.[3] She makes this choice, moreover, as a member of a society with a particular economic and social structure, and in 'Le point de vue du matérialisme historique' Beauvoir reminds us of Engels's argument that it was the advent of private property that led to the enslavement of women. But she herself believes that the idea of private property cannot be understood without reference to deeper, metaphysical concepts and that the oppression of women cannot be shown to derive from it. Women are more than mere economic entities: apart from anything else, their reproductive function has to be taken into account.

Beauvoir considers that she has now shown that far from constituting a 'destiny', biological, sexual and economic factors have concrete reality for any woman only in so far as she perceives them as important 'dans la perspective globale de son existence'.[4] It may not be self-evident what Beauvoir means by this, but undoubtedly underlying her position here is Sartre's series of powerful anti-determinist arguments in *L'Être et le Néant*: men and women are basically free to view and evaluate the 'brute facts' of their existence, be these biological, environmental, or whatever, in any perspective that they freely choose to adopt (a huge rock is an obstacle only if we wish to move it: it is an aid if we climb it to admire the landscape).[5] Hence only explanations in terms of the fundamental choices made by individuals can be regarded as adequate accounts of human behaviour. Biology, psychology and Marxism all have contributions to make to our understanding of women, but it is a different *kind* of account altogether that Beauvoir wishes to give.

In the first section of the historical part of her essay Beauvoir gives her answer to the question of the origin of male dominance. The biological and economic situation of primitive tribes was the context of this development, but the key factor was a metaphysical one, namely the thrust for transcendence that characterises the human species: 'ce n'est pas la vie qui est pour l'homme la valeur suprême . . . elle doit servir des fins plus importantes qu'elle-même' (84). Now, because the species makes heavier biological demands upon the female than upon the male, because in maternity 'la femme demeurait rivée à son corps, comme l'animal', she was never able to share fully in male activities or projects and was therefore bound to occupy an inferior place on the scale of values that men created. All four subsequent sections of 'Histoire' are designed to show how the initial male victory of Existence over Life, Nature and Women was perpetuated, as well as the complex ways in which male dominance evolved over the centuries. It is to be noted that as an essentially *metaphysical* account of the origins of the oppression of women, Beauvoir's view can be taken to subsume both biological and economic explanations and to escape certain types of objection—for instance, ones concerning historical timing—that other theories might be open to. However, it does inherit the flaws that we recorded in the last chapter in her treatment of the crucial concept of transcendence itself, and it may be thought to be abstract and tenuous. Once more, Beauvoir's explanation is more of an assertion than a hypothesis supported by evidence, at least in the context of *Le Deuxième Sexe*.

Of course, once the assertion is made she can go on to interpret all kinds of phenomena in the light of it. Thus, faced in the second section of 'Histoire'[6] with the problem of accounting for early agricultural communities where women were accorded great respect, even veneration or worship, by men, she argues rather feebly that 'quand . . . il la pose comme l'essentiel, c'est lui qui la pose et il se réalise ainsi comme l'essentiel dans cette aliénation qu'il consent' (94). (Must not women have consented to *their* alienation in the first place?) Nevertheless, Beauvoir soon passes on to patriarchies, which she sees as representing the stage of human development when men gained sole and permanent ascendancy (104). Drawing on evidence from a wide range of societies now, she is able to show in her third section how women's fate from this point onwards was closely linked with questions of private property. Abstract rights, she points out, are no measure of the real position occupied by women in a society, as the example of developments in Roman times demonstrates. She argues in her fourth section that the Christian era brought no significant improvement in women's condition, whatever one might expect from religion, and that their lot in the Middle Ages was a particularly hard one. Furthermore, although from the Renaissance onwards a certain number of women managed to reach the intellectual and social heights, the great mass still had no access to education and culture, let alone power, under the *ancien régime*.

Beauvoir's final historical section is the most detailed and substantial, reviewing women's situation from the French Revolution to 1949. She sees the Revolution itself as having achieved relatively little for women, but in any case their cause in France was greatly retarded by the civil code proclaimed between 1804 and 1810. Increasing mechanisation and industrialisation in the nineteenth century, however, was a major factor favouring the emancipation of both the working classes and women. Women were still seriously exploited over a long period, but gradually their very participation in production, together with more extensive use of contraception, and even abortion, which freed them from the slavery of reproduction, brought about a change in their social and political status. In most parts of the world in the twentieth century considerable progress has been made in the struggle for freedom and equality for women, and the process will continue: 'Il semble donc que la partie soit gagnée. L'avenir ne peut que conduire à une assimilation de plus en plus profonde de la femme à la société naguère masculine' (170). Nevertheless, although women are beginning to enjoy both abstract rights and concrete opportunities, this is a transitional period and the world is still in the hands of men: 'entre les deux sexes, il n'y a pas aujourd'hui encore de véritable égalité' (178). The whole weight of history and tradition is still bearing down upon women and they need to make a far greater effort of will than men do to gain and retain independence in modern society.

Part II of *Le Deuxième Sexe* forms an important stage in Beauvoir's argument, being an attempt to show 'comment la "réalité féminine" s'est constituée'. Its least satisfactory aspect is probably the non-historical, metaphysical explanation with which it begins, but this does little to undermine subsequent analyses. Once Beauvoir starts, in a characteristically bold way, to marshal evidence and scrutinise historical facts for the reality that lies behind them, then the force of her central thesis becomes extremely difficult to resist. At the fairly high level of generality on which she is dealing with history here—and while any less detail would have risked making the section too insubstantial to be worthwhile, much more would have overloaded it—many of the assertions about particular periods are bound to have an elusive quality, if only because the process of checking them would be such a difficult one. Yet Beauvoir undoubtedly makes out a strong case for the view that no really significant part in the unfolding of history has been played by women, whom men have always confined to a limited, secondary role in society. This panoramic view of the development of human civilisation provides a framework within which she can go on to describe the more specific manifestations and implications of male dominance.

From the fact that men have always held the power, for instance, it follows that the myths that seem to be so essential to the human race will be myths created by men:

Tout mythe implique un Sujet qui projette ses espoirs et

ses craintes vers un ciel transcendant. Les femmes ne se posant pas comme Sujet n'ont pas créé de mythe viril dans lequel se refléteraient leurs projets: elles n'ont ni religion ni poésie qui leur appartiennent en propre. (192)

And since man's attitude towards woman, who is one of the principal incarnations of the Other, is characterised by ambivalence, Beauvoir tries to show in Part III, 'Mythes', how many different concepts women have represented for men over the centuries. Thus as an embodiment of Nature women stand for the source of all life, but also for contingency and death, so that Beauvoir talks of 'l'hésitation du mâle entre la peur et le désir' (208)—a hesitation that produces conflicting myths concerning virginity and sex, as well as a paradox in male attitudes to beauty: 'souhaitant saisir dans la femme la nature, mais transfigurée, l'homme voue la femme à l'artifice' (219). There is ambivalence, too, in the myths of motherhood, which express disgust and hostility as well as tenderness. Man projects onto women all that he is not himself, so that they embody his dreams, become his inspiration, but at the same time they represent his failure to realise those dreams. To the extent that men succeed in enslaving women, they are enslaved in their turn; for instance, in marriage. Women deceive their husbands because this is the only form that their freedom can take, and because men effectively drive them to it: 'il veut que la femme soit sienne et qu'elle demeure étrangère; il la rêve servante et sorcière à la fois' (266). In general, then, woman is 'tout ce que l'homme appelle et tout ce qu'il n'atteint pas' (277). But if she is everything to him at one time or another, 'elle est Tout sur le mode de l'inessentiel: elle est tout l'*Autre*' (277).

To this general account of myths concerning women, Beauvoir adds a chapter analysing the particular attitudes adopted by five male writers.[7] Each of the writers she examines reveals his own chosen form of transcendence in his view of women, and the views are well assorted:

Pour chacun d'entre eux, la femme idéale sera celle qui incarnera le plus exactement l'*Autre* capable de le révéler à soi-même. Montherlant, l'esprit solaire, cherche en elle la pure animalité; Lawrence, le phallique, lui demande de résumer le sexe féminin dans sa généralité; Claudel la définit comme une âme-sœur; Breton chérit Mélusine enracinée dans la nature, il met son espoir dans la femme-enfant; Stendhal souhaite sa maîtresse intelligente, cultivée, libre d'esprit et de mœurs: une égale.[8]

In fact, it is almost incidental that the attitudes Beauvoir discusses here are those of writers. Her interest lies in the men behind the books and she is prepared, where appropriate, to draw on knowledge of their lives. Only Stendhal emerges with any credit, although even in his books the heroines tend to help the male characters to fulfil their destinies.

In a brief final chapter to Part III, Beauvoir argues that myths about women provide an essentially static representation of 'l'Éternel Féminin', which reality is not allowed to undermine. Ideas like that of 'le mystère féminin' are very advantageous to men, who use myths to ensure that women continue to think of themselves as 'l'inessentiel'. In so far as her view is that men should abandon this process and treat women as fellow human beings, Beauvoir's thesis is obviously to be applauded, but there are questions to be raised about her whole treatment of myths. The first chapter, in spite of its fairly extensive range of mythological and religious references, is in no sense an empirical investigation of myths. It opens with an extremely abstract metaphysical account of men's needs in relation to the Other, and throughout Beauvoir is clearly *illustrating* a particular view of man rather than examining an area of human expression in its own right. The lack of anything resembling scientific rigour in her approach to myths is very apparent in the way in which she provides herself with a framework into which *any* image of woman can be fitted:

> Il n'est pas une des figures de la femme qui n'engendre aussitôt sa figure inversée (260-61);
> Elle figure d'une manière charnelle et vivante toutes les valeurs et antivaleurs par lesquelles la vie prend un sens (270);
> Du bien au mal elle incarne charnellement toutes les valeurs morales et leur contraire (277).

It is hardly surprising that even Beauvoir should admit that this makes it difficult to say anything at all about the matter! Nor is it surprising, in view of the fact that women 'mythically' represent, among other things, 'le Rêve' and are a source of poetic inspiration to men, that she should show some slight traces of regret at the thought that reality might take over: 'plus les femmes s'affirment comme des êtres humains, plus la merveilleuse qualité de l'Autre meurt en elles' (192).

The fact is, as the chapter on writers confirms, that Part III is about 'myths' not in the narrow, stricter sense of the term, but in the extended sense of any discernible pattern of attitudes towards women espoused by one man or some men. Yet one still feels that Beauvoir's central plea for a view of women based upon concrete reality could have been conveyed much more crisply and directly. Some of the main points about the role that myths play in the oppression of women finally emerge sharply enough in the short third chapter, but in certain ways it actually adds to the confusion over Beauvoir's approach to the topic: if woman is always 'l'Autre absolu', how can she *ever* represent 'Harmonie, Repos, Terre nourricière'?[9] The strength of Part III lies in the intrinsic richness of Beauvoir's simple notion that men's images of women are ambivalent, which produces the most fascinating examples and seems, at a certain level of generality, to be indisputable. The question is whether this insight can ultimately be reconciled with her main line of argument in the essay. In any case, her treatment of myths is lacking in order and system, giving the impression that she has not fully assimilated and structured the abundant material that was originally to have constituted the core of her study.

In the second volume of *Le Deuxième Sexe* Beauvoir directly examines the nature and quality of women's life in this man's world, 'l'expérience vécue'. The opening sentences of the section on 'Formation' perhaps sum up better than any in the first volume her central thesis:

> On ne naît pas femme: on le devient. Aucun destin biologique, psychique, économique ne définit la figure que revêt au sein de la société la femelle humaine; c'est l'ensemble de la civilisation qui élabore ce produit intermédiaire entre le mâle et le castrat qu'on qualifie de féminin. (285)[10]

Drawing now on her own personal experience, on published memoirs, fiction, psychological and sociological surveys, theoretical works of various kinds, she first takes us through the initial stages in the upbringing and development of a woman—childhood, adolescence, early womanhood, sexual initiation—and explains the phenomenon of lesbianism. The chapters entitled 'Enfance' and 'La jeune fille' are among the very best in the whole book. Anticipating a great deal of research that has been carried out since 1949, Beauvoir shows very convincingly that the key to how girls develop is to be found not in any 'mystérieuse âme féminine' but in the manner of their upbringing in a society geared to male supremacy. She offers her own explanations —social or cultural ones—of the phenomena covered by psycho-analytical concepts like penis envy and the Electra complex, and in-dicates how biological facts acquire the particular significance they have because of the system of values within which a girl is obliged to situate them (for instance, 'c'est le contexte social qui fait de la menstruation une malédiction'; 354). The pressures upon girls to consider them-selves as sex-objects or to see their lives as centring on their quest for a man is very well brought out and the 'difficult' behaviour of adolescent girls is elucidated with great sensitivity. Especially important here, as throughout the essay, is the vicious circle in which women are seen to be caught, for Beauvoir never evades the point that in many respects women have actually *become* inferior because men have consistently regarded them and treated them as such. Only rarely in these chapters does she overstate her case—for example, in claiming of the adolescent girl that 'c'est blessée, honteuse, inquiète, coupable, qu'elle s'achemine vers l'avenir' (369); or in talking of 'les automutilations si fréquentes à cet âge' (409). And if the odd detail seems to locate her analysis more precisely in time and space than is compatible with its general validity, we need to remember that it is implicit in the whole of the second volume that Beauvoir is limiting her comments almost exclusively to the situation in Western countries, and concentrating very largely on France.

Taken together, the two chapters 'L'initiation sexuelle' and 'La lesbienne' offer an extremely thoughtful examination of female sexuality that is much wider than the titles suggest. It is important to recognise how remarkable it was for a woman, or even a man, to write so frankly and openly about these matters in France in 1949. In her memoirs Beauvoir gives us some idea of the odium and abuse she incurred simply for daring to treat the topic at all (FCh, 260-63). Yet the dispassionate nature of her approach is beyond dispute and the tone of her writing entirely unexceptionable. As far as the actual content of the chapters is concerned, although it is not too difficult to find substantive points that later research has thrown into doubt, and although her judgement and emphasis could not be said to be faultless, this is an unusually lucid and balanced analysis, even in the light of the numerous studies that have been published since. Beauvoir's comments on the sexual vocabulary of 'possession', on feminine 'passivity' ('Se *faire* objet, se *faire* passive c'est tout autre chose qu'*être* un objet passif'; 445), on the different ways in which lesbianism may be adopted are excellent. And her ideal for sexual relations between individuals, based upon attraction, generosity, reciprocity and freedom, can only be admired. Once more some of her remarks relate very specifically to conditions in France at the time—she herself suggests that in certain respects the situation in America is much better—but all of the material is supported and tightly held together by her general view that a woman's sexuality needs to be seen in the context of 'tout l'ensemble de sa situation sociale et économique' (478) and that, having no significance in isolation, it manifests 'l'attitude globale du sujet en face de l'existence' (483).

On the whole, the chapter on marriage ('La femme mariée') is a great disappointment. It is crammed full of examples and quot-ations that are frequently fascinating in their own right, but very many of which could have been omitted or shortened without loss to the argument. Moreover, Beauvoir's very conception of her task here is inadequate, and the quality of her individual perceptions or comments is quite astonishingly uneven. For any reader seeking one of the earlier accounts of both the obvious and subtle ways in which marriage can work to the disadvantage of women, or of exactly how it may be seen as an instrument of male dominance, this chapter has a great deal to offer. Indeed, much of what has become commonplace in feminist studies only in recent years is already contained in Beauvoir's pene-trating analysis of the housewife's condition, and there are truly brilliant sequences on housework and cooking in particular. But in the end the chapter is no more than a description of the very worst forms that marriage *can* take. Beauvoir's attack on the institution as such—'le principe du mariage est obscène parce qu'il transforme en droits et devoirs un échange qui doit être fondé sur un élan spontané' (II,48)—carries no weight for a number of reasons. For one thing, she acknowledges that she is attacking 'le mariage traditionnel' and that modern marriage is becoming 'une union librement consentie par deux individualités autonomes' (II,9). Then a number of her judge-ments, especially on 'l'amour charnel' ('il est très rare qu'il dure pendant de longues années'; II,50) and love ('Généralement ce n'est donc pas par amour que se décident les mariages'; II,24), suggest that her general grasp of what is common or even possible in marriage is exceedingly poor. She seems rather confused, what is

more, on the whole question of the relationship between individuals and social institutions. Why should it be a 'paradox' that
marriage has 'à la fois une fonction érotique et une fonction sociale'
(II,89)? And within Beauvoir's own broad philosophy does it make
sense to claim that 'ce ne sont pas les individus qui sont responsables
de l'échec du mariage: c'est . . . l'institution elle-même qui est
originellement pervertie' (II,128)? Perhaps the most charitable point
to make is that her view of marriage has to be seen in conjunction with
her beliefs that work is the key to women's liberation and that the
having of children is the 'meaning' or 'goal' of the institution itself.

Unfortunately, Beauvoir's examination of motherhood ('La mère')
is even less satisfactory, in that it has none of the breadth or depth of
subsequent studies on the topic. The first fifth of the chapter is
devoted to her liberal views on abortion, which most feminists would
happily endorse but which shed little light on motherhood as such.
Then Beauvoir reviews in order the different stages that a woman goes
through from the onset of pregnancy to having to deal with growing
children. On most of these stages she has nothing of significance to say
at all. Apart from making one or two dubious assertions ('Même si la
femme désire profondément l'enfant, son corps se révolte d'abord
quand il lui faut enfanter'; II,160), she is content to structure her
remarks around the trite point that different women react in different
ways according to the circumstances. Perhaps these 'facts' are intended
to provide some kind of justification for her controversial claim that
the 'maternal instinct' does not exist (II,178), but such an assertion
obviously requires a much more systematic and detailed defence than
it finds here. Beauvoir's metaphysical interpretation of the phenomena in question in terms of the child's 'Otherness' is badly lacking in
plausibility, and her affirmation that maternal devotion is only rarely
entirely authentic seems singularly arbitrary. On the other hand, she
offers a timely reminder of the different ways in which the mother's
dissatisfactions may be worked out on the child, thereby forefully re-
butting two widespread fallacies: that maternity is in itself enough to
satisfy a woman, and that the child is sure to be happy in its mother's
care. But she fails to spell out in any detail at all her own proposal that
both parents should be much less involved in raising their children
than they are at present, and that a child should be 'en grande partie
pris en charge par la collectivité' (II,200).

In 'La vie de société' Beauvoir explores the social pressures that come to bear upon the housewife by virtue of the fact that in certain situations and certain respects she must 'keep up appearances'. The significance of clothes for a woman is especially well explained and Beauvoir shows how the struggle to be well-dressed and well-groomed becomes more of a burden with age. She also describes how the housewife's loneliness leads to complicity rather than friendship with her peers and why the taking of a lover does little to solve the real problems. 'Prostituées et hétaïres' is a serious, if brief, study of both high-class and common prostitutes, almost on a sociological basis. It is to Beauvoir's credit that she tackled this topic at all, and it has to be acknowledged that she goes *some* of the way towards illustrating her surprising thesis about the prostitute: 'en elle se résument toutes les figures à la fois de l'esclavage féminin' (II,248). She succeeds in showing that the phenomenon of prostitution can be understood only in the context of the general attitude towards women that prevails in society, and suggests some interesting links with the position of the successful woman film star.[11] The final stages of a woman's life are described in 'De la maturité à la vieillesse', which is rather more general than earlier chapters and consists of little more than a series of broad assertions concerning the pitfalls of maturity and old age. Nevertheless, the chapter contains a few astute observations and there is clearly some truth in the view that while, with her main duties carried out, the older woman at last finds her freedom, 'elle découvre cette liberté au moment où elle ne trouve plus rien à en faire' (II, 289). Beauvoir's review of the different aspects of women's situation ends, therefore, on a predictably gloomy note: 'A aucun âge de sa vie, elle ne réussit à être à la fois efficace et indépendante' (II,305).

There is some repetition in 'Situation et caractère de la femme', where she attempts to pull together the threads of her argument in this section of her essay, but she gives a slightly different slant to her material by considering what general characteristics may be ascribed to women as a result of their situation in society. Beauvoir again points out that a vicious circle is involved: 'on lui coupe les ailes, et on déplore qu'elle ne sache pas voler' (II,317-18). Many alleged feminine propensities and traits are seen to flow from the fact that women submit to male domination only with great reluctance and are poised 'à mi-chemin entre la révolte et l'esclavage' (II,328). Revolt is, in fact, the only way in which a woman can authentically 'assume' her freedom, and now Beauvoir passes on to certain women who adopt the opposite course of accepting their unfavourable position by finding a justification for it.

In 'Justifications' she looks first at narcissism, arguing that it is a stage that needs to be passed through during adolescence and that it can bring no deep satisfaction to mature women. Very little is added in this chapter to what Beauvoir has already said about narcissism and it seems that she is overstretching in implying that it can be a whole outlook on life rather than a component in the attitudes of many women. Similar comments may be made about Chapter 2, 'L'amoureuse'. She admits that very few women devote their whole existence to love (II,379), and since it is also clear that she is examining only one type of love—'l'amour idolâtre' as opposed to 'l'amour authentique'—the application of her analysis looks very limited. It is true that, given male 'sovereignty', a woman's conception of love is likely to differ from a man's and Beauvoir teases out some possible consequences of this fact very skilfully. Some of these consequences are entirely incompatible with others, however, and one cannot help feeling that her recognition of male dominance has again led her to formulate generalisations on the basis of all of the very *worst* results that women's condition can produce. Those who believe that 'authentic' love is less rare than Beauvoir claims will see this chapter as a kind of special pleading. In the next, 'La mystique', she argues that a woman turns to mystical experience 'si les circonstances lui interdisent l'amour humain, si elle est déçue ou exigeante' (II,416). But when she is obliged to place Saint Teresa of Avila in a quite separate category from other mystics, and acknowledges that 'la ferveur mystique, comme l'amour et le narcissisme même, peuvent être intégrés à des vies actives et indépendantes' (II,428), one realises yet again that her targets in 'Justifications' are peculiarly indistinct ones.

Beauvoir might have been better advised to pass directly from 'Situation' to the final substantive part of Le Deuxième Sexe, 'Vers la libération', where she argues that there is only one way in which a woman can employ her freedom authentically, 'c'est de la projeter par une action positive dans la société humaine' (II,428). In 'La femme indépendante' she repeats that the vote and other legal rights are not enough to ensure real freedom for women, which can only come through economic independence and therefore through work: 'C'est le travail qui peut seul lui garantir une liberté concrète' (II,431). But if work and legal rights are necessary conditions for the liberation of women, they are certainly not sufficient. Working women in the economically oppressed classes receive none of the help they require from their husbands and from society to become the equals of men. Having made this vitally important point, Beauvoir goes on to devote the rest of her chapter to the privileged women who gain social and economic autonomy through their profession. Her analysis of the psychology of the independent woman in 1949, of the particular stresses and strains that she labours under, is exceptionally perceptive and well-founded. Beauvoir shows clearly how the successful professional woman is torn between contrary forces; how difficult it is for her to have casual sexual relationships or reconcile her career with her marriage; and how motherhood is a near-impossibility in the prevailing circumstances. She also goes back to the question of education, to argue that feelings of inferiority are bred into girls, who tend to set their sights too low and fail to take the kind of 'grip' on the world that men have.

Summarising her views in her Conclusion, she points out that men are now creating a new war between the sexes in reacting so badly to women's struggles for transcendence. She admits that some women are trying to have the best of both worlds, 'misant sur leur vieille magie et sur leurs jeunes droits' (II,485), but sees this as an excusable reaction to an ambiguous situation. In general, she refuses to blame one sex more than the other:

> les deux sexes sont chacun victimes à la fois de l'autre et de soi . . . chaque camp est complice de son ennemi; la femme poursuit un rêve de démission, l'homme un rêve d'aliénation. (II,486-87)

In any case, within this broad scheme of things irremediable injustices are absolutely inevitable and Beauvoir gives her own version of what a society in which men and women were strictly equal would amount to:

> les femmes élevées et formées exactement comme les hommes travailleraient dans les mêmes conditions et pour les mêmes salaires; la liberté érotique serait admise par les mœurs, mais l'acte sexuel ne serait plus considéré comme un 'service' qui se rémunère; la femme serait *obligée* de s'assurer un autre gagne-pain; le mariage reposerait sur un libre engagement que les époux pourraient dénoncer dès qu'ils voudraient; la maternité serait libre, c'est-à-dire qu'on autoriserait le birth-control et l'avortement et qu'en revanche

> on donnerait à toutes les mères et à leurs enfants exactement
> les mêmes droits, qu'elles soient mariées ou non; les congés de
> grossesse seraient payés par la collectivité qui assumerait la charge
> des enfants, ce qui ne veut pas dire qu'on *retirerait* ceux-ci à leurs
> parents mais qu'on ne les leur *abandonnerait* pas. (II,494)

But such conditions have not yet been achieved in any country and
could come about only as the result of an 'évolution collective'. One
cannot expect a spontaneous act of generosity on the part of the
oppressor, but new situations have led to a partial emancipation and
women must ensure that progress continues to be made. No one need
worry, Beauvoir assures us, that this will lead to a colourless world.
There will always be differences between men and women and these
will in no way be undermined by equality of status. It is in the context
of their natural differences that men and women must assert their
fraternity.

With *Le Deuxième Sexe* Beauvoir found, for the first time in her
non-fictional writings, both a topic of her own and a broad way of
tackling it that command great interest, however one may react to
existentialism in general. As we have seen, her views here ultimately
rest upon Sartrean arguments repudiating determinism and establishing the reality of human freedom. But much of her descriptive
account of women's condition can be separated from such arguments
and considered in its own right. She herself was later to state that she
would no longer wish to place the phenomena described on the same
basis as she did in 1949:

> Théoriquement, j'ai dit déjà que si j'écrivais aujourd'hui *Le
> Deuxième Sexe* je donnerais des bases matérialistes et non idéalistes
> à l'opposition du Même et de l'Autre. Je fonderais le rejet et
> l'oppression de l'autre non sur l'antagonisme des consciences, mais
> sur la base économique de la rareté. (TCF,614)

As she observes, however, such a change would alter little, if anything, in the subsequent direction or detail of the book. (Similarly,
her inadequate explanation of how male dominance came about in the
first place in no way undermines all that she goes on to say about its
nature.) Although Beauvoir's approach to her topic, in contrast to that
of others, is initially a metaphysical one, the book's significance lies
not in its foundations but in its superstructure: the examination of the

oppression of women across an extremely wide range of areas of human activity. This range in itself is one of the main reasons why *Le Deuxième Sexe* is one of the most important and far-reaching books on women ever published. It is to Beauvoir's eternal credit that, once she had been alerted to the existence of a 'condition féminine', she immediately recognised that the implications of the oppression of women extend into every aspect of human culture or civilisation and need to be traced in detail, for the benefit of all. Unfortunately, her detailed execution of this highly ambitious project leaves a good deal to be desired, for the book cannot be said to be very carefully composed, or even, on the whole, particularly well-written. There is little to criticise in its general structure as such, but none of the seven major parts is satisfactory in its entirety, as each is fairly seriously flawed either in organisation or by the markedly uneven quality of its individual chapters. While almost every section contains some fertile ideas and valuable insights, argument of the highest quality is rarely sustained for long, since Beauvoir frequently overloads her discussion with examples and quotations. Memorable sequences on the stylistic level are disappointingly few and far between.

Nevertheless, underlying the over-abundance of detail and holding the diverse parts of the study together is an apparently simple thesis: that 'womanhood' or 'femininity' is a cultural rather than a natural construct. If the metaphysical basis of the work is not indispensable, this thesis is central and crucial. In the latest volume of her memoirs, Beauvoir not only continues to insist that it is correct, but also claims that it has been confirmed by scientific research carried out since 1949 and needs only to be supplemented by the parallel assertion that: 'On ne naît pas mâle, on le devient' (TCF, 614). The unresolved debate that rages about the respective roles of heredity and the environment in human development suggests that the general issues underpinning her position are much more complicated than she implies, but even if we allow her to take certain broad philosophical points for granted, her principal thesis about women still raises problems. Beauvoir's view would be a fairly trivial one if she were merely arguing that the *idea* or *concept* of womanhood is a product of culture rather than nature, for what idea is not? She must, therefore, be taken to mean that women themselves are as they now are because of the kind of culture or civilisation to which they belong, rather than by virtue of the natural differences between themselves and men. It is plain that part of the point is to deny that they have a nature causally determined by anatomical or genetic factors. But then *exactly* what is the force of the cultural factors that are said to make women what they are? There cannot be a causal relationship here either, since women, like men, are free to choose themselves.

We come back at this stage to the point that Beauvoir is never clear on, the question of women's complicity in their condition, or the degree to which they are to be held responsible for their situation. We saw that in the last section of the book she is disinclined to blame one sex more than the other (II,486), and it is possible to show that such an attitude underlies all of the parts of the text where she is not carried away by her polemical fervour. Yet we are *still* left with theoretical problems of some significance, for this makes it no easier to explain Beauvoir's earlier use of terms like 'disposé', 'prédisposé', even 'obligé' to describe women's reactions. If human beings are free rather than causally determined, no intermediate concepts of this kind have any validity. She claims that men invite women to follow 'la pente de la facilité' (II,489), but it is extremely doubtful whether, within her system of beliefs, sense can be made of the idea that one choice is easier than another. After all, she and Sartre hold that tasks or situations can only be difficult in relation to prior choices or projects already formed. She does indeed appear to assume that most women make the same prior choice ('la femme poursuit un rêve de démission'; II,486), but completely fails to explain why this should be so if there is no feminine nature as such. In the end, the notion of 'situation' that she hopes to substitute for that of such a nature cannot do what she requires of it, since women are said to be free and can therefore see and read their 'situation' in totally different ways. A contradiction that she became aware of as early as 1940—when she knew she was right to urge, against Sartre, that 'du point de vue de la liberté . . . les situations ne sont pas équivalentes', but realised that to maintain this position she would need to 'abandonner le terrain de la morale individualiste, donc idéaliste, sur lequel nous nous placions' (FA, 498)—is still present at the heart of *Le Deuxième Sexe* and constitutes a weakness in the very basis of Beauvoir's view of 'la condition féminine'. It also mars the moral dimension of her treatment of the question, since the 'mauvaise foi' that she ascribes to many women cannot be properly understood until we have a better idea of its contrary, authenticity, and this necessarily remains obscure—doubly so—as long as she talks only of a woman 'assuming' her 'situation'.[12]

There is a case, however, for not taking Beauvoir's main formula concerning femininity too literally. Feminism, after all, is nothing if not a rallying cry, an appeal for changes in society and people's attitudes. At least to this extent, Beauvoir is surely right to urge that we abandon thoughts of 'l'éternel féminin', since almost everything relating to the way in which women are regarded and treated—and thereby to what women actually *are*—is capable of being modified by human beings. And she is probably right, too, to remark that this is a belief held by all feminists (TCF,623). Looking at *Le Deuxième Sexe* in this more positive or 'practical' light, one sees just how important a book it is for modern feminism. As Beauvoir suggested in 1976, it is not so much that it was influential in the setting up of Women's Liberation as that it was available as a source once the movement began.[13] Yet on the whole it is far more theoretical than most subsequent feminist works and is not, in fact, an especially militant book. When Beauvoir spells out what she thinks real equality for women would amount to, there is relatively little that the non-feminist could reasonably object to, apart from the vague suggestion that the collectivity would take charge of children. Conversely, even the mildest feminist is likely to be aware that while she *over*-estimates the effectiveness of work as an instrument of liberation (her suggestion that women should be *obliged* to earn is perhaps less significant than the fact that in 'Vers la libération' she almost totally ignores the huge majority of working women who have non-professional jobs), she seriously *under*-estimates the potential of radical or defiant action—be it on the relatively trivial matters of make-up or clothes, or in protests and manifestations on a larger scale—at least as part of a general strategy.

In her memoirs as well as in a whole series of revealing interviews and articles published since the end of the fifties,[14] Beauvoir has made it perfectly plain how her own attitudes towards feminism have changed since 1949 'sur le plan pratique et tactique'. She believes that the relative optimism of *Le Deuxième Sexe* has proved totally un-justified and that, as far as women are concerned, striving for social revolution is not enough: 'je pensais autrefois que la lutte des classes devait passer avant la lutte des sexes. J'estime maintenant qu'il faut mener les deux ensemble' (TCF, 624). Since about 1970 she has been militating in a variety of ways—and with a variety of organisations,

113

including the Mouvement de Libération des Femmes—on most of the standard feminist issues. She now thinks that action comes first and theory later—'nous devons tirer notre théorie de la pratique et pas inversement'[15] —but this is not to say that she is not alive to divergences within women's movements. In *Tout compte fait,* for instance, she talks of a number of major disagreements amongst feminists. Opinions are divided on the question of the family and she frankly notes that her own position is a slightly uneasy one: 'Comme beaucoup de féministes, je désire l'abolition de la famille, mais sans trop savoir par quoi la remplacer' (TCF, 626). On the question of sexuality, without being in the least opposed to lesbianism, she ranges herself with those who accept that men still have a role to play in women's lives: 'Je répugne absolument à l'idée d'enfermer la femme dans un ghetto féminin' (TCF, 626).

This last point takes us near to the core of a fundamental matter concerning Beauvoir's position and one that brings her into serious theoretical conflict with certain other feminists. Because she clings to her view that there is no pre-determined 'nature féminine', she feels obliged to deny that there are specifically feminine qualities or values (TCF, 628). In connection with *Le Deuxième Sexe,* Suzanne Lilar and Jean Leighton, among others, have strongly argued that this particular view is part of a general flaw in Beauvoir's attitudes, which consists in accepting the traditional masculine values associated with 'transcendance' as the true ones and denying that there could be any intrinsic virtue in the 'immanence' or passivity that is commonly linked with womanhood.[16] This is an important issue not only because it immediately raises practical questions of feminist tactics and strategy, but also because, in the other direction, it leads back to inadequacies in the theoretical foundations of *Le Deuxième Sexe*. If a 'situation' is really all that women have in common as women, then what does 'assuming' it amount to? Or what is there for women to revolt on behalf of, that does not involve their becoming more like men? There is the odd little sign of hesitation about feminine values in the book—Beauvoir once suggests that we simply do not know to what extent the liberated woman 'demeurera singulière' (II, 481)—but by and large, if we look to the end of the oppression that she so graphically records, Beauvoir wants and expects women to be less different from men than they are now and to be doing more of the things that men do, rather than anything new of their own or distinctive of women. Her views on this may actually have hardened since 1949: 'Refuser les "modèles masculins" est un non-sens'(TCF,628). It seems that while she has thought out the consequences of the absence of a fixed feminine nature rather more carefully than many feminists, she has also been more inclined than most, perhaps for personal reasons, to embrace 'masculine' values.

Yet to regard Beauvoir as anything other than a genuine feminist of the first rank would be to do her an absurd injustice, for she should continue to be viewed with the very greatest respect whenever and wherever women's liberation is being discussed. In a number of ways, both direct and indirect, the influence of *Le Deuxième Sexe* has undoubtedly been much greater than is commonly acknowledged and although it could not possibly be considered as Beauvoir's best book, it will almost certainly turn out to be, on the social and historical levels, her weightiest. In any case, she has pointed out on a number of occasions that the countless letters she has received since its publication and the contacts she has subsequently made with women from all walks of life show that it has helped many individual women to become aware of themselves as women and to struggle against what would otherwise have been their inevitable fate: 'Si mon livre a aidé les femmes, c'est qu'il les exprimait, et réciproquement elles lui ont conféré sa vérité' (FCh, 268).

Notes

[1]   Bracketed references in the body of this chapter are to the two-volume 'Idées' edition of *Le Deuxième Sexe,* but this is an abridged version of the original text, to the first volume of which we shall need to give certain references in these notes.

[2]   1949 edition, p.77.

[3]   1949 edition, p.93.

[4]   1949 edition, p.104.

[5]   Jean-Paul Sartre: *L'Être et le Néant*, p.562.

[6]   Pages 85-104 of the 'Idées' edition, which, strangely, includes this in the first section and misnumbers the remaining sections accordingly.

[7]   Neither this nor the final chapter of Part III (that is, pp.312-95 of the 1949 edition) is included in the 'Idées' edition.

8 1949 edition, p.381.

9 A point made with some force in Suzanne Lilar: *Le Malentendu du Deuxième Sexe*, Chapter 5.

10 Some of the second volume proper is included in the first volume of the 'Idées' edition.

11 In this connection, attention may be drawn to Beauvoir's brief essay, *Brigitte Bardot and the Lolita Syndrome* (*Esquire*, Aug. 1959; Deutsch, Weidenfeld & Nicholson, 1960; French translation in *Écrits*, pp. 363-76), in which she argues that Bardot is (or was earlier in her career) a new embodiment of an old myth, a modern version of 'l'éternel féminin', destined to be far more popular in America than in France.

12 If this reading of *Le Deuxième Sexe* is correct, then Beauvoir's philosophical difficulties run exactly parallel to those of Sartre in, for example, his discussion of Jews. In *Réflexions sur la question juive* he attempted to define Jews strictly in terms of their 'situation', yet in the very last interview that he gave he was to acknowledge that this is an error and that there is 'une réalité juive' over and above the Jew's situation (*Le Nouvel Observateur*, 1980).

13 'Le Deuxième Sexe vingt-cinq ans après', interview with John Gerassi, *Society*, 1976; reprinted in *Écrits*, pp. 547-65.

14 Most of these are published in Part III of *Écrits*. For a detailed analysis of the evolution of Beauvoir's feminism since 1949, see Jacques Zéphir: *Le Néo-féminisme de Simone de Beauvoir*.

15 Interview with Gerassi, *Écrits*, p.560.

16 Suzanne Lilar: *Le Malentendu du Deuxième Sexe*; Jean Leighton: *Simone de Beauvoir on Women*. This criticism is entirely consistent with weaknesses that we detected in Beauvoir's handling of the very concept of transcendence in *Pyrrhus et Cinéas* (Chapter 4).

6 Socio-political Essays

In 1951 Beauvoir had occasion to reread all of the books of the Marquis de Sade, when she was invited to write a preface for a volume devoted to him. Feeling that his life and works illustrated features of the human condition in an important way, she wrote an essay, 'Faut-il brûler Sade?', which was first published in *Les Temps modernes* in December 1951 and January 1952, then as the first of three pieces collected in *Privilèges* of 1955.[1] Arguing that neither his writings as such, nor his sexual perversions are particularly remarkable in themselves, she claims that it is the relationship that he created between the two that deserves attention, for his activities represent the conflict between the individual and society in its most extreme form. His true originality, according to Beauvoir, consists in the decision that he made as an adult to turn his sexuality into an ethic and to express this in his fiction. In her essay she offers us her own brief account of Sade's life, an interpretation of his eroticism, some comments on his literary works, and an examination of his philosophical or moral doctrine.

She sees him as having discovered early in his life that 'entre son existence sociale et ses plaisirs individuels une conciliation est impossible' (16). Being a young aristocrat, he belonged to a class that no longer exercised real power but was subject to an illusion of sovereignty. After the scandal of 1763 his attitude became one of defiance: he was now prepared to urge the superiority of 'evil' over 'good'. It was in the middle of his long period of imprisonment between 1778 and 1790 that he began writing, in order to express this defiance and to indulge his imagination. There was no solidarity between himself and other men at any point in his life, however, and it is precisely his radically introverted nature that makes his case so significant. For in spite of strong sexual appetites, he was unable to forget himself or lose himself in sex and unable to seize the real existence of others as embodied consciousnesses: 'C'est . . . l'alliance d'appétits sexuels ardents avec un "isolisme" affectif radical qui m'apparaît comme la clé de son érotisme' (32). His only satisfactions were to be had in the imaginary world, which explains his commitment to literature. His work is in part an endeavour to justify or excuse himself. In fact, his very *need* to write severely limits his achievements, in that he lacks the 'recul indispensable à un artiste' (50). Nevertheless, his insights into the nature of sexuality and the significance of perversions make him a precursor of psychoanalysis, and his ceaseless questioning of himself a great 'moraliste'.

On the philosophical or ethical level, having completely rejected the idea of God, Sade turned the new cult of Nature against its adherents by seeing Nature as evil rather than good, yet still inviting us to follow it. According to Beauvoir, he realised that the ideology of his time was no more than the product of a particular economic system, and wished to dispel 'les mystifications de la morale bourgeoise' (65). We as individuals can assert and maintain our concrete selves only through crime and must *make* ourselves criminals in an act of defiance performed not out of desire, but from free choice: 'par la violence de son affirmation, devenant réel pour l'autre il dévoile aussi l'autre comme existant réellement' (77). Sade's solution cannot be valid for all—'il est socialement du côté des privilégiés' (80)—and he fails to examine the possibilities of concrete collective action in the world. But at least he attacks 'toutes les réponses trop faciles' and, by disturbing us, forces us to re-examine the question of the relationships between people.

'Faut-il brûler Sade?' belongs to a type of examination of the life and works of an author associated with the 'existentialist psychoanalysis' that Sartre describes in *L'Être et le Néant*. In this context, it is understandable that Beauvoir should not address herself directly to the question of whether Sade's books are 'pornographic'—her implicit answer is clearly that this is not how they should be regarded—and that she should devote very little space to the matter of the artistic quality of his works, about which she admits to the most serious reservations. The lack of information about Sade's childhood is a problem, however, since the 'original choice' that individuals make of themselves must, within the Sartrean framework, go much further back than the period in which Beauvoir has Sade making his adult decision to turn sex into a morality. We are asked to admire a choice without knowing what lies behind it. In any case, not only are quotations from Sade's works (often given without references) selected on a basis that requires much more justification, many of the assertions about Sade himself deserve to be treated with suspicion (particularly in the light of Beauvoir's admission that 'dans ses livres il s'invente plus qu'il ne se dévoile'; 29), and some are manifestly speculative or unverifiable. How can we possibly be sure of why he decided to have three children (20), or of Beauvoir's crucial point that he was unable to forget himself even during sexual activity? Yet if it is to the very *coherence* of Beauvoir's reading of Sade that we should look for its explanatory power, it has to be said that her claim that he experienced no solidarity with others does not fit at all well with what she tells us of his position during the Revolution (25), or of his revulsion against oppression of the masses (63). Whatever light her interpretation of Sade casts upon his published works, it is extremely doubtful whether she succeeds in justifying her view that 'il nous aide à définir le drame humain dans sa généralité' (13). By the end of the essay, the truths about human kind that he is being said to reveal are especially vague, and the affirmation that 'l'érotisme apparaît chez Sade comme un mode de communication' (79) is paradoxical to say the very least!

A less striking feature of the essay is the fact that the socio-political dimension that Beauvoir gives to Sade's situation—he is one of 'les derniers rejetons d'une noblesse décadente' (28-29)—is neither very carefully worked out, nor at all well integrated into her main argument. Yet this is the aspect of the study that she stressed in 1955 in the Preface to *Privilèges*. Suggesting that Sade attempted a curious synthesis between the attitudes of the nobility and the bourgeoisie, she now saw him as much as a forerunner of Marx as of Freud: 'En posant comme irréconciliables les intérêts du tyran et ceux de l'esclave, il a pressenti la lutte des classes' (7-8). This difference of emphasis is to be accounted for by an important change in Beauvoir's views that took place soon after she wrote her essay on Sade. For some time Sartre had been trying to develop his earlier existentialism in the direction of Marxism, and early in 1952 he drew close to the French Communist Party. She herself, however, was hesitant about following the same path and this probably explains why 'Faut-il brûler Sade?', while resting upon the same 'bases idéalistes' as *Le Deuxième Sexe,* bears rather confusing traces of an entirely different type of approach to her topic. It was not until 1953 that, under the influence of Lanzmann as well as of Sartre, Beauvoir was to recognise the need for a more overtly Marxist stance on both the theoretical and practical levels: 'je liquidai mon moralisme idéaliste et finis par reprendre à mon compte le point de vue de Sartre' (FCh II,23).

Early in 1954 the editorial team of *Les Temps modernes,* becoming concerned that the term 'la gauche' was being devalued, embarked upon a campaign to clarify its meaning in various ways. Beauvoir's particular assignment was to define current *right-wing* ideas, and the article that she published in the journal in the middle of the year, 'La pensée de droite, aujourd'hui', is the second essay collected in *Privilèges.* Seeing her task as similar to the one she undertook in connection with myths about women—'en ce cas aussi, il s'agissait de mettre à nu les vérités pratiques—défense des privilégiés par les privilégiés—qui dissimulent leur crudité derrière des systèmes et des concepts nébuleux' (FCh II,60)—she read as much conservative polit-ical theory as possible, but concentrated her attack on an eclectic mixture of ideas that she saw as 'le fonds commun des idéologies modernes de la droite' (85).

Her longish essay begins with a review of the 'situation actuelle de la pensée bourgeoise', in which Beauvoir contends that under a new threat from the Left, all that right-wing theorists can do is to define their position 'à partir du communisme, contre lui, d'une façon purement négative' (90). Furthermore, the bourgeoisie of to-day is 'tout encombrée par l'idéologie qu'elle s'est forgée au temps où elle était une classe montante' (92), for reason is universal and cannot properly be used to justify the privileges of one particular class against the rest of humanity. Those on the Right cannot afford to acknow-ledge the class struggle and attribute communist views to resentment or envy, arguing that it is the mentality of the oppressed that needs to be changed, not their situation. They postulate the existence of an élite and hold one or other of a number of views of history which all exclude the possibility of change or progress. Their very idea of human kind is formed 'à partir de la particularité bourgeoise' (141), and the whole point of right-wing morality is to 'nier les masses au profit de l'Élite' (148). Aestheticism, too, is a means of justifying the estab-lished order and a way of scorning those that it oppresses (153). Bourgeois wisdom encourages us to *accept* things as they are and bourgeois institutions regulate the relationships between human beings in such a way as to ensure that there is no real communication between them. Nature, with its 'immuable fatalité' is one of the great idols of the right, since it discourages us from trying to change the course of the world. Right-wing theory is a mass of contradictions, for because truth and values are essentially universal, 'il est impossible à la

121

bourgeoisie d'assumer par la pensée son attitude pratique' (182). It is no more than a 'contre-pensée'.

'La pensée de droite, aujourd'hui' is Beauvoir's first major excursion into political theory proper and has undoubted interest as an account of the views that she takes those on the Left to be most characteristically opposing. As an exposure of the kind of 'mauvaise foi' to be detected in the very worst versions of right-wing theory, moreover, it may have provided—may still provide—targets and ammunition for those on the Left who are unfamiliar with the more outrageous doctrines of their political adversaries, and it may even convert certain waverers. But the essay is essentially polemical and certainly does not constitute serious, rigorous political argument. Beauvoir's description of right-wing theory is often caricatural (are there supposed to be no arguments at all in favour of conservatism that are worthy of serious discussion?), and she does nothing to help her case by presenting it as monolithic. Raymond Aron was quick to point out that one of her many mistakes is to 'confondre bourgeoisie (au sens marxiste) et Droite'.[2] She sometimes visibly stoops to the alleged level of her opponents (looking for the personal motives of right-wing intellectuals, while protesting that this should happen to those on her own side), and is in no position to criticise the dogmatic tone of those on the Right, when her own tone in the essay is often a rather unpleasantly ironical, even sneering one. Her material is fairly well structured, although there is some repetition, but it is striking that the lively, spirited nature of her first section, where she is offering her own analysis of a certain situation, contrasts strongly with that of subsequent parts, which are almost entirely dominated by *summary* of views that are frequently simply taken to be self-defeating.

The final essay in *Privilèges*, 'Merleau-Ponty et le pseudo-sartrisme', is another occasional piece. In June 1955 Maurice Merleau-Ponty, who had formerly collaborated with Sartre and Beauvoir on the editorial board of *Les Temps modernes,* published *Les Aventures de la dialectique*, in which he attacked Sartre's 'ultra-bolshevism', and Beauvoir immediately replied with this particular article. She argues that the doctrine to which he objects is not that of Sartre, but a 'pseudo-sartrisme'. Not only does Merleau-Ponty distort the ontological basis of Sartre's thought, he also misreads the important articles 'Les Communistes et la Paix'. His interpretation of Sartre's attitude to political action is quite mistaken and he is demonstrably wrong in his claim that Sartre no longer believes in the Revolution but bases his political choices only on 'des mobiles subjectifs'. In the final section of her piece Beauvoir mounts a direct assault on Merleau-Ponty's own political position of 'a-communism', falling back on some of the characterisations of the Right in her previous essay, condemning 'reformism' (that is, working for change 'dans les cadres du régime parlementaire'), and affirming the commitment to 'l'action révolutionnaire' which she shares with Sartre. By the nature of things, her defence of Sartre cannot be systematic enough here to constitute a useful summary of his doctrine, much less give us greater insight into it. It may even be misleading, in that she writes as if Sartre had never changed his views on anything, which—to judge only by her own comments in her memoirs—is evidently not the case. Neither is the essay calculated to bring out clearly what are in fact rather important divergences as well as similarities in the fundamental philosophical positions of Sartre and Merleau-Ponty. Beauvoir's sole concern is to rebut the latter's specific charges against Sartre and to undermine his general political stance. Although she undertakes her task in a scholarly manner and without undue animosity, it is hardly to be expected that her essay should have very much significance outside the context of the heated political disputes in France in the nineteen-fifties.

In fact, *Privilèges* as a whole is a very unsatisfactory work. The essay on Sade does suggest serious and fruitful lines of inquiry concerning an author who may have been rather neglected at the time. There is very little reason to believe, however, that either of the subsequent essays merited publication in book-form once they had already appeared in *Les Temps modernes*. Moreover, in spite of Beauvoir's claim—'Écrits à des époques et dans des perspectives différentes, ces essais répondent néanmoins à une même question: comment les privilégiés peuvent-ils *penser* leur situation?' (7)—the three pieces do not fit together at all well. 'Faut-il brûler Sade?' belongs to an earlier phase of her thought and does no more than offer odd glimpses of the broadly Marxist framework that she was later to adopt as her own, for instance in 'La pensée de droite, aujourd'hui'. And even if the matter of privileges is at the heart of both of these essays—which is doubtful in the case of the first—this could certainly not be said of the third, which would not have the remotest link with this question if Beauvoir had not gratuitously charged Merleau-Ponty with conservatism in the final section. The significance of *Privilèges* is that it constitutes a kind of still photograph of Beauvoir passing through a transitional stage in her development. The modification of her political stance in the early fifties was accompanied (as in the case of Sartre) by a shift of emphasis in her basic philosophical views whereby the notion of 'situation' came to encroach more than ever upon that of freedom ('tout ne vient pas de la *liberté* mais de la situation'; 220). This causes certain theoretical tensions in *Privilèges* as a whole, for even in the second and third essays one feels that Beauvoir has not yet completely adjusted to her fresh perspectives or settled comfortably into her new positions.

Nevertheless, she soon began to feel more at ease politically: 'Après des années à contre-courant, je me sentais de nouveau soutenue par l'histoire; et j'avais envie de m'y mêler davantage . . . de vieilles consignes se réveillaient en moi: servir à quelque chose' (FCh II, 72). In September 1955 she undertook her eagerly awaited six-week trip to China with Sartre. Since 1949 they had vaguely believed that the Chinese way to communism would be more flexible and more in- fluential than the Russian (FCh, 250), but the visit made an especially strong impression upon Beauvoir:

> Pour la première fois je touchai l'Extrême-Orient; pour la première fois je compris pleinement le sens des mots: pays sous- développé; je sus ce que signifiait la pauvreté à l'échelle de 600 millions d'hommes; pour la première fois j'assistai à ce dur travail: la construction du socialisme. (FCh II, 79)

Anti-communists were by now directing much of their fury against China rather than Russia and it seemed particularly important and useful to attempt to dispel misconceptions by writing a book about the country. On her return to France Beauvoir worked long and hard on relevant books, documents and statistics and *La Longue Marche* was published in June 1957.

In 'Préliminaires' she claims that China in 1955 is in a transitional phase—'Il s'agit de passer de la révolution démocratique à la révol- ution socialiste' (25)—and is undergoing a transformation in a quite distinctive manner. It must progress slowly, step by step, not destroying the past, but building upon it. The present moment in China being no more than 'un passage, une limite', it is impossible to report on it in the usual way by exploring a stable state of affairs. It can only be understood by reference to the future: 'Il est vain de prétendre décrire ce pays: il demande à être expliqué' (29).

Chapter 1, 'Découverte de Pékin', is something of a mixed bag of elements. It opens with an account of the city itself, in which Beauvoir blends informative descriptions, a little history and personal impressions to great effect. Her brief review of the economic structure of the country as a whole, on the other hand, seems somewhat misplaced and reads rather like an official government document. Some of her reactions to Peking are rather naïve—'Ici chaque personne, chaque chose est à sa place' (51)—but her comments all indicate that it is essentially the surge towards the future that impresses her.

In her chapter 'Les Paysans', Beauvoir points out that while Lenin was among the first to acknowledge the importance of the peasantry, Mao Tse-tung went still further: 'dans le cas de la Chine . . . la paysannerie devait être le principal facteur de la révolution' (86). Stressing the significance of the land redistribution of 1950-52, she claims that part of the aim was to awaken class-consciousness among the peasants and illustrates the psychological problems involved. One of the most original and successful features of the Chinese Revolution is said to be that the leaders wished the people to make it their own and found ways of involving them actively. This enabled the move from land redistribution to mutual-aid teams, then to lower-stage and higher-stage co-operatives to be made fairly smoothly, although Beauvoir acknowledges some of the diffficulties entailed ('il y a encore conflit entre les intérêts particuliers et l'intérêt collectif'; 106). She takes us through the major political measures adopted and relates what she saw for herself in three villages (102-09). Collectivisation is both necessary to the economy of the state and advantageous to the peasants, but it is inseparable from the waging of the particular form of class war that prevails in China. The mistakes made in Russia and elsewhere will be avoided in China.

Until the technical revolution is complete, social factors will continue to have great economic significance in China, and it is because family communities were something of an obstacle to collectivisation that the Marriage Law of 1950 was vital to the country's progress. Beauvoir argues in Chapter 3, 'La Famille', that China is not suppressing or devaluing the family, but simply replacing the traditional (feudal) structures that were oppressive. Women in particular suffered under the old family system and Beauvoir devotes considerable space here to describing, with graphic examples as well as generalisations and statistics, just how appalling their situation was. It took the Marriage Law, codifying new communist practices, to envisage 'une famille conjugale fondée sur l'égalité des époux et leur droit à disposer d'eux-mêmes' (139). Severe resistance is being encountered on this issue, however, and at least in the rural areas attitudes towards the family still bear the marks of the traditional system. Peasant women need to be paid for their labours, as men are: 'C'est par l'extension des coopératives que s'accomplira l'émancipation de la paysanne chinoise' (145). In the cities the situation is already much better for women, who no longer have to engage in a sex war. At the end of the chapter, perhaps rather belatedly, Beauvoir passes on to the question of children, arguing that vast improvements have been made in relation to their health and education and that they are no more 'indoctrinated' than in other countries. In general, the family remains the cornerstone of society (155).

In her fourth chapter, 'L'Industrie', Beauvoir explains why industrialisation is in both the immediate and long-term interests of the whole Chinese population. She sketches the evolution of the class war in China, emphasising how the country was dependent upon foreign capitalists, and describing the truly terrible condition of the country's workers before the People's Republic came into being. It is not expected that the process of socialising the economy will be completed for another fifteen years, but industry is already flourishing in Shanghai and in Manchuria. For the moment priority has to be given to heavy industry and here Soviet aid is invaluable. Another urgent need is to train a large number of engineers and technicians, but although the workers played only a secondary role in the Revolution, 'c'est le prolétariat qu'on considère aujourd'hui comme son avant-garde' (207). Beauvoir provides much detail on how workers are paid and their living and working conditions, expressing the hope that their circumstances will soon be improved. Understandably, she seems somewhat uneasy about certain features of the present position (workers do not have the right to strike, for instance), and again can only hope that the unions will soon take on the role of defending the interests of their members. Yet she believes both that the regime has already radically transformed the workers' condition and that the policy being followed will lead to further improvements and greater freedom (220).

Chapter 5, 'La Culture', is twice as long as any other in the book and deals with a wider range of phenomena than one might expect. Beauvoir claims that politics and culture have always been closely interrelated and that in modern China culture is as much an agent of change as an expression of the human condition. The regime is trying at the same time to combat superstition and to extend educational provision. There has been a massive adult literacy campaign since 1949 and the next stage is seen as political instruction. For the time being, control of the press is necessary, since the powers of understanding of the public are still very limited. Beauvoir explains how and why over the centuries in China there has been a clear distinction between 'classical' and popular culture, pointing out that this raises a policy problem for the new regime: 'ce qui fut populaire peut-il prendre aujourd'hui une dimension nationale?' (251). And how far should the bourgeois elements of culture accumulated from the end of the nineteenth century onwards be preserved? In fact, 'La vieille civilisation chinoise est . . . activement revendiquée par les Chinois' (252), and the only question is to what extent it has been assimilated in the different intellectual and artistic domains. Currently the real issue is not the relationship between Marxism and 'les anciennes sagesses' (like Confucianism), but between Marxism and other modern philosophies. Up to 1956, every doctrine other than historical materialism was banned, but a considerable change has just begun to take place and no popular democracy has ever taken liberalism so far: 'En théorie du moins il n'existe plus aucune restriction à la liberté de penser' (276).

In a long section on literature Beauvoir shows that 'les privilégiés l'ont monopolisée plus radicalement qu'en aucune autre civilisation' (276-77). The new regime is endeavouring to steer writers in the direction of Marxism-Leninism and to have them criticise earlier Chinese literature and Western literature in that perspective. She notes that the material conditions of writers have never been better and argues that the demands made upon them by the government are understandable, although the visibly edifying books being produced really constitute no more than 'une pré-littérature' (310). She claims that most intellectuals have rallied to the new regime and is greatly encouraged by a change in the party line in spring 1956, which opens up 'les chemins de la liberté' (311). She also applauds the steps taken to simplify and standardise written Chinese as measures designed to 'démocratiser concrètement la culture' (321). As far as theatre and painting are concerned, the new forms required to express 'la nouveauté du monde' have not yet been discovered. Beauvoir is indifferent to the deterioration and imminent disappearance of the products of 'l'art populaire', but clearly believes the actions taken to preserve ancient Chinese forms of medicine alongside Western forms to be right. She records that the problem in the sciences is simply how to increase the number of scientists and raise their level, but concludes that 'Actuellement en Chine le problème de *l'extension* de la culture passe encore avant celui de son *élévation*' (351). Chinese culture is undoubtedly being westernised, but Beauvoir sees its originality as lying in front of it rather than behind it.

In Chapter 6, 'La Lutte défensive', Beauvoir reminds us that Communist China's struggle against Chian Kai-shek and the Nationalists continues and that this explains the regime's attitude towards military service and defence in general. She also points out that the assimilation of national minorities has been a major task since 1949. Her main concern, however, is to defend the government's policies on internal dissent in China. She believes that the particular progress required made resistance inevitable, but claims that 'Aucun citoyen en Chine n'est inquiété pour ses "opinions"' (366). Prisons are more humane institutions in China than in the West, and the worst reproach to be levelled against the system of camps for 're-education through work' is that it is not effective. She explains at length why Christianity has had so little success in China and strongly vindicates the conditions that the regime imposes upon its tolerance of Western religions. The last two substantive chapters of the book—describing the Peking festivities of 1st October and recording Beauvoir's impressions of four major Chinese cities (Nanking, Shanghai, Hangchow and Canton)— contain relatively little political commentary as such, although she does express admiration for Mao himself and the style of his leadership (414), as well as giving her analysis of the political situation in some of the cities. There is much here that is guide-book material, but when Beauvoir is clearly registering her own experiences and perceptions, the descriptions are often excellent. While Chapter 7 brings China more vividly to life for us, Chapter 8 gives us a far better idea than previously of the great variety in the country's geography and urban environments.

La Longue Marche is a markedly different type of work from *L'Amérique au jour le jour*. Yet Beauvoir's admission that it is a less

lively book should not be allowed to obscure the fact that in certain parts she is prepared to have it resemble a traveller's diary and that, more generally, the deliberately personal element in the work is an important ingredient. Here as elsewhere, she shows us not only how sharp her powers of observation are in a foreign country, and how eager she is to understand the significance of what she sees, but also how evocatively she can describe a setting or scene, be it a whole city, a view from a train window, or the hustle and bustle of activity in the streets. Sections of *La Longue Marche* really do give the uninitiated a strong desire to see China for themselves and experience what Beauvoir experienced. Nevertheless, she has more than once referred to the book as an expression of her political commitment during the nineteen-fifties and this is the feature that broadly dominates the text. She wished to 'réfuter certaines erreurs et exprimer certaines idées politiques',[3] and the work is first and foremost a long, extremely serious attempt to explain the situation of China in 1955-56 and justify the direction in which the new regime is guiding the country.

In spite of Beauvoir's repetitive and heavy-handed way of presenting her historical perspective here, her central belief is that it is reference to the *future* that is essential to an understanding of modern China. The result of this, as she herself foresaw, is that her book rapidly became out of date in certain respects. She was perhaps particularly unfortunate to be writing about China when she did, in that the relatively liberal and relaxed policies that prevailed in 1955-56 were very soon to be superseded by intensified repression, which made what she had to say, for example, about the position of Chinese intellectuals appear peculiarly ill-judged. Her general comments on China's more recent evolution, in *Tout compte fait,* not surprisingly show considerable bewilderment and some traces of disillusionment (TCF, 562-68). In any case, it needs to be acknowledged that some of Beauvoir's appeals to the future in the text itself look very much like last lines of defence, for at a number of points she can do no more, in the course of answering criticisms of China, than fall back on the *hope* that matters will soon improve (in relation to the family, workers' freedom, writers' freedom, ideological quarrels, and so on). Whether or not these hopes have been realised, they show her belief in China to be a *faith* as much as a reasoned assessment. This is rather borne out, too, by what she says concerning her sources of information. Beauvoir went to China as one of about fifteen hundred guests of the Chinese government and although very critical of the official documents distributed to delegates, she seems happy enough to put her trust in items printed in certain journals, even though these come ultimately from the same source (18-21). However much she used her own eyes and ears and consulted independent experts in France, her view of China corresponds to a remarkable degree with the official one. Frequently, the only reservations that she is prepared to entertain about particular policies are those that the government itself admits to, and therefore has answers to. Virtually all criticisms are cat-egorised as anti-communist prejudice, and for the most part Beauvoir's defence is simply a matter of counter-assertion, of pitting one dog-matic view against another. There is never any suggestion that there may be *some* truth in objections that have been raised and her tone often approaches the abusive.

Various reviewers have, of course, detected factual errors or ques-tioned particular artistic judgements that Beauvoir makes,[4] and there are manifestly points at which her admiration for the regime is carried to ridiculous lengths. More generally, certain recurring patterns in her argument are intrinsically suspect. The claim that as long as the right social and political ends continue to be pursued, everything will eventually work out well for the individual involves a belief in the idea of 'le bien général' of which she was fiercely critical in 'La Pensée de droite, aujourd'hui'. And if it is true, as she suggests, that the regime adopts the policies it does not by reference to moral principles, but as the best practical means to certain political ends, then it is not clear how much praise is appropriate for any measures that happen to favour freedom (like the campaign for the emancipation of women). Indeed, the least persuasive sections of the text are those where Beauvour tries to defend policies like the drastic curbing of the freedom of the press (240), or the purging of 'counter-revolutionaries' (363). Finally, it is noticeable that she regularly oscillates between positions implying that China is doing something radically new or different and that it is simply doing what any other regime in China would have done (484), or even what every other country already does!

Changing her whole vision of the world by convincing her that Western comfort is an exception and a privilege (FCh II,96), Beauvoir's visit to China certainly produced a more worthwhile book than *Privilèges*, for *La Longue Marche* contains a vast amount of material of various kinds about China, as well as some most memorable descriptions. Judging by reactions to the book in France and America, moreover, it was a timely essay, in that a deeply sympathetic account of the country's aims and achievements was badly needed at this stage. Yet in it Beauvoir does appear to place herself in as extreme a position as those she castigates in *Privilèges*. Her praise for China is so unqualified, her views so obviously one-sided, that *La Longue Marche* runs some risk of being counter-productive. In any case, one may have sympathy with the general beliefs that lie behind the work without thinking that she has chosen the most persuasive way of propounding them.

As early as August 1958 Beauvoir's desire to write something on the topic of old age was a strong one (FCh II,212). But it was in May 1967, having abandoned her attempt to write a novel on the theme, that she decided to compose a long essay that would be 'touchant les personnes âgées, le symétrique du *Deuxième Sexe*' (TCF,183). She wished to reply to some criticisms of her remarks on the subject at the end of *La Force des choses*, but above all to investigate a problem that intimately concerned her: 'Femme, j'ai voulu élucider ce qu'est la condition féminine; aux approches de la vieillesse, j'ai eu envie de savoir comment se définit la condition des vieillards' (TCF,183). Beauvoir prepared herself for this task in her usual way, reading almost everything available in French and English, yet developing her own views and emphasis. *La Vieillesse* appeared at the end of January 1970, shortly after the publication of an important French report on the social problems of old people, which gave her book an unexpected topicality.

It is another very lengthy work, structured in roughly the same way as *Le Deuxième Sexe*. Part I ('Le point de vue de l'extériorité') consists of chapters on the biological, anthropological, historical and contemporary sociological aspects of the topic, while Part II ('L'être-dans-le-monde') explores the nature and quality of the experiences of old people as seen from their own point of view. Beauvoir makes her own general position clear in the Introduction. She considers that there is a conspiracy of silence about old age; that capitalist society treats old people as outcasts and therefore wants as little attention drawn to their existence as possible—something made easier by the fact that we all have the gravest difficulty in believing that we shall grow old in our turn. Exploitation, social fragmentation and the existence of a privileged class are at the root of the scandalous material situation of old people, which only radical reorganisation of society will remedy: 'tout est à reprendre, dès le départ' (18).

Acknowledging that old age (like femininity) is 'un fait culturel', Beauvoir first describes in detail, with the aid of the most recent knowledge and statistics, what ageing amounts to physically and physiologically. But since the implications of the biological processes involved are governed by the type of society to which the aged belong and their particular place within it, we need to examine how societies have treated their old people at different times and in different places. This will give us some idea of which features of their condition are inevitable and the extent to which society itself can modify it. Looking in Chapter 2 at primitive tribes, and relating what is known about their treatment of old people to the circumstances and structure of the community as a whole, Beauvoir detects no single pattern. The old person in these societies, however, is invariably regarded as *l'Autre*, with all the ambivalent implications that this entails (137). Whatever the status of old people, it is not one that they themselves have earned, but one assigned to them by the rest of the community. Biological forces inevitably make them non-productive, though communities with different resources react to this economic fact in different and revealing ways: 'C'est le sens que les hommes accordent à leur existence, c'est leur système global de valeurs qui définit le sens et la valeur de la vieillesse' (140).

In Chapter 3 Beauvoir uses standard historical sources in reviewing attitudes to the old as a social category across the centuries, but she also refers to works of literature ('le point de vue des poètes') for insights into how individuals have viewed the fate that awaits them. Old people as a group have never exercised a major influence upon the course of history, although they have sometimes been accorded an important role in society by the active adults. History from biblical times to the twentieth century shows that well-organised and stable communities have used the experience of the old, while in troubled times or divided societies younger adults have been entirely domin-ant. The sweeping changes that took place in the nineteenth century improved the lot of some old people, but this only accentuated the gap between the privileged and unprivileged, exploiters and exploited. The fate of the aged in the poorer classes has always been worse than any records reveal and since the privileged can no longer ignore them, they are obliged to downgrade all old people: 'Plus que le conflit des générations, c'est la lutte des classes qui a donné à la notion de vieillesse son ambivalence' (342).

Chapter 4 is a searing indictment—based upon some personal testimonies, but above all an abundance of facts and figures—of the way in which many Western countries treat their old people. We are all to blame: 'C'est la classe dominante qui impose aux personnes âgées leur statut; mais l'ensemble de la population active se fait son complice' (343). The majority of capitalist states set the level of pensions in relation to strict economic interests rather than taking account of the needs of those involved, with the result that most old people are given only just enough to survive on (384). Accommodation is a problem, yet the provision for them in homes and hospitals is entirely inadequate. The sudden change from an active life to retirement brings serious psychological problems, especially for men, and especially for manual workers. Radical changes are required to break the vicious circle whereby those least well situated have fewest means of counteracting their misery, although even old people who are financially well placed suffer from feelings of uselessness. The situation of the old is an eloquent condemnation of a whole social system, 'un système qui ne fournit à l'énorme majorité des gens qui en font partie aucune raison de vivre' (438).

In Part II Beauvoir is no longer concerned with how old people can be seen from the outside, but with the way in which they themselves experience their condition. She shows in Chapter 5 why old age takes us all by surprise. It is what Sartre calls 'un irréalisable', since we are unable to experience inwardly exactly what we are, outwardly, to other people: 'cette situation que je *vis* est au milieu du monde une forme objective qui m'échappe' (II, 25). And because we do not have direct, 'transparent' experience of age, we can choose either to be old before our time or to stay young to the end. Either choice will be an expression of our relationship with the world in general. Yet we still have to live through the physical manifestations of ageing and Beauvoir strongly attacks the 'spiritualist' view that our decline has great compensations. She discusses sexuality in old people at considerable length, with numerous detailed examples from the lives of well-known figures, illustrating her point that, in this domain as elsewhere, a whole range of responses to reality are possible. Rather than passively undergoing a biological 'fate', we are constantly choosing our image of ourselves and acting accordingly.

Beauvoir next examines old people's view of time, activity, history and death. Memory is so unreliable and fragmentary that our past is not available to us in any helpful sense. In fact, the longer we live, the more we are in its grip. Furthermore, the future for old people looks brief and closed, while time itself seems to pass more quickly. In many cases this is enough to paralyse all activity, especially as the world is now changing so swiftly that the 'experience' of old people is no longer highly valued. Physical decline is rather less of a problem for intellectuals than for others, but even for scientists, philosophers and writers the weight of the past slows down, or even halts, their activity. History shows itself as a force in the case of the politician, who, however successful, is often overtaken by it. Men and women identify themselves with the times in which they conceived and executed their projects, and when these times are over they become merely survivors from a past age. It is not surprising, therefore, that although death is another 'irréalisable' (II, 249), many old people prefer it to further struggling and suffering. Yet others choose to hang on desperately, even after losing all apparent reason for living.

A major problem of old age, Beauvoir argues in her seventh chapter, is that once we have no more major projects, the world becomes an infinitely less interesting place in our eyes, setting up another vicious circle: 'l'inaction décourage curiosité et passion et notre indifférence dépeuple le monde où nous n'apercevons plus aucune raison d'agir' (II, 267). Although old people are able to use their age as an excuse for many things, they pay dearly for this privilege, by being considered inferior in all respects. This can lead to self-disgust and depression or sullenness, but above all it makes the old defensive. They are anxious and mistrustful, depending increasingly upon routine or self-imposed obligations, clinging to their possessions and money. If relations with their children, and especially their grand-children, are good, this can be a comfort, but there is often hostility in old people's attitudes towards later generations, because of the way in which they themselves are treated. Although in a few cases old age results in a kind of enrichment of liberation, very few indeed have the opportunity of seizing the possible advantages of their position. The general situation of the old is liable to produce a whole variety of mental illnesses, which Beauvoir lists and describes.

In Chapter 8 she shows, by recounting the old age of six famous men and one famous woman, how people's choices in their earlier years combine with contingent events or circumstances later to give a particular quality and shape to their old age. In her Conclusion she contends that, in present conditions, old age is a kind of parody of adult life. Only a handful of 'privilégiés' are able to continue pursuing the ends that gave meaning to their lives, and the gap between their position and that of the vast majority of old people is enormous. Our society's policy on old people is scandalous, but even more scandalous is the way in which it exploits most people before old age, for this is what makes them age prematurely and decline so rapidly and painfully: 'La vieillesse dénonce l'échec de toute notre civilisation' (II, 398). If people were given an education that was 'pratique et vivante', and were encouraged to participate much more in the life of the collectivity, then old age would not imply degradation of any kind, but would involve a wide range of possibilities and its own equilibrium. These are conditions that have never prevailed in any country and a thoroughgoing transformation of the present system is needed.

In *La Vieillesse,* as in *Le Deuxième Sexe,* Beauvoir sees the deplorable situation of a very substantial but oppressed proportion of the population as a 'fait culturel' rather than an inevitability. Demolishing the screen of comforting myths and lies that hide this fact, she once more locates an aspect of Western society that we have no reason to be proud of and tells us exactly why. The book displays a concern to understand how old people think and see the world that is wholly admirable, and her comments on, for instance, sexuality in old age (II, 63-115) or the 'anti-social' conduct of old people (II, 305-10) reveal a depth of sympathy that is an example to all. More generally, her insights into the psychology of ageing in Chapters 5, 6 and 7 are invaluable and perhaps all the more penetrating for being presented in a somewhat personal, intuitive manner, rather than a dry, rigorously empirical form.

Unfortunately, not all of these virtues are in evidence in Part I, where the angle of approach followed in *Le Deuxième Sexe* does not prove especially successful. The chapter on the biology of ageing is no more than a brief summary of existing knowledge, and Beauvoir fails to convince us that her long anthropological and historical survey (which takes up a third of the whole book) is indispensable to an understanding of the reality of old age. Even if it is true that her analysis is original (TCF, 184-85), the conclusions to Chapter 2 are neither precise nor surprising, and in the loosely structured Chapter 3—which she admits does not constitute a history of old age: 'nous avons seulement décrit les attitudes des sociétés historiques à l'égard des vieillards et les images qu'elles s'en sont forgées' (339)—an uneasy combination of historical fact and passages from literary works leads nowhere in particular. Because *La Vieillesse* is a campaigning book, the chapter on the position of old people in contemporary society, which is really the heart of the matter, should have attracted much of the space devoted to history. It is not short on hard information, but on some points (for instance, retirement) Beauvoir's assertions are flatly contradicted by experts, and, in any case, anyone can recognise over-generalisations and exaggerations in her material. Her deeply gloomy views apply with much more force to the very last stages of a person's life than to old age as a whole, and she is obviously wrong to infer from the point that we all bear responsibility for the plight of the old that everyone looks down upon old people and treats them badly on the personal level: 'C'est d'une manière sournoise que l'adulte tyrannise le vieillard qui dépend de lui' (347). Beauvoir is scarcely more careful in her attack on a whole social *system,* for her admission that certain capitalist countries (Sweden, Norway, Denmark) treat their old very well directly undermines her sweeping observations about how a society of exploitation necessarily rejects those who can no longer work.

Part II also has its faults. Beauvoir substantiates her claim that written accounts of ageing emanating from the privileged classes have general significance (II, 11), but often fails to persuade us that detailed accounts of the old age of *famous* people are entirely to the point. Does not the considerable space devoted to the sex lives of certain celebrities divert her attention from other very important aspects of old people's perception of their bodies? How can the fact that the vast preponderance of cases cited are those of writers be justified? And does the study of three politicians add anything to the argument? The most penetrative features of her compassionate attempt to understand the old emerge in between, almost in spite of, her examples of famous people, which rather shift the centre of gravity of the book. There is no contradiction between the points that a society's treatment of its old is a function of its general nature and that the old age of some very privileged people is largely a function of their choices earlier in life, but an adequate explanation of how the two theses fit together is required and the second should occupy no more than a secondary place in the work.

If *La Vieillesse* succeeds in its aim of picking out those aspects of old people's condition that society can modify, it does so only sketchily, while dwelling at inordinate length on tangential matters. It is a rich source of information and anecdote about old age, into which Beauvoir at times blends her own experience and intuitions as well as some of the philosophical arguments of Sartre, yet even on its own terms its omissions are significant ones. Only in Chapter 4 is direct and explicit account taken of the great mass of unprivileged old people, or their plight dwelt upon in any detail. In view of Beauvoir's later views on the best way to fight for women's emancipation, it is already surprising that she should be content to advocate a radical transformation of the whole of society as a solution to the problems of the old, but her failure to spend any time at all considering what is to be done here and now is, by any standard, difficult to understand. Even her indications of how old people would be treated in the ideal society are extremely vague. The strength of *La Vieillesse* lies not in any practical proposals that it makes, but in the very fact that it draws our attention to a social question that can easily be neglected, implying that much *can* be done and preventing us from averting our gaze with an easy conscience.

Notes

[1] The 'Idées' edition of *Privilèges*, from which page references are taken here, is entitled *Faut-il brûler Sade?*

[2] 'Mme de Beauvoir et la pensée de droite', *Le Figaro littéraire*, 1956.

[3] Interview with Madeleine Chapsal, *Écrits*, p.393.

[4] See, for example, G. F. Hudson: 'Mme de Beauvoir in China', *Encounter*, 1959; I. Epstein: 'Bright light on China', *Mainstream*, 1958.

PART III
Fiction

7 *Quand prime le spirituel* and *L'Invitée*

On a number of occasions in the early nineteen-thirties Beauvoir began writing novels, but she abandoned each of her attempts before producing anything that she might submit to a publisher. In 1935, however, she embarked upon a series of five interlinked stories, the unifying theme of which was 'la profusion de crimes, minuscules ou énormes, que couvrent les mystifications spiritualistes' (FA,256). The collection was ironically entitled *La Primauté du spirituel*. She herself was in revolt against the spiritualism that had oppressed her for so long and wished to express her disgust 'à travers l'histoire de jeunes femmes que je connaissais et qui en avaient été les victimes plus ou moins consentantes' (QPS,vii). Beauvoir completed the work in 1937, but by the time it had been turned down by both Gallimard and Grasset she had other projects in hand and was content enough to forget it. It was finally published under the modified title *Quand prime le spirituel* in 1979, when she decided that it was not without its qualities and shed a certain light on her other writings.

The first story, 'Marcelle', sketches the childhood, adolescence and early aspirations of the heroine, then describes in rather more detail the nature and failure of her marriage to a worthless, playboy 'poet'. Marcelle's self-indulgence as a child soon becomes thoroughgoing self-deception as she covers up her strong sensuality, first with fantasies and then with a belief in the special destiny that governs her life. Her job as a social worker is little more than a way of biding her time until the right man comes along, as is her involvement with the movement attempting to bring culture to the working classes. As her 'mystérieuse féminité' asserts itself more, she becomes engaged to one of the organisers of the movement. Although she still fails to acknowledge her sensuality, when her fiancé proves not to have a passionate nature she loses interest in him and becomes infatuated with an aspiring poet, whom she takes to be her man of destiny. They marry and for a while her voluptuousness receives full, if somewhat tormented, expression. Denis, however, soon turns out to be an indolent parasite and eventually leaves her for someone else. Undeterred,

Marcelle immediately chooses martyrdom, constructing another personal image with which to maintain her self-deception:

> peut-être la souffrance seule pourrait-elle combler enfin son cœur. 'Plus haut que le bonheur', murmura-t-elle . . . Pour la seconde fois elle eut la merveilleuse révélation de son destin. 'Je suis une femme de génie', décida-t-elle. (44)

The strength of 'Marcelle' lies in its portrayal of the persistent 'mauvaise foi' of a shallow young woman of bourgeois origins. Since the story is narrated for the most part from the viewpoint of the central figure herself, this theme cannot be spelled out explicitly and Beauvoir's technique consists in juxtaposing details which fit together only on the assumption that Marcelle's motives and ideals are not what she claims they are. At some points the device is rather too obvious, but on the whole Beauvoir manages this main feature of the tale with skill, and her examination of the self-deception of her character, even of a certain *type* of woman, is penetrating and forceful. Relative lack of detail, however, makes the account of the earlier stages of Marcelle's life much less substantial and convincing than that of her marriage. The latter suffers from compression and has its melodramatic moments, but it contains telling sequences, like the description of Marcelle's wedding night, while a specific problem with the first half is the flimsiness of Beauvoir's explanation of the *origins* of Marcelle's 'mauvaise foi'. As we have simply to accept that the character chooses this stance early in her childhood, our interest in Marcelle remains limited until we become involved in the more carefully delineated relationship with Denis.

Although the heroine of 'Chantal' is also a victim of self-deception in some measure, this is not quite the main feature of the second story, which relates the first year of a young Sèvres graduate's initial teaching appointment, in the provincial town of Rougemont. Chantal's attitudes are certainly marked by contradictions. She hopes for professional and even social success, yet sees herself as an anti-establishment figure in the school, fraternising with two of her pupils rather than with her colleagues. Furthermore, her love of culture is evidently something of an affectation, for it emerges that she is happy to have finished studying (49) and does not enjoy intellectual conversations (55). In these and other respects Chantal is undoubtedly deluding herself to some unspecified extent. More essential to the story, however, is the general point that, whether self-deceived or simply cynical, she is not what she claims to be. The way in which Chantal refuses to help her favourite pupil Monique, when the latter becomes pregnant, shows both that her views are more conventional than she pretends and that she is much less concerned about the welfare of her pupils than she would have them believe. Above all, she is relieved not to have been implicated in the scandal: 'Ils auraient pu me compromettre' (100).

Beauvoir brings these points out well by relating two and a half of the six sections almost exclusively from the standpoint of another of Chantal's pupil's, Andrée. While part of Chantal's account of events —including the beginning of the story—is cast in a diary-form that is quite appropriate to her new situation, Andrée's viewpoint is introduced much later, in a rather more disorientating manner (for a short time we are not aware that the person she refers to as 'Plattard' is in fact Chantal). This is an effective way of forcing us to see Chantal from the outside and to contrast her view of things with that of someone else. Andrée sees through Monique's boy-friend Serge in a way that Chantal never does, as well as exposing the hopelessly romantic character of the teacher's vision in a number of other respects. In the eyes of the reader, therefore, Chantal's viewpoint is doubly undermined, for she continues to regard Andrée as an unintelligent, unimaginative girl. Because of Beauvoir's juggling with conflicting perspectives, the story rather lacks a strong focal point and the key relationships in it are not explored in sufficient detail or depth to fascinate us. What all of the main characters have in common, however, is that they feel cramped or stifled in the town of Rougemont. The satirical portraits of social life in the provinces and petty squabbling in the local *lycée* are not enough to pull the story together, but they are vivid in themselves and make Beauvoir's revolt against provincialism one of the most memorable features of the tale.

'Lisa' is a brief but interesting study of the mentality of a highly sheltered post-graduate student, who lives as an assistant teacher in a Catholic institution for rich young girls on the outskirts of Paris. Lisa's commitment to philosophy has gone and her central concern is to excite the interest of the brother of her more independent and free-thinking friend, Marguerite. Beauvoir exposes Lisa's immaturity by tracing her reactions to the trivial incidents of one of her days of freedom in a city that still overwhelms her: 'Les rues de Paris, les passants avaient toujours ce visage ennemi' (117). Lisa is both cruelly disappointed at her failure to win over her 'friends' and stimulated to the point of fantasy by casual encounters in the street, as well as by an appointment with her dentist. She returns meekly to Auteuil, however, and quickly realises how little significance what has happened to her has in the context of her everyday life at the school. Although it is somewhat easier to sympathise with the heroine here than it was in the earlier stories, the institutional background to 'Lisa' is not entirely satisfactory. It is difficult to believe that someone of Lisa's age and education—even one whose studies had been conducted under the watchful eye of Mlle Lambert—would accept such a humiliating position so submissively (' "vous savez que le règlement interdit de passer plus d'une journée par semaine hors de la maison" '; 109). Nevertheless, Beauvoir's portrayal of the vague and unstable romanticism of certain protected young women is convincing, and some of the set-pieces in the story—notably, detailed descriptions of work in the Bibliothèque Nationale and a session in the dentist's chair—are particularly successful.

The key to 'Anne' resides in the fact that no part of the story is narrated from the viewpoint of the heroine. Beauvoir's central purpose is to show how the individuality and freedom of a girl of twenty is ignored by the other main characters, into whose minds we *are* allowed to penetrate. Anne's mother, Mme Vignon, is only concerned, allegedly in the name of deep religious principles, to ensure that her daughter remains 'moral' and respectable in all ways: 'c'était atroce de torturer cette enfant, mais il fallait penser à son salut, non à son bonheur' (145). Her friend Chantal at least helps her to recognise 'combien il se mêlait de prudence bourgeoise au souci que Mme Vignon prenait de son âme' (166), but she herself, in encouraging Anne to rebel against her mother, is using Anne to solve her own problems: 'elle avait besoin d'une réussite éclatante pour oublier tout à fait Rougemont' (156). Torn between these two forces, Anne attaches great importance to her relationship with Pascal Drouffe. He, however, in spite of his efforts to be honest, is confused and self-deceived. While he idealises Anne and their relationship in certain respects, he does not have genuine love for her and uses the excuse of the situation of his mother and sister (Marcelle) in order to avoid becoming engaged. Perhaps under the pressures involved, Anne breaks down and dies, of encephalitis or a brain tumour. Mme Vignon, Pascal and

Chantal all draw some kind of consolation from her death: Pascal interprets it in vague philosophical terms ('la vie s'accomplit par la mort et la mort est source de vie'; 186); Mme Vignon sees it as God's will; and Chantal sees in it a way of making herself into a more mysterious, romantic figure: 'désormais des ombres mystérieuses passeraient parfois sur son visage, ses gestes, ses paroles, auraient de subtiles résonances' (192).

The story is again technically interesting in the way in which it makes us read between the lines. Beauvoir skilfully plays off one viewpoint against another as she did in 'Chantal'—here Chantal is critical of Mme Vignon's view of Anne as well as of Pascal's, while Mme Vignon deplores the influence of both Pascal and Chantal, and Pascal thinks that he understands Anne better than either of the two women. Over and above this, Beauvoir gives a distinctive tone to each of the three main 'narrators' (a short section of Part IV is related from the standpoint of Marcelle), but in each separate case one which encourages the reader to detect forms of 'mauvaise foi' in the words and attitudes on display. Mme Vignon is the first of a line of portraits that Beauvoir was to draw of the repressive mother who transfers her own psychological problems to her daughter; and Chantal's narrative continues to show us the deeply selfish and insecure young woman that we saw in the second story. However, the figure of Pascal (who is an especially important person for many of the women characters in this collection) is not very well delineated, and far too little is made of Anne's death, which scarcely seems to relate to preceding events at all. While the separate parts cohere neatly in relation to the main events, there is a void rather than a fascinating mystery at the heart of the story, since we have no reason for identifying particularly strongly with Anne, who remains relatively unknown to us.

The final story, 'Marguerite', is similar in content to the opening one. It relates, this time in the first person, the childhood and early adulthood of Marguerite Drouffe. Though less sensual than her older sister Marcelle, she too has to struggle against her background in order to understand sexuality; she too soon loses faith in God; and she too works for the movement Contact Social. Moreover, she becomes just as captivated by Denis Charval as her sister was and, after a break, goes on seeing him when he is no longer with Marcelle. Ostensibly in the name of philosophical principles, he introduces her to drink and the night-life of Montparnasse, but although her naïve belief in him represents too violent a swing from the extreme of narrow bourgeois morality to that of empty bohemian rhetoric, Marguerite's commitment to Denis eventually goes far beyond a submission to the charm of the sordid. Her devotion is certainly more genuine and less self-centred than was her sister's rather patronising attitude and—for all its short-sightedness—can be seen as having a certain nobility (237). She is shaken out of it by a similar shock to that sustained by Marcelle, whom he finally decides to go back to. The last part of the story stresses that it was only when she had outgrown her obsession with Denis that she could develop autonomously and begin coming to grips with the real world: 'j'ai voulu montrer seulement comment j'ai été amenée à essayer de regarder les choses en face, sans accepter d'oracles, de valeurs toutes faites; il a fallu tout réinventer moi-même' (249).

In spite of some vivid sketches of bizarre characters and shady nightclubs (like 'Marcelle', it comes to life more when Denis enters the scene), and despite Beauvoir's relatively high opinion of it, the story is a rather conventional, undistinguished one. It is rather too tidy and structured to have the open-ended quality of the first tale and although it begins to raise questions of its own—notably, concerning the risks run by a woman who invests all of her faith and hopes on one man ('ma vie était transfigurée, elle avait retrouvé enfin ce sens qu'elle avait perdu le jour où j'avais perdu Dieu'; 228), these are left unexplored. With Marguerite promising to face up to the world more positively than any of Beauvoir's other heroines, the ending allows the collection to close on an apparently constructive note. But this convenient optimism is vague and weak in relation to the pitfalls described in the rest of the story, let alone the rest of the book. Grasset's reader, Henry Müller, made a very astute remark about the stories in this connection: ' "Vous vous êtes contentée de décrire un univers en décomposition, et de nous abandonner au seuil d'un monde nouveau sans nous en indiquer très exactement le particulier rayonnement" ' (FA,375).

Beauvoir was surprised that her collection should have been taken as a deliberate evocation of certain settings and situations in the period after the First World War, yet this may indeed be its major merit in general. As she suggests, *Quand prime le spirituel* certainly begins exploring a number of the themes that were to dominate her later fiction—especially that of 'mauvaise foi'—but it cannot be said that the attack on spiritualism provides a single strong focal point for the various stories. At different times she herself has claimed that the satirical and didactic sides of the work are 'trop accusées' (FA,258) and that the satire 'bien que pertinente, restait timide' (QPS,vii). The more important fact is that the target itself remains particularly vague. It was doubtless a very real one for Beauvoir, and comparison with her memoirs shows how extensively she drew on her personal experience in creating her characters ('Anne' is clearly based on Zaza's tragedy, and Beauvoir admits to liking the early part of 'Marguerite' because it is largely her own story). Nevertheless, the crucial process of characterisation is in one way or another inadequate in most cases. This is probably not simply because she was lacking in technique at this point—her handling of narrative, whilst promising a great deal, repeatedly shows a certain lack of control and consistency—but also because she had not yet found a properly substantial and coherent topic. It is also true that the book falls between two stools. At some stage since 1937, at least a few changes seem to have been made to the text (Marcelle was formerly called Renée and 'Lisa' was originally the first, not the third story in the collection; FA,256), but although a broad chronological progression has been preserved and although the interlinking of the tales becomes more prominent in later stages, the book has neither the range and variety of a good collection of separate stories nor the continuity and harmony of a novel.

While her stories treated a theme that preoccupied her, Beauvoir had approached it through characters for whom she felt at best very limited sympathy and she soon came to recognise their lack of relief: 'Je n'avais pas prêté la chaleur de ma vie à ces histoires où des héroïnes anémiques évoluaient dans un monde falot' (FA,259). A suggestion by Sartre that she should begin putting more of herself directly into her fiction at first filled her with horror. This constituted a critical turning-point in her career, however, for during the autumn of 1937 she started drafting an account of the childhood of a character with whom she identified fairly closely. Although she was persuaded by Sartre and Brice Parain a year later that this account was inferior to her earlier tales, the foundations were laid for the story that was eventually to appear as L'Invitée, Beauvoir's first published novel and, indeed, her first published work of any kind.

Musing, in La Force de l'âge, over why she took so long to find a subject on which she really had something to say, Beauvoir claims that literature comes into being only when things go wrong in life: 'la première condition c'est que la réalité cesse d'*aller de soi*; alors seulement on est capable de la voir et de la donner à voir' (FA,417). One obvious factor that she has in mind, as far as *L'Invitée* is concerned, is the breakdown of the attempt made by Sartre, herself and Olga Kosakievicz in 1936 to form a balanced and lasting 'trio' ('Nous pensions que les rapports humains sont perpétuellement à inventer, qu'*a priori* aucune forme n'est privilégiée, aucune impossible: celle-ci nous parut s'imposer'; FA,279). But other major sources of the novel's events to be found in Beauvoir's own life include what she had come to regard as her over-dependence upon Sartre, and her related failure to face up to the 'scandal' and the menace of others' existence in general. Part of the fascination of *L'Invitée,* at least for readers of her memoirs, lies in seeing how skilfully she has woven together these elements and further personal experiences (including, for instance, her illness in 1937) in an apparently simple story.

In the final version of the novel much that Beauvoir had originally intended to describe in detail is taken for granted. Nowhere in the book do we learn anything substantial about the childhood of the heroine, Françoise Miquel,[1] or about the circumstances in which she first met the man she loves, Pierre Labrousse, an actor and producer of some standing in Paris theatre circles. Their relationship is an outstandingly close one and they have already been together for some eight years when *L'Invitée* begins, yet their happiness comes to seem precarious when they encourage a young girl from Rouen, Xavière Pagès, to live in Paris at their expense and share in their life. Françoise is soon surprised at the seriousness with which Pierre takes Xavière's views, moods and 'principles', particularly as the girl turns out to be an unpredictable, selfish and awkward companion. The intensity of Pierre's interest in Xavière is such that his attitudes and reactions no longer coincide exactly with those of Françoise, and the latter's distress and frustration gradually build up until she falls ill and is confined to her bed for a number of weeks. During this period her belief in Pierre's love and her own affection for Xavière are both revived and Part I ends with Françoise determined to make a success of the new triangular relationship: ' "Ce n'est pas une forme de vie ordinaire, mais je ne la crois pas trop difficile pour nous" ' (264).

For a time things appear to be working out well for the trio, principally because Françoise is now making as much effort as Pierre to understand Xavière and to stay on the most intimate terms with her. But the delicate balance is disturbed by Pierre's jealousy when Xavière first spends an evening with, then later has sex with, another man. The resulting antagonism between Pierre and Xavière has profound consequences for Françoise. When Xavière deliberately and defiantly burns her own hand in a night-club, Françoise is suddenly made to realise that the very existence of another mind like Xavière's represents a permanent and unalterable source of hostility in the world. And when, in another striking sequence, Pierre is reduced to peering through a keyhole in order to see what Xavière is doing, she is also brought to recognise the abysmal depths to which their ambitious project of a harmonious trio has sunk. Although, in spite of everything, she goes out of her way to bring about a reconciliation between Pierre and Xavière, she is met by further treachery on the latter's part and begins to feel that the appropriate response is hatred. While she is away on holiday, however, Pierre loses interest in Xavière and by the time he is obliged to go off to war relations between Françoise and Pierre are back on a perfectly even keel. This does not prevent Xavière from holding on to her own interpretation of what has happened, with the result that when she comes to have some reason for regarding Françoise herself as guilty of treachery, Françoise is unable to bear the thought that Xavière's private version of events will continue to exist and she kills Xavière in a deliberate act of self-affirmation: 'C'était sa volonté qui était en train de s'accomplir, plus rien ne la séparait d'elle-même. Elle avait enfin choisi. Elle s'était choisie' (503).

Yet it would be misleading to pretend that this account of *L'Invitée* constitutes an adequate summary of the novel's narrative content, even at a fairly high level of generality. It is a linear review of developments affecting the central trio in the book and, as such, perhaps corresponds in significant measure to Beauvoir's early conception of her tale (FA,386). But, for one thing, no reference has yet been made, by name, to the only two other characters of any importance in the book, Élisabeth and Gerbert. Élisabeth visibly has less talent than her brother Pierre and has been living under his shadow for some years. And since she knew Françoise before Pierre did, she has further cause for resenting the closeness of these two, quite apart from the fact that her own love-life is much less satisfactory than theirs. It is for these reasons that Élisabeth at one point plays a crucial role in the plot by maliciously encouraging Gerbert to make approaches to

Xavière. For Gerbert, the young friend and protégé of Françoise and Pierre, is the 'other' man who unwittingly excites Pierre's jealousy and thereby marks the beginning of the end of the trio. Furthermore, Françoise, who in the first chapter of the work turns down the opportunity of an affair with Gerbert, eventually makes love with him while they are away on holiday together near the end. It is Xavière's discovery of the relationship between them and her consequent conviction that Françoise has wilfully and vindictively stolen Gerbert from her that precipitates the final act of murder.

As well as adding to the complexity of the plot, the two secondary characters, introduced largely on the advice of Sartre, give another dimension to the narrative of the book. In *L'Invitée* we see events and people mostly through the eyes of Françoise, but on three occasions Beauvoir adopts the viewpoint of Élisabeth and on one occasion that of Gerbert. Although she was already experimenting with narrative viewpoint in *Quand prime le spirituel,* a lack of consistency was often noticeable in her technique. Only later did she and Sartre come to define an artistic principle that has remained as a constant throughout her career as a novelist, namely the view that at any given point in a work of fiction the narration must be such that it could have been written, or at least 'thought', at that time by one of the characters in the story. In connection with *L'Invitée* Beauvoir puts the point in this way:

> J'observai la règle que nous tenions, Sartre et moi, pour fonda-
> mentale et qu'il exposa un peu plus tard, dans un article sur
> Mauriac et le roman français: à chaque chapitre, je coïncidais avec
> un de mes héros, je m'interdisais d'en savoir ou d'en penser plus
> long que lui. (FA,386)[2]

Whatever the intrinsic merits of this particular artistic stance, it is one that we can never afford to ignore in examining Beauvoir's fiction. In *L'Invitée*, the narrative written from the standpoint of Élisabeth and Gerbert has the important effect of making us doubt, in a way that we might otherwise never have done, whether Françoise's view of the trio and her version of events can be taken to be the whole truth. As Sartre claims in his article, 'dans un vrai roman, pas plus que dans le monde d'Einstein, il n'y a de place pour un observateur privilégié'.

The restrictive aspect of this narrative principle accounts for a number of characteristic features of *L'Invitée*. It governs, for instance,

Beauvoir's treatment of space and time. Since there can be no independent descriptions of surroundings in the novel, the view of any given setting must reflect the general outlook and particular mood of one of the characters at the time concerned. Some such angled descriptions in *L'Invitée* are outstanding: Françoise's complacent opening account of the theatre at night contrasts revealingly with her lugubrious view of the flea market in Chapter 6; and not only does her hotel room seem a different place to her according to what is happening to the trio, we also have one fascinating glimpse of the room through the eyes of Élisabeth (87). Again, for indications of the time elapsing in the story the reader is wholly dependent upon any thoughts on the matter that Beauvoir may plausibly attribute to her narrators, and to relevant comments made in recorded dialogues. Sometimes these sources provide precise information, and sometimes not. Thus, for example, we know that the events of the book take place over one year, but there is no precise allusion to the question of the time-gap between the end of Part I and the beginning of Part II. This sort of result is an inevitable and distinctive consequence of Beauvoir's decision to approach time only through the perceptions of her characters and a good illustration of her belief that the reader's active participation is required for the work of fiction to come to life. In introducing elements of uncertainty or ambiguity into the story, refusing to place her characters strictly in relation to some prior philosophical system and giving events the concrete but elusive quality of real subjective experience, she is clearly trying to ensure that her novel has the characteristics for which fiction is praised in 'Littérature et métaphysique'.[3]

Other noteworthy properties of the novel also help to ensure that the reader's attention is scarcely ever distracted from the personal thoughts, actions and reactions of the protagonists. Although the story of *L'Invitée* takes place in the year between the Munich Crisis of September 1938 and the outbreak of the Second World War, references to the momentous political circumstances of the time are infrequent and usually insubstantial. In a long novel, there are only some twenty-five references of any kind to the crisis in Europe, nearly half of them falling in the relatively rare sections of the book narrated from the point of view of Élisabeth or Gerbert, both of whom take the approach of war more seriously than do the central trio. The significance of the penultimate chapter of the book, which centres on Pierre's call-up, owes nothing to the war as such, but attaches simply to the fact that Pierre is going away. Beauvoir herself has admitted that the war merely provided her with 'un excellent prétexte pour l'éloigner' (FA,392). It is also remarkable that the bonds or pressures of social situations and functions exercise absolutely minimal influence upon the five main figures in the story. We learn very little about their background, family or education; not one of them is married; and their work allows them an unusual degree of freedom, while scarcely bringing them into contact with the non-artistic sections of society at all. The central drama of the novel is played out without any crucial reference to history or society, in what Françoise sometimes sees as a kind of magical isolation: 'Elle avait envie de le briser, ce cercle magique où elle se trouvait retenue avec Pierre et Xavière et qui la séparait de tout le reste du monde' (345). In short, *L'Invitée* focuses sharply on the complex and shifting relationships between three individuals, and slightly less sharply on two other characters who stand outside, but in close contact with, the trio.

Any account of the central relationship between Françoise and Pierre is necessarily bound up with judgements concerning Françoise's general frame of mind when *L'Invitée* opens. The self-satisfaction that she displays in the first chapter and her frequent references to regrets that she does not have may possibly predispose us to wonder whether all is quite so perfect between Pierre and herself as she suggests. In any case, the story eventually shows her experiencing not only a degree of alienation from Pierre that at first seems unthinkable, but also all of the horrors that she here regards herself as somehow immune to, particularly illness and war (15) and the 'scandal' of the existence and potential hostility of other minds (18). It is clear that at the beginning of the novel Françoise is largely incapable of seeing herself from the outside. Yet this is not an adequate reason for believing that her relationship with Pierre is entirely based upon illusion. We are not, of course, obliged to accept that they themselves have attained the ideal of reciprocal recognition of freedom that Pierre spells out later (376), but some of the attempts that have been made by critics to devalue the bond between them are certainly misguided. In view of the degree of sincerity and frankness manifest in their discussions, to suggest, for instance, that there is any serious lack of communication between Françoise and Pierre is paradoxical in the extreme.[4] And there is simply no truth at all in the contention that the story warns against the 'bad faith' involved in relying on ratiocination and language, as opposed to feelings or 'real emotions'.[5] Like many views of the couple, this one might carry more weight if their ties were to be broken or permanently weakened in the course of the book. But in the penultimate chapter they are shown as being as close as ever, and this on exactly the same basis as before. In spite of all that happens in the novel, it is only by some highly abstract or strange criterion that one might qualify the union between Françoise and Pierre as seriously defective.

What is true, however, is not only that the relationship does not always go smoothly, but also that it is possible from the first to detect certain cracks in an edifice that Françoise regards as rock-solid. One passage in the second chapter, among others, strongly suggests that there is something evasive about the way in which she dismisses temporary 'malaises' (37). And only weeks later she comes to believe that individual moments may be precisely what matter after all, in that she and Pierre now seem to have the form of love without its substance. Her doubts about the quality of Pierre's love persist in one form or another until he breaks the charmed circle by losing interest in Xavière. We do have to suppose, therefore, that what happens in the story represents a considerable deviation from the usual route followed by their relationship. And this at once raises the question of why and how.

If *jealousy* were the principal source of Françoise's anguish, as some have supposed, we should need to explain why it has apparently never surfaced before, since Pierre has had a number of affairs with other women and is even in the middle of one when the novel begins (29). Admittedly, this may be the first time that he has become involved with a woman who was first Françoise's friend, and it is true that at certain points the two of them appear to be fighting over Xavière. (Françoise's reaction when Pierre and Xavière announce that they love each other is revealing: 'Elle n'était pas jalouse de lui, mais cette petite fille soyeuse et dorée qu'elle avait adoptée par un aigre petit matin, elle ne la perdait pas sans révolte'; 252.) Yet since the relationship between Françoise and Xavière is not a lesbian one, we are already beginning to leave the usual meaning of 'jealousy' behind. In fact, the whole treatment of sex in the book militates strongly against the idea that *L'Invitée* is centrally about jealousy in the normal sense. We learn virtually nothing at all about sexual relations between Françoise and

Pierre, and very little indeed about those between Pierre and Xavière (the text is not explicit, for instance, on whether they actually make love together while Françoise is away on holiday). Pierre is certainly jealous when Xavière has sex with Gerbert (although, as Merleau-Ponty points out, Françoise would scarcely have suffered for him at this point had she herself been simply jealous about his relations with Xavière),[6] but the important point is that jealousy is seen in the book as only a superficial manifestation of deeper metaphysical battles between individuals. For Beauvoir as for Sartre, sexuality is no more than one expression of our being-in-the-world.

Indeed, the suggestion that the story is an illustration of one precise aspect of Sartre's theory in *L'Être et le Néant*—that *any* harmony established between two people will be shattered by the advent of a third person—is more helpful, although it cannot constitute an adequate explanation in itself. The fact is that the distinctive characters of the participants in this particular trio play a vital role in the outcome of events. Pierre's womanising expresses not simple lust but a certain 'manie de conquêtes' (82), and to the extent that his conduct is self-indulgent he must bear some of the blame for the breakdown of the trio. But, equally, everything might have been very different had Xavière not been the kind of person she is. She comes between Françoise and Pierre in a way that no other woman apparently has because she represents the Other *in its most extreme form*. Not only is she a singularly unsuitable target for Pierre's mania for conquests, being unwilling to be subjugated without receiving an absolutely single-minded commitment in return, she is also 'un vivant point d'interrogation', just the person to force Pierre and Françoise to re-examine their love in a way that they have perhaps been failing to do. There could be no question of including in the novel any narrative from Xavière's point of view, since she must be as opaque to the reader as to the couple, with her every word and action requiring inter-pretation and never-ending re-interpretation.

An equally crucial feature of *L'Invitée*, however, is the fact that we are by no means inclined to exonerate Françoise herself from all blame, even though the story is told predominantly from her point of view. From the first we are aware that she has a desire to 'annex' others that has its parallels with Pierre's 'manie de conquêtes': 'rien ne donnait jamais à Françoise des joies si fortes que cette espèce de possession' (23). Her assumption that an inexperienced young girl from the provinces—whom she regards as essentially child-like—could easily share the sophisticated reactions and values of Pierre and herself is intrinsically unsatisfactory, but one of the ironies of the story is that the little girl Françoise was so confident of 'annexing' should eventually come to hold the older woman at her mercy: 'Xavière . . . était soudain devenue l'unique réalité souveraine' (364). This phenomenon, in fact, reveals a fundamental weakness in Françoise's character that lies at the very heart of the novel. In spite of her early recognition that she has been over-dependent on Pierre ('Le tort qu'elle avait, c'était de reposer sur Pierre de tout son poids'; 138), she goes on, after her illness, to devote so much of her time and energy to winning Xavière's confidence and love that we can only conclude that her need for some kind of approval or confirmation from others shows a deep lack of confidence in herself and tends to the self-destructive. The last few chapters of the book chart her delayed awakening to this failing and her long-overdue attempts to assert herself as an individual.

A reading of *L'Invitée* with this kind of emphasis takes in all phases of the story, and provides an angle of approach to the murder of Xavière. The motive for the murder has nothing to do with Pierre, but lies in Françoise's perception of the importance of Xavière's view of her. Earlier in the novel she has already shown a concern over Xavière's private image of her and in the final chapter, just when she has grown accustomed to the idea that she has broken the spell and defeated Xavière, events conspire to give Xavière an interpretation of Françoise's conduct that will leave her definitively convicted of treachery: 'Elle existe en chair et en os, ma criminelle figure' (501). With her new determination not to be 'une femme résignée', Françoise is unable to tolerate this situation and kills Xavière, in order to destroy a particular image of herself: 'son image devenait si hideuse qu'il lui fallait ou se détester à jamais, ou briser le sortilège en supprimant celle qui l'exerçait. Ainsi faisait-elle triompher sa vérité' (FA,387). It may well be that this constitutes no real solution to the problem, that 'Xavière morte éternisera l'image de Françoise qu'elle portait en elle au moment de mourir',[7] but what should not escape us is that the act of murder continues and completes one main line of development in the story. From being scarcely conscious at all of her own image, Françoise finally attains such awareness of it that she is prepared to kill to prevent it from being distorted.

Françoise's perspective, however, is not the only one in the book and at this point we need to take account of the roles of Élisabeth and Gerbert. As Gerbert rates only a single (short) chapter to himself, his narrative as such is of relative little importance. His ability to see the comic side to the antics of the trio (318,320) is a useful corrective to the intensity of Françoise's chapters, as is his judgement on the 'tricheries' of Françoise and Pierre (327). In his preoccupations and his very youth, he makes a much more suitable companion for Xavière than are the couple, although nothing about him is developed in any detail. Nevertheless, the pattern of his separate relationships with Françoise, Pierre and Xavière pulls the threads of the story together well and his presence gives us a valuable point of reference outside the trio. It is interesting, for example, that Françoise and Pierre are prepared to lie to him to exclude him from the activities of the trio (126) and that Françoise is quick to offer to 'give him back' to Xavière at the end (499).

Élisabeth's presence in the story, too, constitutes something of a challenge to the couple's view of themselves. Although not entirely lacking in lucidity, she is manifestly guilty of 'mauvaise foi' in many areas (her affair with Battier; her painting; politics; the approach of war), and we cannot accept her belief that the trio is a major obstacle to success in her own life. At the same time, seeing Françoise and Pierre from her standpoint undoubtedly causes us to modify our view of them in some measure. Not only do they deliberately exclude her from the trio, as they do Gerbert, they also make surprisingly little effort to help her out of a condition that they diagnose so accurately. Being very different from Françoise and in some respects a foil to her (FA,390), Élisabeth sharpens our perception of the heroine. For example, the surprise that she expresses early on about Françoise's fidelity to Pierre both gives the reader food for thought and sets off interesting echoes later in the book. There is a minor tragedy in *L'Invitée* in Élisabeth's failure to enjoy the relationship that she might have had with her brother Pierre (472), and both the psychological depths that Beauvoir plumbs in this character and the absorbing quality of certain confrontations not strictly related to the main plot—between Élisabeth and Battier, or Élisabeth and Guimiot—make us realise how much more colourful the novel is for her presence.

Indeed, in general the treatment of human relations in *L'Invitée* is characterised by a richness that belies any suggestion that Beauvoir was merely seeking to give flesh and blood to Sartre's theories. Close parallels, some general and some very precise, can easily be found between the book and the third part of *L'Être et la Néant*,[8] but there remains a fundamental difference between Sartre's deeply pessimistic account of 'les relations concrètes avec autrui' and the broad pattern of human contacts traced in *L'Invitée*. In spite of the conclusion, and in spite of its Hegelian epigraph ('Chaque conscience poursuit la mort de l'autre'), the novel is by no means a record of universal failure in human relations. Xavière temporarily disturbs the harmony between Françoise and Pierre but she certainly does not destroy it—there may be greater value than ever in the unity that they achieve once more before the end of the book. And however little Françoise's relationship with Gerbert may mean to her, she is never less than sincerely affectionate towards him and they grow very much closer together in the course of the story. Even the ending, depressing though it is, does not go quite to the bitter limit of Sartre's analysis, as Hazel Barnes points out,[9] since Françoise's hatred is not directed at *all* others. Xavière represents the Other in the most extreme form that this concept can take, yet we have to acknowledge that Beauvoir also records some quite different ways in which the Other may exist for us. It is not surprising, after all, that the novel should implicitly qualify some of Sartre's radical views on this topic, for we have seen that in an essay like *Pour une morale de l'ambiguïté* Beauvoir consciously set out to build something positive, including authentic human relationships, upon the grim foundations of *L'Être et le Néant*.

It is not difficult to resist the temptation of laying too much emphasis on the murder at the end of *L'Invitée,* for although Beauvoir claims that it was 'le moteur et la raison d'être du roman entier' (FA,389), she also acknowledges that its implausibility makes it 'le point le plus faible du livre' (FA,387). In admitting that, while hostility between people often gives an ugly and evil aspect to life, 'motiver par là un assassinat, c'est une autre affaire', she indicates her own unwillingness to take the extreme metaphysical implications of the conclusion too seriously, just as she affects to disregard its ethical aspects ('Peu m'importe qu'elle ait tort ou raison'; FA,388). The key to how the murder can possibly be the 'raison d'être' of the novel is to be found in Beauvoir's stress on the cathartic value that writing about it had for her personally: 'en tuant Olga sur le papier, je liquidai les irritations, les rancunes que j'avais pu éprouver à son égard . . . je retrouvai ma propre autonomie' (FA,388). In this sense, the ending may be regarded as simply one illustration of the extent to which the autobiographical nature of *L'Invitée* imposes limitations or constraints upon the book as a whole. The transposition of events from Rouen to Paris constitutes another example, for turning two young, unknown provincial teachers into leading Parisian personalities was not an unqualified success: 'l'aventure infernale, poignante, parfois miraculeuse de la solitude à trois s'en trouva dénaturée' (FA,392). Again, the fact that Xavière embodies only the more recalcitrant, capricious side of Olga makes it very hard to understand how Pierre and Françoise could have been so drawn to her (FA,278-79). And if Beauvoir's determination not to present, in Pierre, a precise likeness of Sartre led her to amalgamate features from two or three sources, it also produced a character somewhat lacking in density, even in coherence: 'je n'ai su ni créer un personnage ni tracer un portrait' (FA,391).

The lack of narrative from the point of view of either Xavière or Pierre, then, has its drawbacks and other features of the telling of the story are also rather unsatisfactory on the artistic level. If Élisabeth's chapters are fairly well integrated into the main plot, Gerbert's single section of narrative in the second part of the book stands out as something of an oddity, and it encompasses a variety of tones or styles—from poetic description to childish slang—that seriously undermines its credibility as the thoughts of one character. Moreover, although Beauvoir usually traces changes in her heroine's state of mind in the most minute detail, there are still puzzling juxtapositions or leaps in Françoise's narrative. To take just one example, the harmony of the trio at the beginning of Part II, Chapter 2 is destroyed too trivially and far too quickly (299) for the change to be convincing. Beauvoir is also a little over-generous towards herself in claiming that her basic narrative principle is respected throughout the novel: there are many places in *L'Invitée*—especially at the beginning of a chapter or section—where she is manifestly summarising events for the reader, although her character would have had no occasion to do so. One might equally take leave to doubt her assertion that the book reads like a detective story, even if it does have its own kind of tension and, occasionally, suspense. To say that it is too long is perhaps a naïve comment, but certain types of conversations and certain patterns of events (no fewer than seven chapters end with Françoise and Pierre alone together discussing what Xavière has done, or some other issue relating to her) recur so often that some loss of interest on the reader's part is inevitable from time to time.

In general, however, the merits of L'Invitée heavily outweigh its defects. Even the very length and repetitiveness of the novel find a certain justification in Beauvoir's determination not to over-formalise her story, but to give it the relative shapelessness and the texture of life itself:

> Tandis que le philosophe, l'essayiste, livrent au lecteur une re-construction intellectuelle de leur expérience, c'est cette expérience elle-même, telle qu'elle se présente avant toute élucidation, que le romancier prétend restituer sur un plan imaginaire.[10]

In this context, it is an obvious strength rather than a weakness that certain issues—like Françoise's motives in making love with Gerbert (FA, 393)—should remain unresolved at the end of the book. There is no 'objective' truth about the trio in L'Invitée, any more than there is about Beauvoir, Sartre and Olga, but only various subjective view-points which yield different, and sometimes conflicting, perspectives. The principal fascination of L'Invitée, after all, lies in its examination of individual feelings and relationships rather than in any positive conclusions or moral message that can be drawn from the characters' behaviour. If the book is somewhat amorphous, Beauvoir describes the thoughts and emotions of her protagonists with remarkable sensitivity, analysing reactions to particular situations, 'renverse-ments des alliances' and shades of feeling with a penetration that constitutes the novel's overriding excellence.

Not that on the artistic level proper the broad achievements of L'Invitée are inconsiderable. In spite of flaws in the narrative, the relativity that Beauvoir's basic aesthetic principle introduces into the story is a notable feature of the book. She is right to argue that L'Invitée is no 'roman à thèse' and yet it is eminently successful in giving concrete embodiment to certain philosophical perceptions associated with existentialism. In one of the key philosophical sequences, where the 'scandal' of the existence of others is under discussion, Françoise captures the spirit of the novel when she explains why she is 'touchée d'une manière si concrète par une situation métaphysique':

> 'Mais c'est du concret, dit Françoise, tout le sens de ma vie se trouve mis en jeu.'

'Je ne dis pas, dit Pierre. Il la considéra avec curiosité. C'est quand même exceptionnel ce pouvoir que tu as de vivre une idée corps et âme.'

'Mais pour moi, une idée, ce n'est pas théorique, dit Françoise, ça s'éprouve, ou si ça reste théorique, ça ne compte pas.' (375-76)

And this snatch of dialogue, in addition to showing that the author was far more concerned to catch the colloquialisms and rhythms of everyday speech than to create elegant conversations, reminds us that another of her aesthetic preoccupations in *L'Invitée* was to turn verbal exchange into a kind of action (FA,393). In fact, together with the further point that something important must also be going on elsewhere while a dialogue is taking place, this principle is perhaps the main factor in Beauvoir's tangible success, in her first novel, in making metaphysics so readable.

In *La Force de l'âge* Beauvoir strongly emphasises how much her own views and preoccupations changed even while she was writing *L'Invitée*. As early as January 1941 the novel was already 'de l'histoire ancienne' for her, and by the time it was about to appear she had come to regard it—though doubtless largely in order to protect herself against possible failure—as no more than 'une frivole histoire d'amour ' (FA,637). The war had altered her perspectives quite drastically and her thoughts were now of 'de vastes romans engagés' that would incorporate a social and historical as well as a personal dimension. By the middle of 1943, in fact, she had virtually completed her second novel, *Le Sang des autres*.

Notes

1 Two chapters that Beauvoir had originally intended to include in *L'Invitée* are published in *Écrits*, pp. 275-316.

2 The article by Sartre that she refers to is 'M. François Mauriac et la liberté', (*La Nouvelle Revue Française*, 1939; reprinted in Sartre's *Situations I*), in which he attacks Mauriac for being an omniscient narrator and adopting the point of view of God in relation to his characters.

3 See Chapter 4.

4 It is hard to know what B.T. Fitch understands by 'communication'when he argues that 'Leur façon de s'extérioriser par la

parole est un bien pauvre substitut pour la communication' (*Le Sentiment d'étrangeté chez Malraux, Sartre, Camus et Simone de Beauvoir*, p.159).

5   Jean Leighton: *Simone de Beauvoir on Women*, pp.59-60.

6   M. Merleau-Ponty: 'Le Roman et la métaphysique' in his *Sens et Non-sens*, pp.51-82.

7   Merleau-Ponty: op.cit., p.65.

8   See, for instance, Hazel Barnes: *The Literature of Possibility*.

9   Barnes: op.cit., p.135.

10   'Littérature et métaphysique' (in *L'Existentialisme et la sagesse des nations*), p.91.

8 *Le Sang des autres* and *Tous les hommes sont mortels*

When Beauvoir began working on *Le Sang des autres* in October 1941, she knew that there was no possibility of seeing it published before the end of the German Occupation, since it referred to the French Resistance. She speaks in *La Force de l'âge,* however, of a 'dissociation entre le sujet profond du livre et les épisodes où je le coulai' and says that it was only as she started to write that she conceived the idea of using contemporary political situations. Her central aim, as she noted at the time, was one that arose directly out of the themes treated in *L'Invitée:*

> 'Je voudrais que mon prochain roman illustre le rapport à autrui dans sa vraie complexité. Supprimer la conscience d'autrui, c'est puéril. L'intrigue doit être beaucoup plus liée aux problèmes sociaux que dans le premier roman. Il faudrait aboutir à un acte ayant une dimension sociale (mais difficile à trouver).' (FA,625)

On one level, *Le Sang des autres* is a love story, recounting the beginning, development and end of a relationship between Jean Blomart and Hélène Bertrand. Breaking with her strategy in *L'Invitée,* but observing the same broad principles of narration ('à chaque chapitre, je coïncidais avec un de mes héros'), Beauvoir relates this story from the point of view of both protagonists, adopting alternately that of Blomart (in the odd-numbered chapters) and that of Hélène. Seven chapters—rather more than half of the book—are devoted to Blomart's narrative, much of which is in the first person and which situates him throughout in the headquarters of a Resistance movement just outside Paris during one single night of the Occupation. He spends the night at the bedside of the dying Hélène and, in describing his thoughts and feelings during her final hours, he goes back over his past ('autour de moi, ce sont mes souvenirs qui se pressent; c'est mon histoire qui se déroule'; 45-46), relating the early stages of his acquaintanceship with Hélène and his attempt to rebuff her (Ch.3); how they came together and he came to tell her, albeit untruthfully, that he loved her (Ch.5); how the war brought about a rift between them (Chs. 7 and 9); and how they became reconciled in the Resistance, by which stage Blomart genuinely loved her and only reluctantly allowed her to go on the mission that was to lead to her fatal injury (Ch. 11). In the last chapter he describes her very last moments and his own reactions to her death. Hélène's own narrative—written almost entirely in the third person and never from any specified time or place other than those at which the events described take place—offers a different perspective on the relationship and fills in some gaps for the reader.

If *Le Sang des autres* is barely recognisable from this account, however, it is because there is another equally important dimension to the book. Its social, political and historical content provides not only the context of the love story and a number of factors that weigh heavily within it, but also some of the work's central themes. Most of Blomart's first chapter is concerned with his social background, his decision to leave his bourgeois family in order to become a worker, and his early involvement with the Communist Party, which results in the death of Jacques, the younger brother of his friend Marcel. Subsequent chapters from Blomart's viewpoint bring in, in varing degrees of detail but always prominently, the main political issues of the thirties, the Second World War itself and the situation or dilemmas facing the French under the Occupation. It is true that the first half of Hélène's section of the narrative is singularly apolitical—she actually argues that political matters are of no significance in relation to the personal concerns of the individual. But from the beginning of Chapter 8 onwards history and politics begin impinging forcefully upon her life as Blomart is mobilised, she herself is obliged to flee from Paris as the German army advances, and she later samples some of the worst aspects of the Occupation. Somewhat belatedly, she joins forces with Blomart in the Resistance and eventually loses her life in the cause of anti-Fascism. In addition to all of this, the novel as a whole is set within the framework of a political decision, for Blomart is asked on the first page to say whether the next sabotage mission against the Germans will go ahead or not, and gives his decision only in the very last sentence of the book.

Analysis of the development of Blomart involves some disentangling of a narrative that is technically complex, not least chronologically:

Toutes les dimensions du temps se trouvaient rassemblées dans cette veillée funèbre: le héros la vivait, au présent, en s'interrogeant à travers son passé sur une décision qui engageait son avenir. (FA,622)

The different stages of his life, as he recalls the past, are presented in broadly chronological order and his separate chapters are often given extra continuity by the repetition of key phrases from the end of one chapter at the beginning of the next. His account of his past is occasionally interrupted by events in the present—a movement or sound from Hélène on her deathbed, or someone coming into the room—but much of the complexity of Blomart's narrative arises out of links and contrasts that he is constantly making in his own mind. These give Beauvoir great scope in her handling of his story, enabling her to use a greater variety of techniques than before: 'je ralentissais, j'accélérais le mouvement du récit, j'usais de raccourcis, d'ellipses, de fondus; j'accordai moins de place aux dialogues' (FA,622). In conjunction with two other prominent stylistic devices (Blomart's mixture of first-person and third-person narration, and the fairly frequent italicising of certain asynchronous sequences or single sentences), this makes for an outstandingly complicated and confusing beginning to the book, where Beauvoir undoubtedly expects too much of her reader too soon.

The opening of Blomart's review of his past, for example, is much less sharp and clear than it might have been (Beauvoir herself was to comment that she had failed to justify 'le sentiment de culpabilité qui pèse sur toute sa vie'; FA,623). But as the story unravels, we become immersed in Blomart's early moral preoccupations with social privilege, remorse, the 'scandal' of existence and 'la faute d'être un autre'. His description of the painful break with his family is convincing enough, and if the death of Jacques, for which Blomart holds himself personally responsible, is a little melodramatic, Beauvoir finds ways of conveying the horror that it provokes in Blomart and makes it a weighty symbol of the way in which our actions have more consequences than we intend. When Blomart subsequently abstains from all political action and devotes himself to trade unionism ('une vie sans compromis, sans privilège, qui ne devait rien à personne, et qui ne pouvait pour personne être une source de malheur'; 89), the two main strands of his narrative begin running in parallel, since he is

163

simultaneously making sure that he gives no encouragement at all to Hélène (99).

Beauvoir is right to admit that her account of Blomart's unionist period is thin and vague, but there is great strength in the middle sections of the book, which give pointed embodiment to many of the theoretical problems raised in her moral essays. The illustration, on both the personal and political levels, of the familiar existentialist maxim that 'abstention' from action is itself a form of action, is particularly powerful and poignant. It is also very well integrated into Blomart's story, for Hélène's pregnancy by someone else, which comes about when she is driven away one night by Blomart, not only eventually draws them together, but also brings Blomart to the realisation that 'la faute n'était en aucun acte . . . elle était la pâte même de mon être' (147). Yet even as he stills the remorse that he might have felt about Hélène, the Other begins to impinge upon their temporarily stable relationship, both in the form of individuals affected by their intimacy (Hélène's former fiancé Paul and Blomart's girl-friend Madeleine) and in the form of people suffering in parts of Europe where Blomart has strongly advocated a policy of non-intervention (158).

It is perhaps not implausible that Blomart should next pass through a phase of passivity and resignation ('Je me laissais ballotter avec indifférence par tous les caprices du hasard'; 198), or even that he should find it a relief to have to do no more than follow orders as a wartime soldier. But the dream-like state in which Beauvoir has him experience the fighting and killing (240-41) is not easy to reconcile with his normal sensitivities; and his claim that war is merely one more example of the metaphysical scandal of existence (204) is not altogether consistent with the firm determination to play his part that causes his break with Hélène. Yet when Blomart's earlier sense of shame returns with the defeat of France and he becomes an extremely militant leader in the Resistance ('toute monnaie était bonne même celle-ci: le sang des autres. On ne paierait jamais trop cher'; 249), Beauvoir once more shows her gift for inventing and exploring concrete examples of the moral problems that she discusses elsewhere. She squarely faces up to the difficult issues of sabotage and reprisals and portrays Blomart as ultimately attaining—thanks in part to the reassurance contained in Hélène's last words—not peace of mind, but 'le courage d'accepter à jamais le risque et l'angoisse, de supporter mes crimes et le remords qui me déchirera sans fin' (314). His guiding principle at the end is seen to be the freedom of the individual on which Beauvoir was to lay so much stress in *Pour une morale de l'ambiguïté,* and in the name of it Blomart is finally able to give the order for the violent Resistance work to resume.

The chapters related from Hélène's point of view contrast with and complement Blomart's narrative in almost all respects. Her story is told with no deviation from the chronological order of events and in a style which, while containing more imagery and colourful description, is marked by very few special technical features (the first person is occasionally used, but most sparingly). Above all, Hélène's perspective and values are totally different from those of Blomart and it says much for Beauvoir that she not only foresaw our need for regular relief from the hero's convoluted and tortured thought-processes, but also succeeded in projecting us, in every other chapter, into the mind of a spoiled and selfish young woman. Towards the end of Chapter 2 the opposition between their outlooks on life is brought out explicitly in a dialogue where Blomart confesses that 'ça me gêne toujours de chercher mon propre avantage' and Hélène argues that this is what everyone does all of the time, and quite rightly (65). It is important to recognise, however, that the contrast in personality and character never operates wholly in Blomart's favour. Hélène has qualities that are almost entirely missing in Blomart—spontaneity, a zest for life, a capacity for certain emotions, perhaps even a particular kind of determination—and ones to which he himself is quick to respond. In spite of, or perhaps because of, her extravagant behaviour, he finds her 'charmante' and respects in her 'un courage qui forçait l'estime' (77).

Hélène does, after all, illustrate some significant features of the human condition as Beauvoir sees it. For instance, her earlier loss of faith (57) probably lies behind her rather desperate search for love and justification. She experiences a kind of emptiness or metaphysical anguish familiar to many characters in existentialist fiction ('On est là. Pourquoi là, justement? Moi. Qui? quelqu'un qui dit moi'; 69), which disappears when she believes that Blomart loves her (182). Blomart himself recognises that this is no valid solution to her problem (201) and for most of the novel his own attitude to love is very different from Hélène's. Here, as in *L'Invitée*, Beauvoir is raising questions concerning the nature or significance of love, its relative importance to the two sexes, and the risks of over-dependence in women (Marcel's wife Denise who is in many ways contrasted with Hélène, also illustrates this last theme). Looking at the book as a whole, one might say that on the topic of love it is Blomart who comes around to Hélène's view, for by the end his love for her is intense and unqualified. But what is fascinating is that she seems finally to win him over by going directly against his wishes (in order to save his life), in spite of the distinct possibility that he will hate her as a result. It is debatable whether this action is a supreme example of Hélène's selfishness or one revealing the very depth of her love. In any case, in spite of himself Blomart is strongly impressed by her sincerity and courage at this point (237-39).

By contrast, on the political plane Hélène undergoes a conversion that brings her much closer to Blomart's position by the end. The detailed description of the flight from, and return to, Paris in 1940 (in her memoirs Beauvoir actually breaks off at one point, saying that what happened is recounted in her novel; FA, 507), and the sketches of life under the Occupation (Chs. 10 and 12) are undoubtedly among the most realistic and vivid in the whole book. Her experience at this time, in conjunction with her depression over the break with Blomart, leads Hélène to her own period of resignation, in which she sees herself as a passive pawn, subject to the forces of history: 'elle regardait passer l'Histoire qui n'était pas la sienne, qui n'appartenait à personne' (260). She proposes to go to Berlin with a rich German industrialist until she realises that she has been lying to herself and that she has her own particular place in history (301). There is no doubt that Hélène is responding at this stage to the suffering of those around her (notably that of her friend Yvonne and the mother in the street), and in the end she is more than content to risk and lose her life for the Resistance cause. What is less certain, nevertheless, is whether her eventual commitment to anti-Fascism is of the same nature as that of Blomart. Her new stance appears, characteristically, to be more of a reaction to individual distress than a carefully thought-out choice. Perhaps this is precisely where, in the context of the novel, its value lies, yet one is bound to have some slight reservations about a decision made, apparently spontaneously, in Blomart's presence and perhaps specifically in his name: 'Je te choisissais. Je ferais encore le même choix' (311).

Another character to discover 'solidarity' in the final stages of the book is the rather eccentric painter and sculptor Marcel Ledru. One of

Marcel's main functions in the novel is to show us some of the implications for the artist of the social and historical circumstances with which Blomart himself is trying to come to terms. When Marcel discovers, before the war, that he cannot do without a public, he abandons art and spends his time playing chess. In painting frescoes for his compatriots in a prisoner-of-war camp, however, he sees the fascination of creating works of art for a particular public and later becomes involved in the Resistance because, as he says, 'Je veux choisir mon public' (287). It is hard to agree with Beauvoir that he has 'plus de relief' than her other characters, for his presence in the novel is somehow less real than, for instance, that of his wife Denise, for whom we feel some sympathy, in spite of the fact that she is the only one of the main figures with any social or material ambitions. In any case, Beauvoir herself recognises that the symmetry between Marcel's development and that of Blomart is strained: 'Voilà encore un des reproches que je fais à ce roman: la composition en est serrée, mais la matière pauvre; tout converge au lieu de foisonner' (FA, 624).

In fact, Beauvoir suggests in her memoirs that Blanchot was right to classify her novel as a 'roman à thèse' which betrays reality by failing to register its ambiguities: '*Le Sang des autres* ... aboutit à une conclusion univoque, réductible en maximes et en concepts' (FA, 623). She is unduly harsh on her own work in claiming that this fault marks the book throughout, but criticisms that the ending itself is contrived and 'closed' are difficult to dismiss. There is of course a certain historical justification for the way in which she has everyone pulling together in the Resistance: Blomart, Hélène, Communists, workers, Marcel, Denise, Madeleine, and the French bourgeoisie as represented (somewhat caricaturally) by Blomart's father. But the ending does little more than paper over certain conflicts that have been given great emphasis earlier in the book. The class struggle is the most obvious case, but even the serious clash of perspectives that opposed Hélène and Blomart early in the war may have a validity that is belied by Hélène's convenient shift of opinion towards the end. In other words, some of the questions asked in the novel are far better than the answers that Beauvoir felt obliged to give at the time. The objection that if the Resistance fails, then those participating will have committed 'crimes inutiles' (248) receives only the most inadequate of responses. And if Hélène's final exoneration of Blomart ('Tu n'avais pas le droit de décider pour moi'; 310) is meant as some sort of resolution of his remaining dilemmas, it is a poor one, since he himself has earlier seen the weaknesses in such a view, both in relation to Marcel's treatment of Denise (166) and in relation to his own attitude to Hélène: 'La laisser libre, c'était encore décider pour elle' (170).

As with a number of Beauvoir's other stories, however, the ending can be read in different ways according to the stress laid upon various elements. Blomart's major problem, it may be argued, is one that cannot in any case be resolved by a particular moral or political stance, since his preoccupation with responsibility and guilt has to be seen as excessive. From early on we see him admitting that his deep concern with 'le remords et la faute' is something of an obsession (40, 137); more than once Marcel accuses him of being 'présomptueux' in taking so much upon his own shoulders (142, 156); and in a sharp little discussion on leadership near the end (where Blomart wants to go on a dangerous mission, to salve his own conscience), Denise forces him to acknowledge that his qualms are a result of his bourgeois background (289). Moveover, the ending of the novel makes it clear that he has still not found peace of mind, but is merely giving temporary assent to a necessary evil. To this extent it is implicit at the end that the 'philosophical truths' Blomart discovers in the course of the story— that 'j'étais en faute à jamais, depuis ma naissance et par-delà ma mort' (152), or that 'chaque homme est responsable de tout, devant tous' (159)—lead nowhere at all. One can well understand Beauvoir's comment that his final position is 'par-delà tous les raisonnements et tous les calculs . . . Il renonçait à démêler le nœud gordien: il tranchait' (FA, 620). Whether this 'leap' is entirely easy to reconcile with Blomart's character as portrayed in the rest of the novel is another matter. It is true that he is very impatient with Jacques's theoretical doubts near the beginning (30), but he also regrets the fact that the young man does not arrive at his commitment to communism 'à coup d'arguments raisonnables' (39). Furthermore, we need to remember that we are dealing with a character who is the articulate spokesman and leader of a trade union movement as well as of a Resistance group, and that he is thought to be the appropriate person to judge the literary merits of Denise's first novel. In short, the concept of Blomart as essentially a man *obsessed* with guilt may make us less inclined to take the Resistance message as such as the key to the ending, but it does raise difficulties of its own.

Nevertheless, these considerations go some way towards explaining why Beauvoir should have been irritated to see *Le Sang des autres* characterised as 'un roman sur la résistance'. It is less clear why she should now be quite so hard on a book that by no means fails to achieve her main objective of illustrating the true complexity of human relations, including their social dimension. The novel has its faults— most of them, as we have seen, bound up with the laboured, tangled nature of Blomart's narrative and the over-schematised or didactic treatment of certain themes—but it has much to offer in the area where matters of personal relationships begin to overlap with ethical questions. Hélène's story actually centres on her reaction to, and confrontations with, other individuals, but Blomart's chapters too contain excellent sequences on crucial aspects of personal relations. More generally, Blomart's story vividly registers the paradox of 'cette existence vécue par moi comme ma liberté et saisie comme objet par ceux qui m'approchent', which Beauvoir takes as her starting-point in her moral essays and here regards as her principal theme (FCh,59). (While the stylistic device of swapping from first-person to third-person narration and vice versa is not used entirely in the way that Beauvoir explains, it undoubtedly contributes to this end.) Some of the most lasting impressions left by the book are of the ways in which our very existence on the earth necessarily affects others, for better or worse, and of how the consequences of our actions escape us. Whatever its defects, or indeed its other merits, *Le Sang des autres* is outstanding as an extended illustration of these points.

In the late summer of 1943, with *Le Sang des autres* finished but unpublishable before the Liberation, Beauvoir began writing her third novel. She was to break off this work for some three months, however, in order to compose her only play, *Les Bouches inutiles*. Since attending the rehearsals of Sartre's *Les Mouches* she had wanted to try her hand at drama and in April 1944 a suitable subject presented itself in a historical work on Italy by Sismondi. Transposing the topic to fourteenth-century Flanders, she completed the play in July. *Les Bouches inutiles* tells the story of the town of Vaucelles, which has thrown off the yoke of the Duke of Burgundy in the name of freedom and independence, but has been besieged by his forces for a year. At the beginning, Jean-Pierre Gauthier has just slipped back through enemy lines with the message that help will be forthcoming from the French King, but not for three months or so. Since there are food supplies to nourish the whole population of the town for only some

three weeks, the council, headed by Louis d'Avesnes, decide that the
'useless' members of the community—the sick, the aged, women and
children—shall be cast out. This causes Jean-Pierre, who has previously turned down an offer to join the ruling council—'Je garderai
mes mains pures' (41)—to recognise (like Jean Blomart) that there is
no way of evading his responsibilities. Largely by exposing the plot to
seize power hatched by Louis's son and François Rosbourg, he persuades the council to change its decision. The play ends with everyone
in the town about to participate in an all-or-nothing attempt to
overcome the besieging forces.

The plot has considerable dramatic potential and the play is full of
incident and confrontation. A number of major women characters—
the most important being Louis's wife Catherine—constitute the
main representatives of 'les bouches inutiles' and thereby come
directly into conflict with the men, from the end of the first act.
Another significant theme is that of love, which Beauvoir tries, with
mixed success, to link with the political action. The council's decision
somehow spurs Jean-Pierre to declare his love for Clarice for the first
time; Clarice undergoes, through love, a conversion very like Hélène's
in *Le Sang des autres;* and Catherine claims that Louis's love for her
will prove to be a lie if he goes through with the sacrifice. Yet the loves
and lusts of Georges, Jeanne and Jacques add nothing essential to the
plot. The same might be said about the malevolence and ambition of
Georges and François, whose roles are suspiciously like those of
standard theatrical villains (although thematically they are meant to
represent the way in which tyranny soon spreads throughout a
society). In general, it is perfectly clear that Beauvoir's main aim is to
air in a play those moral issues that had preoccupied her in *Pyrrhus et
Cinéas* and *Le Sang des autres*, most notably questions concerning
freedom, choice and our needs or rights in relation to others.

A further dimension is added to these matters here, however, since
there is an identifiable community as such—the town of Vaucelles—
which enters strongly into the equation and raises questions of a new
type. What is best for the town in the long run (130)? What exactly
will remain of the town if the useless are expelled (116)? What will be
the effect of Vaucelles's fate on other towns (135)? The eventual
collective decision to mount a charge on the Burgundians is a stirring
one and constitutes a fairly satisfactory solution to some of the theoretical problems raised. Negatively, it avoids certain obvious incon-

sistencies, for as Jean-Pierre says, 'Si un seul homme peut être regardé comme un déchet, cent mille hommes ensemble ne sont qu'un tas d'ordures' (132). It can also be construed as the only decision fully consistent with the principle of personal freedom: 'Nous luttons pour la liberté, c'est elle qui triomphe par notre libre sacrifice' (141). Furthermore, because of the uncertainty of the outcome, it neatly supports Beauvoir's view that important choices are accompanied by Kierkegaardian 'Fear and Trembling'. Nevertheless, the ending, like the play as a whole, fails to come to grips with the specifically political issues involved. ('L'erreur a été de poser un problème politique en termes de morale abstraite'; FA,674.) If Vaucelles is run democratically and if the town is seeking to survive in order to spread the principle of autonomy or freedom, then its constitutional decision to sacrifice 'les bouches inutiles' is not entirely indefensible on strict political grounds. Interestingly, Louis's argument that freedom is undermined by the fact that the victims themselves have not chosen to make the sacrifice (132) is one that Blomart rejects, however reluctantly, at the end of *Le Sang des autres*.

Les Bouches inutiles was first produced in Paris in November 1945. While a number of critics stoutly defended its dramatic merits, it was for the most part very badly received. It lasted for about fifty performances, but considering the interest in existentialism at the time, it cannot be regarded as having achieved success on the stage. The first act contains some fine scenes and generates interest in a variety of ways. Above all, the dialogue is spare and sharp, creating out of particular situations characters whose attitudes and reactions we become involved in and want to know more about. Unfortunately, Beauvoir seems much less in control of her material in Act II, which tends to oscillate between philosophical discussions containing slightly longer, somewhat declamatory speeches, and rather frantic action verging on the melodramatic. The evidence of the first part of *Les Bouches inutiles* does not bear out Beauvoir's judgement that she cannot compose good theatrical dialogue,[1] but the play as a whole suggests that she is testing herself or meeting a challenge rather than writing because she has something new to say. She appears to be happier with fiction because she can actually enter the minds of her characters and expose their workings with a wider range of resources. In any case, in her next novel she was to go back to doing this in the ways that she had been adopting since her earliest stories.

Like *Le Sang des autres, Tous les hommes sont mortels*—completed at
the end of 1945 and published in 1946—is narrated from the point of
view of one male and one female character, although the form of the
book is rather different. The novel begins with a one-hundred-page
'Prologue' centring on Régine, an ambitious, highly egocentric
actress who is enjoying some success with a play in the French
provinces. She becomes intrigued by the mysterious and listless figure
of Raymond Fosca, succeeds in reviving his interest in life, and
persuades him to return to Paris with her. As soon as she can bring
herself to believe his claim that he is immortal, she sets out to make
him love her 'comme il n'a jamais aimé, comme il n'aimera jamais'
(69), in the belief that this will give her superiority over all of her rivals
and ensure that her memory persists for ever. However, Fosca discovers again what he has apparently had to accept on many previous
occasions, that he is unable to live and love like an ordinary mortal.
All that Régine can do is to persuade him to tell her the story of his
life, in the hope that the blow will be lessened if she understands how
immortality is a curse. The five parts of the rest of the novel correspond
to the five major phases into which Fosca divides his life, and at the
end of each we are taken back very briefly to Régine to see her
reactions.

Born near the end of the thirteenth century in Carmona in Northern
Italy, Fosca is anxious to see justice and equality in the town and
eventually becomes its ruler by assassinating his predecessor. Frustrated by the realisation that he himself may die before his work is
complete, he takes an immortality potion. With the advantage of his
own invulnerability and by tyrannically exacting all the required
sacrifices from the people of Carmona, he ruthlessly furthers the cause
of the town in the face of war, famine and plague. More single-minded
than ever when he loses all of his family, he wages military and
commercial battle against the cities of Genoa and Florence, until he
finds that he needs to make common cause with them in order to fend
off the forces of the Duke of Milan. Taking peace as his goal now, he
enables Carmona to flourish economically for many years, believing
that unification of the country is the highest priority. Even Italy comes
to seem too small a unit, however, when he is forced to accept that its
fate cannot be divorced from what is happening in the rest of the
world: 'On ne peut rien faire à moins de régner sur le monde entier'
(225). After some two hundred years in Carmona, he leaves Italy to

throw in his lot with the Habsburgs.

Fosca gives Carmona to the Holy Roman Empire and soon becomes chief advisor to the Emperor Charles V. Engaging in endless financial and military struggles, supporting more and more repressive measures in the name of justice and happiness for everyone, he eventually finds that no progress is being made and begins to turn to the New World as the only part of the globe where 'on peut créer et construire' (291). Yet on his first visit to Central and South America he discovers what irremediable damage his policies have been responsible for there: 'Nous avions détruit un monde, et nous l'avions détruit pour rien' (312). He abandons politics and wanders off around the world alone. In the middle of the seventeenth century Fosca joins forces with an explorer, Pierre Carlier, who is trying to find a way across the uncharted territories of the North American continent to the Pacific. But Carlier comes to resent his help and even his very presence before he dies and the disillusioned Fosca goes on to spend a very long period in a humble Indian village.

In the eighteenth century he is 'rescued' and taken to Paris, where he becomes involved—though for his own personal reasons—in the great search for knowledge at the time. This interest in its turn fades when he falls in love with Marianne de Sinclair. They marry and live very happily together until she discovers his secret and sees herself as betrayed. By 1830 Fosca is watching over his great-grandson Armand, an ardent revolutionary who is happy to enlist the support of an immortal. Fosca assists the cause in various ways, but is now almost totally alienated from all human goals. As the Revolution of 1848 succeeds, he again wanders off alone. Managing to sleep for sixty years, he is forced to spend thirty years in an asylum when he wakes. It was just after he left the asylum that Régine met him and, having now heard his story, she realises that nothing at all can enable her to stop the march of time or escape death.

Because Fosca's story constitutes approximately four-fifths of the book and takes up all but a few pages of narrative following the Prologue, it is worth emphasising the significance of Régine, whose state of mind is the point of focus at the beginning and end of the novel. The Prologue leads up to and introduces Fosca's tale, but it functions by projecting us into the mind of a character who could easily have been the central figure of a separate work. Régine particularly resembles Hélène in her early loss of faith and her desperate need to be loved, but like so many of Beauvoir's heroines she is also a living illustration of the 'hollowness' of consciousness or the difficulty of knowing what we are, and she sees relations with others as constant competition and conflict. By any standards she is an unpleasant, malicious woman—the man who loves her calls her a 'vampire' (33)—and there is once more the risk that her very pettiness may alienate us so much that we lose interest in her. Perhaps this actually begins to happen at some points (for instance, when she is so vindictive towards her friend Annie; 84), but Beauvoir skilfully ensures that our dominant feeling towards Régine gradually comes to be one of pity.

It is difficult to do other than sympathise with her in her obsessive aversion to death ('"Sauvez-moi, dit-elle. Sauvez-moi de la mort"'; 58), for in some measure this is shown as representing a deeply human 'goût de l'absolu'. But the desire to be unique that grips her more strongly than it does Hélène—it is even suggested that this lies behind her loss of faith, rather than vice versa: '"Il aurait fallu que Dieu n'aimât que moi"' (104)—is something that brings out the worst in Régine. Nevertheless, we recognise the strength of this drive and consequently the depths of her distress when Fosca drifts away from her. Contact with him has already made her begin to see herself from the point of view of eternity (106), but when he acknowledges that he cannot share her ambitions for long and admits that he is just as fond of her friend Annie ('"Comment pourrais-je faire une différence?"'; 111), Régine's anguish is acute. The reader's reaction to it is heightened, moreover, by the irony and poignancy in the fact that her commitment to Fosca eventually causes her to feel even less unique than a relationship with a mortal might have done:

> Un brin d'herbe, rien qu'un brin d'herbe. Chacun se croyait différent des autres; chacun se préférait; et tous se trompaient; elle s'était trompée comme les autres. (112)

The Prologue is almost a story in its own right, with a direct, compelling opening and an effective build-up of mystery around Fosca, the three chapters being narrated strictly from Régine's viewpoint, in Beauvoir's familiar manner. Régine's insecurity and needs are strongly conveyed in sequences where she lucidly analyses her own feelings, and in a series of dramatic scenes—culminating in the party at which she unexpectedly announces her retirement—which show her at odds with other people. Dialogue is unusually important here and if we learn so much about Fosca in these chapters, it is because some of his main attitudes become apparent from his recorded comments. In Chapter 3 the focus of attention shifts markedly towards Fosca, whose story the reader, like Régine, needs to hear in order to understand his change of behaviour. But by this time it is already clear how the character of Régine is appropriate for the role that Beauvoir wishes her to play in the structure of the novel, for she is just the sort of woman to be caught in the same trap as Fosca, that of wanting immortality. Even when she begins to see all that it implies, she is still 'emportée par le torrent' and can only be purged of her yearning by hearing all the details of Fosca's own sad evolution.

Yet in their general attitude towards others Fosca and Régine are as strongly contrasted as Blomart and Hélène before the war. While Régine is utterly self-centred and gives no thought at all to the welfare of other people, for many centuries Fosca works tirelessly for the good of others as he sees it. It is true that at many stages of his life he is prepared to kill, sacrifice, or otherwise use individuals in order to achieve his goals. To this extent his story raises—sometimes explicitly and very powerfully, as in some episodes concerning Charles V—the very moral questions about ends and means that Beauvoir treated in other works of this period. Yet although he is undoubtedly guilty of pride early in his life, Fosca's motives and aims, unlike those of Régine, are always good. Rightly or wrongly, he sincerely believes for a very long time that he can legitimately inflict harm upon some in the name of the eventual happiness of the greatest number. When he eventually abandons this position (after his period as *éminence grise* to Charles V), this is not exactly because he no longer believes that the end justifies the means, but rather because he recognises that his aims themselves were misconceived, that only men themselves can decide what is good for them: 'il est vain de vouloir dominer la terre; on ne peut rien pour les hommes, leur bien ne dépend que d'eux-mêmes' (313). Even this enables him to continue helping people in the seventeenth, eighteenth and and nineteenth centuries, for although the actual causes espoused by Carlier, Marianne and Armand are of little interest to him, he responds to the individuals concerned, taking as his guiding principle that enunciated by the Lutheran monk about to be burned: '"Il n'y a qu'un seul bien, dit-il. C'est d'agir selon sa conscience"' (282).

Fosca, then, discovers what Beauvoir takes to be metaphysical and moral truths about the human condition—truths that she spells out in *Pyrrhus et Cinéas* and *Pour une morale de l'ambiguïté*—and discovers them in roughly the way that a mortal might. In this respect, only the infinitely wider range of experiences from which he is able to distil these truths distinguishes his case from that of an ordinary man. Indeed, part of the fascination of *Tous les hommes sont mortels* lies— uniquely as far as Beauvoir's fiction is concerned—in the way in which it encourages us to seek parallels between much earlier historical periods or circumstances and modern times. For instance, what Fosca learns about the conflicting interests of collectivities of different sizes (Carmona, Italy, the Holy Roman Empire, 'l'Univers') reminds us of Blomart's dilemmas over the different claims of his trade-union branch, his country, and Europe as a whole; just as Armand's problems after 1830 recall those of the Resistance movement. More generally, Fosca's rather confused awareness of the 'monstrueuse mécanique' of history in Part II plainly reflects the impact of historical forces upon Beauvoir and her contemporaries at the end of the nineteen-thirties. In these ways and others, the significance of Fosca's story is fairly clear in relation to Beauvoir's other works, although the great variety and historical sweep of the tale adds a density and resonance to the philosophical points that would be enough in itself to justify their embodiment in a work of fiction.

The distinctive feature of the book, however, is the specific use to which Beauvoir puts Fosca's immortality. That she should succeed in generating so much interest in both the past of an immortal and the effect that his presence has on one mortal character is already note-worthy, when one considers how severely limited are the flights of fancy in her other novels. But it is obvious that the book's impact would be unduly restricted if we were not able to see Fosca's immor-tality as standing for certain attitudes and values commonly adopted by human beings. In fact, from his own comments as well as Régine's subsequent reactions, it is plain from the Prologue onwards that the disillusioned Fosca represents an attitude of crippling resignation or indifference that we all experience from time to time and which expresses itself as an inclination to survey human life as if from a great distance or height; what Beauvoir calls 'le point de vue de Sirius'. (Françoise occasionally slips into it in *L'Invitée*, and for a while even Hélène sees its attractions; SA,272.) On this level, the 'message' of the book is that such a passive and debilitating outlook is not only associated with great sadness, but is also deeply inhuman. If Fosca is such a pathetic, hapless figure after the end of Part II, this is largely because he becomes increasingly conscious that his immortality actually *prevents* him from doing many of the things that mortals can do. He cannot give meaning to his life by consciously adopting a personal, all-consuming goal, as Carlier does. Nor can he believe in a gradual enlightenment and the improvement of the human lot, like Marianne. Worse still, in Armand he meets a mortal who refuses to accept that the inevitability of death is a sufficient reason for ceasing to care how one leads one's life, or that the ebb and flow of history, which eventually turns victory into defeat, finally negates all human achievement. Not only is it precisely the finite nature of life that gives it value for Armand and his companions, they, unlike Fosca, can consent to die in order to affirm human values: 'je ne pouvais pas risquer ma vie avec la leur' (472). When Fosca definitively acknowledges these truths, he simultaneously sees exactly what it is to be human and recognises that he is permanently excluded from the human race: 'je sus que le dernier lien qui m'attachait au monde venait de se briser' (517).

The strangely haunting quality of *Tous les hommes sont mortels* arises out of the rather ghostly nature of Fosca's presence across the centuries and perhaps particularly out of the way in which this affects the personal relationships that he forms. In this last area the book is outstandingly fertile, for in addition to the strong bonds sometimes generated by Fosca's public functions as ruler of Carmona and advisor to Charles V, we have extensive and privileged views of him in his private capacities as husband, father, friend, master and lover. Furthermore, Beauvoir rings the changes ceaselessly, by modifying the circumstances of his ties, giving different characters to those he knows, and having Fosca's general attitude towards relationships alter over the years. Almost all of his intimates are aware of his immortality —he tries to hide it from Marianne, but with disastrous results—and in a curious way this enables Beauvoir to focus sharply on what she regards as essential in human relations. The reader has constantly to gauge the equivalent of Fosca's relationships in purely human terms, but this somehow enhances their significance, as does the knowledge that he is acutely aware of their temporal limits. Thus, for example, his love for Marianne is as convincing and moving as any sentiment described in Beauvoir's novels; his feelings for his son Antoine her most tender portrayal of fatherhood; his affection for Carlier a particularly touching representation of friendship between males; his bond with Bompard an intriguing sketch of the master-slave relationship; and so on. The Prologue, too, where we see Fosca through the eyes of someone trying to relate to him, embodies some cogent points about the essence of personal relations. Here Fosca's susceptibility to 're-awakening' by others is at its clearest (' "Sauvez-moi de la nuit et de l'indifférence" '; 58) and is an obvious and effective metaphor for what Beauvoir calls 'le mirage de l'Autre'; that is, the way in which we continue to need and to be drawn to people, however much our hopes and expectations may be frustrated. Fosca claims that he will always go on making the same 'mistake' (112), and in the context of all the failed relationships depicted in the book, this is an extremely important point for Beauvoir to have him make.

Looking at the novel as a whole, it is difficult to avoid the conclusion that its structure and proportions are somewhat defective. There are some extremely impressive sequences in Fosca's story, which is often excellent in its description of action (battles in fourteenth-century Italy; street-fighting in nineteenth-century France) and its conjuring up of atmospheres (life in Carmona; exploration on the unknown North American continent; backbiting in eighteenth-century *salons*). It is also well set out in sections which emphasise the phases of Fosca's development, with brief intervening passages to keep the story of Régine alive and enable the reader to maintain a certain distance from Fosca. Nevertheless, it is disproportionately long (Beauvoir herself speaks of 'des longueurs, des redites, des surcharges'; FCh,98); tends to be somewhat tedious as a narrative at those points where Fosca's life itself is repetitive; and becomes turgid near the end, when the technique of referring back to earlier episodes is over-used. Furthermore, the marrying of Fosca's narrative and Régine's is not entirely successful. The decision to have Régine recognise that she can expect nothing of Fosca even before he begins telling his story means that her development after the Prologue is minimal. The brief passages about her placed in the interstices of Fosca's story cannot trace a gradual disenchantment or indeed say much at all about her state of mind, and the idea that she is coming to understand immortality better is slightly abstract and tenuous. Even at the end there is a certain vagueness or ambiguity about her position. It is certainly true that far from making life 'moins terrible' as she had hoped, Fosca's story has shattered any remaining hope she may have had of seeing herself as unique (as she sees this coming, Régine wants Fosca's tale to continue only because it delays the onset of her inevitable solitude). But if Beauvoir really intended that Régine should now glimpse the possibility of salvation— 'Elle a entrevu pourtant un salut mais elle n'a pas eu la force de s'y arrêter: il lui aurait fallu s'agripper à sa finitude' (FCh, 97)— then she should have brought this out much more clearly than in a single allusion. For in the context of the horrifying final sentence of the book ('Ce fut quand l'heure commença de sonner au clocher qu'elle poussa le premier cri'), this could refer to almost anything, including suicide:

> il y avait peut-être une issue; furtif comme un battement de paupière, quelque chose effleura son cœur; ce n'était pas même un espoir et déjà cela s'était évanoui; elle était trop fatiguée. (528)

Beauvoir has stressed that in *Tous les hommes sont mortels* she wished to counterbalance the moral optimism of *Pyrrhus et Cinéas* and *Le Sang des autres* by showing death 'non seulement comme une relation de chaque homme à tout, mais aussi comme le scandale de la solitude et de la séparation' (FA,695). Régine's part of the narrative, of course, conveys this signal directly and prominently, because she is so afraid of death and believes that it will nullify everything that she has done and been. It is not so plain, however, that Fosca's story carries the same message. Admittedly, he sees numerous loved ones die over the centuries and in many cases it can be said that they die alone and lonely in some crucial sense. Nevertheless, it is hard to consider death as a scandal in Fosca's tale as a whole, when he himself would so dearly love to die, and when he has learned from Armand and his colleagues that being prepared to die for something is the human being's supreme way of affirming its value. As Beauvoir also points out:

> infinie, notre vie se dissoudrait dans l'universelle indifférence. La mort conteste notre existence mais c'est elle qui lui donne son sens; par elle s'accomplit l'absolue séparation, mais elle est aussi la clef de toute communication. (FA,693)

The fact is that *Tous les hommes sont mortels* is neither pessimistic nor optimistic in any simple sense. Once more the ending of the novel may be read in different ways according to where one places the greatest emphasis: on Fosca, on Régine, or on Armand ('Le récit se conteste sans répit; si on prétendait en tirer des allégations, elles se contre-diraient; aucun point de vue ne prévaut définitivement'; FCh, 98). And that must count as a strength rather than a weakness, for this is above all a highly inventive novel, in which, within a controlled framework, Beauvoir allows her imagination to circle around themes that she has treated more systematically, and more prosaically, else-where. To some extent the function of Régine's narrative is to ensure that the book's roots remain in familiar soil. If the resulting work as a whole is not so tidy or so well consolidated as some might wish, it unquestionably avoids the strident moralistic and didactic tones of both *Le Sang des autres* and *Les Bouches inutiles*, leaving us with exceedingly powerful images of some of Beauvoir's more general preoccupations during the war.

Notes

[1] See the transcript of the film *Simone de Beauvoir* by Josée Dayan and Malka Ribowska (Gallimard, 1979), p.24.

9 *Les Mandarins*

Just as it had taken a setback in her private life to bring Beauvoir to write *L'Invitée*, so it was only when, following the harmony and expectancy of the final years of the war, French political life began to break up around her that she felt a strong urge to write about it:

> Le triomphe du Bien sur le Mal cessa d'aller de soi: il paraissait même rudement compromis. De l'azur collectif, j'avais chu avec beaucoup d'autres dans la poussière terrestre: le sol était jonché d'illusions brisées. (FCh, 360)

Day-to-day politics still bored her, but since the whole world seemed threatened by greater catastrophe than ever, she found all that she had ever believed in called into question. Not yet having the detachment to consider composing any kind of chronicle, she decided in 1949 to write a novel based upon the friendships that had been broken and the common hopes lost since the Occupation: 'Pour parler de moi, il fallait parler de *nous*, au sens qu'avait eu ce mot en 1944' (FCh, 361). She was conscious that for her this entailed concentrating on intellectuals—'nous étions des intellectuels, une espèce à part' (hence the title, *Les Mandarins*)—but she felt that what had happened to intellectuals was representative of what had happened to all French people since the war (FCh, 361).

Because of the length of *Les Mandarins*—it is twice as long as any of Beauvoir's other works of fiction—and the highly intricate nature of its contents, summary of the book as such is unprofitable. But these same factors make an analysis of the broad movement of the story and of the general structure of the work invaluable. Beauvoir claims that the central thread of the plot is 'une brisure et un retour d'amitié entre deux hommes', but since the break concerned does not take place until two thirds of the way through the book, a better starting-point is the fact that this quarrel, like the novel as a whole, is related from two viewpoints: that of one of the men involved, Henri Perron, and that of the wife of the other, Anne Dubreuilh. Obviously, therefore, Robert Dubreuilh occupies a key position in the network of relationships portrayed, and even on the philosophical or thematic level his role is vital, for in some measure both Anne and Henri situate themselves by reference to him. Yet like the equally central Pierre in *L'Invitée*, Dubreuilh remains partly 'opaque' to the reader, for he is given none of the narrative. As in *Le Sang des autres*, the narrative viewpoint alternates perfectly regularly between Henri and Anne. Each of the first two chapters is shared between them, with clearly marked divisions between the parts, but thereafter the changes of viewpoint invariably correspond with the ends of chapters. A rough quantitative balance is maintained overall, with Henri's part of the book occupying only some forty-five pages more than Anne's, in a work of one thousand pages. The sharing of the first two chapters is an appropriate device, since the story starts at the end of the great collective adventure of the Resistance: the lives and fates of Henri and Anne have been closely linked and it is only as the book progresses that their paths diverge in various ways. As that divergence comes about, it makes less sense to look for exact symmetry in their experiences. Nevertheless, there are significant respects in which their stories continue to run in parallel for much of the book.

Les Mandarins begins with the double celebrations of Christmas 1944—for Christmas itself and for the imminent ending of the war in Europe—and the first chapter revolves around the party held in the flat shared by Henri and his mistress Paule. Both Henri and Anne are trying to grasp the implications of their new circumstances after the four long years of the Occupation. The second—and only other shared—chapter is a good complement to the first, in that it shows both of them keeping appointments made at the party and thereby beginning to break new ground in their personal lives by giving in to 'l'attrait de la nouveauté': Henri with Anne's daughter Nadine, and Anne with Scriassine. The first two chapters combine well to illustrate some of the war's more subtle repercussions on the private lives of individuals and to convey the mood in France immediately after the Liberation: the hopes and expectations, but also the fears and regrets. Chapters 3 and 4 trace the development of the views of Henri and Anne over the seven months following Christmas 1944. They are made increasingly conscious of the political complexities of the post-Liberation situation: Henri mainly because they directly impinge upon his work as a journalist and a creative writer, and Anne principally because they affect the lives of Dubreuilh and her daughter.

(Henri and Anne discuss matters in one of their rare moments alone together; 312-20.) Soon they are both faced with important decisions. Should Henri throw the weight of his newspaper *L'Espoir* behind Dubreuilh's new political movement? Should Anne accept an invitation to go to America in connection with her work as a psychiatrist? Both eventually decide, at the end of their chapters, to take the plunge, thereby recognising that the war is way behind them and that entirely new attitudes and positions are now appropriate.

From this point on the patterns become more complicated. For a time Henri gains satisfaction from working as part of a team and devoting himself almost entirely to political journalism. But by the end of Chapter 5 it is clear that he will have to face another vital decision—whether to publish an account of the newly discovered work-camps in the Soviet Union—and one that will prove a critical turning-point, bringing about the collapse of Dubreuilh's new movement and alienating Henri from most of his friends. Significantly, the last third of Chapter 5, which sees Henri beginning a liaison with the aspiring young actress Josette, overlaps chronologically with the early part of Chapter 6, which relates Anne's first trip to America and the start of her love-affair with the writer Lewis Brogan. The general point is that the pressures of the post-Liberation period drive both of them into relationships that constitute some kind of respite from their deepest involvement with their old life and friends in Paris. There is a rather uncharacteristic element of recklessness or unreality in both affairs and, perhaps inevitably, they eventually turn sour. In the meantime, the issue of the Soviet work-camps, representing the new kind of reality that Henri and Anne have to come to terms with in the post-war situation, has a powerful effect upon their lives, leaving them almost overwhelmed by their awareness of the evil in the world and tempting them both to adopt positions of relative inactivity and indifference. Anne, in fact, never recovers from this state and her part of the book ends on a deeply sad note, with her final decision not to commit suicide made because of its possible effects on others rather than from any positive desire to go on living. Henri, on the other hand, has regained his equilibrium by the last stages of the novel, when he is married to Nadine and has a child. His final decision is to stay in Paris (instead of retreating to Italy) and to become involved in politics again. Although his attitude and expectations are now rather different from those of 1944, the future holds out pleasant prospects for him.

183

At the end of *Les Mandarins*, then, it is the contrast between the outlooks of the two 'narrators' that is most noticeable. In fact, this contrast, in spite of fluctuations over the period of nearly four years covered by the text, underlies the novel as a whole. It is entirely characteristic that while Henri's mood at Christmas 1944 is one of great optimism—'L'air gris-bleu était lourd de promesses, l'avenir s'élargissait à l'infini' (23)—Anne finds the Liberation disorientating and worrying: 'soudain, je n'ai plus confiance, en rien' (68). Beauvoir is clearly right to see the conflict between Henri's perspective (which is similar to Dubreuilh's) and that of Anne—'leur point de vue qui est celui de l'action, de la finitude, de la vie, est mis en question par Anne en qui j'ai incarné celui de l'être, de l'absolu, de la mort' (FCh, 369-70)—as reflecting polarities present in *Le Sang des autres* and *Tous les hommes sont mortels*. Yet the embodiment of these antitheses in particular characters is not precisely the same as in other works (Blomart, for instance, manifests both Anne's 'sens de la mort' *and* Henri's desire for action), so that the complex ways in which Henri and Anne represent, respectively, 'la gaieté d'exister' and 'l'horreur de finir' require careful delineation.

We learn at the very beginning of Anne's narrative how she first realised she was condemned to death at the age of fifteen when she lost her faith in God, and how her love for Robert later enabled her to conquer her fear (38-39). Her preoccupation with death, however, has returned since the Liberation, being linked with both a growing awareness of Dubreuilh's vulnerability and an unwillingness to forget those who died during the war, especially her daughter's young fiancé, Diégo (74). At a number of points there is a hint that Anne's remorse over the dead may be excessive in the way that Blomart's sense of guilt was disproportionate, and she admits later that, like many others, she had *general* difficulty in re-adapting to life after the Occupation. Yet her acute consciousness of mortality is none the less real for all this. It is true that although she is not entirely convinced by Dubreuilh's argument that history will justify everything in the end, she manages to go on finding things in the world to love or hate and even reaches the point of acknowledging that those who died during the war have to all intents and purposes been forgotten (II, 468). But then the collapse of her affair with Brogan once more triggers off her fear of death: 'de nouveau, comme en ce jour de mes quinze ans, où j'ai crié de peur, la mort me traque' (II, 493). She realises that Dubreuilh will die before she does and at the end sees death as not just an idea but a reality that colours everything.

Anne's obsession with death itself is in fact just one—albeit the pivotal one—of what Beauvoir calls 'les aspects négatifs de mon expérience que j'ai exprimés à travers elle' (FCh, 367). A related feature of Anne's state of mind after the Liberation is her feeling that the best part of her life is over. She knows that there is truth in Nadine's accusation that she has somehow shut herself off from new experience, going through life without ever removing her 'gants de chevreau glacé', and she is conscious in particular of having enclosed her body in 'une torpeur égoïste' (117). When she fails to break through these barriers in going to bed with Scriassine, she resolves never to make the attempt again. Age—she is thirty-nine—suddenly seems to be the reason for her problems: 'ma vieillesse m'attend, aucun moyen de lui échapper' (126). Hence the first half of the novel sees Anne leading a 'sage petite vie de morte' and having severe difficulty in relating to people other than her nearest and dearest. When she finally plucks up the courage to go to America, her affair with Brogan brings her to life again physically ('Son désir me transfigurait'; II, 39) and for a time she is a new woman. She vows to herself that she will never become like the predatory older women she meets in Paris, and that Lewis will be her last lover. Yet even before things begin to go seriously wrong, she comes to see this attitude as a kind of self-deception:

> Sous ma chair défraîchie j'affirme la survivance d'une jeune femme aux exigences intactes, rebelle à toutes les concessions, et qui dédaigne les tristes peaux de quarante ans; mais elle n'existe plus, elle ne renaîtra jamais, même sous les baisers de Lewis. (II, 375)

In short, although Anne's American adventure actually ends as it does because Brogan is unable to tolerate the situation, it could not in any case have provided her with any more than temporary relief from her deep preoccupation with ageing, decline, suffering and death.

With Henri the general pattern is the very opposite, for we see his enthusiasm return time and again after serious setbacks and feel that his love of live is undiminished at the end of the book, in spite of all that has happened. Following the Occupation, one of his main aims is to gain some personal enjoyment from life: 'Il était temps qu'il s'occupe un peu de lui' (12-13). He is unlike Dubreuilh and most of those around him in this respect, being more than happy to undertake his pleasure trip to Portugal at a moment when they are especially anxious to reconstruct political life in post-war France. It would be harsh to label his attitude a selfish one, however, for as soon as he returns he throws himself into his work as a journalist, begins writing another novel and agrees, against his better judgement, to give Dubreuilh some help in launching his political movement, the S.R.L. Indeed, his commitments rapidly become so heavy that he finds he no longer has the time to do anything for the sheer pleasure of doing it: 'il vivait du matin au soir à contrecœur' (259). In spite of his determination to resist (he has remembered earlier how a previous period of intense activity depressed him and prevented him from writing; 17-18), he has eventually to admit that he has been swallowed up by politics and that this has resulted in a certain inner emptiness. But the causes he espouses are so important that he is prepared to subordinate his personal wishes completely to the need to work on behalf of the oppressed and underprivileged: 'Fini d'écrire, fini de vivre. Une seule consigne: agir . . . Servir, s'unir, agir' (263).

This stance itself is a manifestation of his desire to 'transcend' himself by changing things in the world and he is as impervious as Dubreuilh to Anne's argument that death negates all such effort. Before long he even finds a reason for beginning to write again (this time a play). Nevertheless, he reaches his own low point when it becomes apparent that his unrelenting attempt to be honest has only made him enemies (II, 163); that all his sacrifices have produced nothing of value on the political front; and that his already restricted private life is being used against him. There is little of his old *joie de vivre* left when he finds himself more or less obliged to go back on many of his deepest principles and commit perjury to save the skin of Josette: 'jamais il ne s'était senti plus triste' (II, 320). And by the time this results in his resignation as editor of *L'Espoir*, his reactions have all been dulled:

il était beaucoup moins ému qu'il ne l'aurait cru. En descendant les escaliers, il se dit vaguement: 'C'est la rançon.' La rançon de quoi? d'avoir couché avec Josette? d'avoir voulu la sauver? d'avoir prétendu garder une vie privée alors que l'action exige un homme tout entier? de s'être entêté dans l'action alors qu'il ne s'y donnait pas sans réserve? il ne savait pas. Et même s'il avait su, ça n'aurait rien changé. (II, 333)

Yet in spite of all this, a new Henri arises out of the ashes. His friendship with Dubreuilh is revived; he finds a way of continuing to wage campaigns against injustices without compromising his devotion to creative writing; and to his own surprise he takes to marriage and fatherhood with considerable enthusiasm. While Anne sees her experiences as confirming her gloomiest view of life, Henri's disappointments and losses fail to change his optimistic outlook and his capacity to make new starts.

These two contrasting personal perspectives in *Les Mandarins* are held together by the fact that Henri and Anne have the same friends and colleagues in Paris and, above all, because they are shown as living through the same difficult period of French political history. Henri is directly and actively involved in politics, both through his journalism and through the unswerving commitment to the cause of the working classes that he made during the war (19). Anne is involved more indirectly and passively because the general left-wing sympathies developed in her childhood (69) were focused for her by Dubreuilh, and she follows every single political step that he takes with interest and concern. Through the eyes of both Henri and Anne, moreover, we see how a whole host of other Parisian intellectuals—almost all politically to the Left in one measure or another—react to the important situations and issues of the years immediately following the Liberation. All of the major political events and developments recorded in the story are real—the attempt to found a new political movement; the dropping of the first atomic bombs on Japan; the discovery of the Soviet work-camps; the declining international influence of France and the build-up of the Cold War—but Beauvoir changes timings and adds or modifies smaller-scale happenings in the interests of the shape of her narrative.[1]

It is, in any case, attitudes, decisions and disagreements rather than events as such that constitute the centre of attention, and here too the story has a strong basis in fact, without claiming to be an entirely faithful record of the troubles of the Left after 1944. One cannot, of course, understand the evolution of political positions in *Les Mandarins* without taking the Resistance as a starting-point. All the references back conjure up precisely the kind of heady unity during the Occupation depicted in *Le Sang des autres*, and according to Dubreuilh's retrospective analysis this was what gave them a false start after the war:

> 'Nous avons cru que nous n'avions qu'à profiter de notre élan: alors qu'il y avait une coupure radicale entre la période de l'occupation et celle qui a suivi la Libération.' (II, 338)

Yet from early on we see Dubreuilh himself speaking in much the same terms as he uses later about the negative side to their wartime experiences (62), while Henri recognises from the first that 'La Résistance était une chose, la politique une autre' (19). Henri is rather horrified that a former leading figure in the Resistance, Tournelle, might be suggesting that they should not have resisted at all, but shows a sound sense of proportion in his remarks to the wild Vincent: '"ce n'était pas l'aventure qui comptait: c'était les trucs qu'on défendait"' (247). His stance becomes rather more dubious in this respect as the story progresses (having written a play with the message that the war should not be forgotten, he perjures himself about who was in the Resistance, in order to save the main actress from being persecuted for collaboration), but his strength lies in his general determination to look forward rather than back. In this he is sharply contrasted with his faithful assistant Luc (32); with Vincent, who is still taking violent revenge upon ex-collaborators at the end of the book; and with Lambert, whose view of what others did during the war is coloured by an inflexible desire to return to all of the simple old values. (On a slightly broader scale, Anne notices a similar contrast between herself and Paule: '"Moi aussi pendant quelques semaines j'ai eu l'illusion qu'on allait retrouver l'avant-guerre; mais c'était de la sottise"'; 294.) Already in the different attitudes towards the past, therefore, we can see a whole spectrum of positions within the left-wing group that the novel portrays.

These differences and others are steadily accentuated as the crucial issues of the post-war period crystallise, and particularly as the world political scene comes to be dominated by the two super-powers. Taken literally, some of Scriassine's early prophecies prove to be immoderate ('"Nous serons annexés par Staline ou colonisés par l'Amérique"'; 54), but he foresees the general problems to come more clearly than any other character at the beginning of the book, even on the French domestic front. In fact, in a conversation with Henri during the opening party he accurately predicts the broad lines of the political developments described in the first two thirds of the novel (30-31). The principal communist character in *Les Mandarins*, Lachaume (for whom Beauvoir shows a great deal of sympathy), warns Henri of the possibility that the Communist Party will attack the S.R.L. even before *L'Espoir* becomes the organ of the movement (236-38) and this threat hangs heavily over Henri and Dubreuilh for some time ('"nous serons des ennemis du seul grand parti prolétarien de France"'; 371). In the event, for tactical reasons the S.R.L. actually fires the first shots in a campaign that rapidly becomes personal, but it is the issue of the Soviet labour-camps that finally polarises positions and brings matters to a head. Henri's decision to publish what he knows brings about his break with Dubreuilh; alienates him entirely from the Communists; and soon causes the collapse of the S.R.L. Henri goes on struggling to maintain his earlier independent stance and becomes, like Dubreuilh, more and more of an isolated figure. Interestingly, however, Beauvoir does not allow the break-up of the unity of the Left to strike the final note as far as the political content of the novel is concerned. The very independence that Henri has striven so painfully to preserve makes him an especially useful ally of the Communist Party in the campaign against French colonialist oppression in Madagascar. When Lachaume approaches him, Henri is, understandably, still bitter about the attacks to which the Communists have subjected him. But the simple fact is, as Dubreuilh has him admit later, that his sympathies continue to be with the U.S.S.R. rather than with the United States, and not for the first time Henri is prepared to swallow his pride in order to help (II, 445-46).

If this broad political framework is largely what holds *Les Mandarins* together as a novel, it is by situating Henri and Anne in different ways within it that Beauvoir allows herself to treat a whole range of other themes, some of which have nothing to do with politics as such. Thus Henri's job as a journalist enables her to raise the matter of informing or educating the public and the dilemmas to which the apparently simple aim of telling the truth gives rise (214-15). It also provides a good example, in the financial difficulties of *L'Espoir*, of how money soon comes to be important again after the war (211). More importantly, by also making Henri, like many of the other characters in the book, a creative writer, Beauvoir can explore and explain the personal side of the process of writing in far more detail than she has in her earlier fiction. Not only is this material interesting in its own right, it also leads quite naturally to consideration of the function and value of literature in general. Through Anne's eyes we see how Dubreuilh and, to a lesser extent, Brogan face up to this question, but the immediate access that we have to Henri's changing views on the matter, and the way in which his other commitments are always threatening to squeeze literature out of his life, make it an especially live issue in the novel. It was one that taxed Beauvoir herself:

Mon attitude à l'égard de la littérature était ambigüe: plus question de mandat, ni de salut; confrontés à la bombe H et à la faim des hommes, les mots me semblaient futiles; et pourtant je travaillais aux *Mandarins* avec acharnement. Anne n'écrivait pas mais elle avait besoin que Dubreuilh continuât d'écrire; Henri tantôt voulait se taire et tantôt non: en combinant leurs contradictions, j'obtenais une diversité d'éclairages. (FCh, 362-63)

Just as the pressures upon Henri as a journalist and writer spring from, or at least reflect, the troubled times, so the nature of Anne's work as a psychiatrist and her attitudes towards it are shown to relate directly to what is happpening in the world. And once more the questions aired have general interest and application, even if it cannot honestly be said that the picture of Anne as a psychiatrist is a consistently convincing one.[2] In her attempt to rethink classical psychoanalysis in the light of Marxism, she had come to believe that to relieve patients of their personal nightmares was to enable them to face up to the real problems of the world (92), but in the post-war situation she begins to wonder whether there is not something wrong with trying to assist people to forget the past. She regains some of her earlier faith in her profession when the first war-deportees begin returning to France: whatever the future may hold, these men and women have to be helped to forget (266). Yet her later view of the way in which Paule is 'cured' by Mardrus (to whom Anne has taken her) exposes the deep ambiguity in her attitude:

je connaissais bien le genre d'explications dont avait usé Mardrus, je m'en servais aussi à l'occasion, je les appréciais à leur prix. Oui, pour délivrer Paule il fallait ruiner son amour jusque dans le passé; mais je pensais à ces microbes qu'on ne peut exterminer qu'en détruisant l'organisme qu'ils dévorent. (II, 353)

In so far as Anne's doubts amount to questioning the validity of helping a patient to adjust to a life of 'normality' when the norms themselves may be anything but admirable, Beauvoir can be seen to be raising points about the philosophical and moral implications of psychotherapy that have a very modern ring indeed.[3]

At this point as at so many others in *Les Mandarins*, one can see how matters concerning characters' work are made to blend with specifically private concerns and admire Beauvoir's considerable skill in gathering a number of the threads of her story around one particular episode or character. For whatever Paule's case may signify in connection with psychotherapeutic theory and practice, it clearly has relevance to Anne's personal situation at the time. There are warnings for Anne in the early stages of Paule's mental breakdown over Henri ('"Tu guériras, il faut guérir. L'amour n'est pas tout . . ." Sachant bien qu'à sa place je ne voudrais jamais guérir'; II, 207), and when she sees how psychiatric treatment has left Paule, she is determined not to find herself in the same position if things go wrong with Brogan (II, 356). Indeed, she could be said to maintain this resolve after her last, disastrous trip to America, but the fact that the phial of poison with which she contemplates committing suicide is one that she earlier took from Paule's handbag to protect her reminds us that her own reaction to the break-up of a love-affair is potentially as self-destructive as Paule's. Beauvoir stresses that Paule's cautionary tale shows 'combien il est dangereux pour une femme d'engager tout de soi dans sa liaison avec un écrivain ou un artiste, buté sur ses projets' (FCh, 364), but Henri's work seems of relatively little significance for their relationship. His general attitude towards women is part of the problem, although relations with Paule were bound to change in some degree in the course of ten years, when their affair had begun as such a passionate one. Paule makes the same mistake as a number of Beauvoir's female figures in clinging inflexibly and desperately to the past in her attempt to keep her lover: 'Elle était prête à nier l'espace et le temps avant d'admettre que l'amour pût n'être pas éternel' (47). The self-deception that her insecurity generates, the bizarre and frightening manner in which she loses control of herself, and the appalling contrast in her values after her return to 'sanity' make her perhaps the most striking and disturbing character in the whole book.

The ways in which Anne and Paule both invest too much of themselves in their romances are entirely different but broadly complementary, the two cases together touching on most of the vital aspects of men-women relations as Beauvoir sees them. It is imposssible to understand Anne without recognising that for some twenty years Dubreuilh has been the very centre of her existence: 'Pour moi le monde, c'est lui' (59). It was his wish that they should have a child very quickly and this has somehow created difficulties in the relationship between Anne and Nadine. Anne is acutely conscious, however, that she has not shown her daughter enough love (her early preoccupation with Diégo is partly due to the way in which he brought her closer to Nadine; 99), and she goes some way towards making up for this by her deep concern with Nadine's situation and behaviour. It is largely her recognition of how essential Dubreuilh and Nadine are to her that leads her not to stay in America with Brogan. Nonetheless, within this structure her love for Brogan is very intense and appears to persist even after his feelings change towards her. Anne's sexual re-awakening—there have been no physical relations between her and Dubreuilh for some time—is undoubtedly a major factor, but for her it is by no means the substance of the relationship, which gives a whole new dimension and direction to her life for some two years. She entertains some doubts about whether Dubreuilh has the same conception of love as she does (71-72), or even whether he needs her (II, 358), but her own reaction to what she feels about the two men is at first one of puzzlement (II, 62). Later she takes it for granted that while it is her passion for Brogan that should be characterised as love, certain other things and people in the world are at least as important to her as this, for by this stage love has come to seem an essentially irrational, inexplicable phenomenon. Although she remains doubtful about the degree of control that can be exercised over it, Lewis (like Henri) is convinced that wilful self-indulgence is involved: ' "Sérieusement, reprit-il, pour aimer quelqu'un d'amour, il faut se monter la tête" ' (II,386). When one remembers that in addition to exploring Anne's experiences and recording the tragic course of Henri's liaison with Paule, the book also covers the psychology of Nadine's relations with men in some detail and shows Henri having a brief but colourful affair with Josette, it becomes clear that *Les Mandarins* is in part a richly illustrated rumination on the nature of love.

Moreover, when one also recalls the differing attitudes of the men and the women characters on this topic, it begins to become apparent how much of what Beauvoir is saying through Anne is related specifically to 'la condition féminine'. In spite of having her work—as Beauvoir points out, 'elle n'est que timidement engagée dans sa profession' (FCh, 367)—Anne's life is, as we have seen, bound up with her family to an unhealthy degree. Like the majority of women, in Beauvoir's view, she leads 'la vie "relative" d'un être "secondaire"' (FCh, 367). She acknowledges early on that Dubreuilh is better armed than she is against regrets, and it is doubtless partly because of the vulnerability of her position that she is so sensitive to ageing or physical decline and attaches so much importance to her affair with Brogan. If Paule's position and stance in relation to the same problems are different, they are equally representative of standard 'feminine' dilemmas: 'je conçus Paule comme une femme radicalement aliénée à un homme et le tyrannisant au nom de cet esclavage: une amoureuse' (FCh, 364).

Part of the significance of the third main female character in the novel, Nadine, is that she belongs to a younger generation. Like Vincent and Lambert in particular, she is portrayed as having been deeply scarred by the war at a crucial stage of her development (though she carries the extra burden of having famous parents). She is the only young woman in this category, however, whose struggle with the extreme diffficulties of reaching maturity in the post-war years is shown in any detail. What strikes us most is her general perversity and what Beauvoir calls her 'brutalité sexuelle', although it is clear that a rather confused desire for independence and equality is at stake. Beauvoir claims that in inventing Nadine she sets out to attack a certain type of young woman, but came to find more and more excuses for her attitudes and to regard her as 'plutôt victime que blâmable' (FCh, 364). Like that of Paule, the portrait of Nadine is one of considerable intrinsic interest. If it also completes, within the novel, a gloomy sketch of women's situation in the world, this is no more than one would expect after *Le Deuxième Sexe*, and it is certainly not, in itself, something to reproach Beauvoir with:

> j'ai décrit les femmes telles que, en général, je les voyais, telles que je les vois encore: divisées. Paule s'agrippe aux valeurs traditionnellement féminines: elles ne lui suffisent pas, elle est déchirée jusqu'à la folie; Nadine n'arrive ni à accepter sa féminité ni à la dépasser; Anne se rapproche plus que les autres d'une vraie liberté; elle ne réussit tout de même pas à trouver dans ses propres entreprises un

accomplissement. Aucune, d'un point de vue féministe, ne peut être considérée comme une 'héroïne positive'. J'en conviens, mais sans m'en repentir. (FCh, 365)

Men's situation is, after all, scarcely depicted as being very much rosier during the period in question. It is true that *Les Mandarins* implies that their more direct involvement in the world—outstandingly through work, which in the limited context of this novel invariably entails some form of political commitment—ensures that they do not lead a 'secondary', passive existence and that they therefore avoid some of the traps lying in wait for women. But this also means that they have their own distinctive problems, as the course taken by Henri's life and career shows, for it clearly traces some of the pitfalls that endanger a man trying to live 'correctly' in the world as it is in 1944-48. We have already seen that the political difficulties for non-communist left-wing intellectuals are almost insuperable, but the great achievement of *Les Mandarins* is that through Henri it gives a personal and moral dimension to these difficulties which leaves a more lasting impression upon the reader than the political issues themselves. Henri sets out after the Liberation with the best of intentions and a unique reputation for courage, honesty and integrity. He never takes happily to being regarded as a paragon of virtue, however, and after his setbacks on the political front and attacks on his private life, he swings for a time to the opposite extreme, taking a perverse delight in conducting part of his personal life in a way that he knows all of his friends would disapprove of: 'Il avait tort, radicalement tort, sans réserve, sans excuse: quel repos!' (II, 171). This uncharacteristic phase of flouting his conscience comes to an end when the bad company he has been keeping takes him to the point of committing perjury for Josette's sake. Recognising that he is being offered 'une belle occasion de dire merde à la moralité', he tries to see the matter in this way, but immediately realises that he cannot: 'Ça ne lui allait pas de jouer au démoniaque. Il ferait ce faux témoignage parce qu'il ne pouvait pas faire autrement, c'est tout' (II, 320).

It is not difficult to see the plausibility of the conclusions that Dubreuilh derives from this story:

'Vous savez ce que ça prouve, cette histoire? dit Dubreuilh avec une soudaine animation. C'est que la morale privée ça n'existe pas. Encore un de ces trucs auxquels nous avons cru et qui n'ont aucun

sens . . . Dans un espace courbe, on ne peut pas tirer de ligne droite,
dit Dubreuilh. On ne peut pas mener une vie correcte dans une
société qui ne l'est pas. On est toujours repincé, d'un côté ou d'un
autre.' (II, 343)

Considering that Henri is a man of such good will and yet is led by
circumstances into going back on some of his most cherished moral
principles, it might be thought not only that this is the final message
of his narrative, but also that it matches the general pessimism about
'la condition féminine' in Anne's half of the book, suggesting that, for
all their greater involvement in the world, men are ultimately just as
limited by their general situation as women are. Yet this is to fail to
understand Dubreuilh's precise role in the book and the revealing ways
in which his attitudes differ from Henri's, in spite of the broad
similarity in their outlooks. Significantly, there is something almost
machine-like about Dubreuilh's commitment to work (he has no need
for leisure, as Henri does), but above all his political thinking lays
great emphasis on the movement of history, leaving us in some doubt
whether the individual retains very much importance at all in his
scheme of thinking. Even Anne, who is second to none in her
admiration for him, appears to have some reservations on this score
and she is closer to Henri's positions when the two men are in
disagreement. Dubreuilh, indeed, changes his tactics and his view of
what is possible quite frequently in the book, to the extent that Henri,
at least, learns of his latest stance with some scepticism: 'Il avait appris
à ne pas prendre aveuglément Dubreuilh au sérieux' (II, 455). Thus
Dubreuilh's assertion that there is no 'morale privée', no 'salut personnel', cannot be regarded as the last word in the novel. In fact, his
whole perspective changes once more at the very end, when he claims
to be reverting to the kind of viewpoint he held in the mid-thirties
(II,454).

Paradoxically, the effect of giving false testimony is somehow to
purge Henri of all that has gone before. His affair with Josette is
certainly doomed from this point and his period of relative moral
irresponsibility thereby comes to an end. By the close of the book he
has rediscovered some kind of personal morality (we have seen that he
deliberately disregards the abuse that has been heaped upon him by
the Communist Party, and his patience and consideration in dealing
with the awkward Nadine are exemplary), confirming Beauvoir's

comment that a major theme of the book is Kierkegaardian 'repetition': 'pour posséder vraiment un bien, il faut l'avoir perdu et retrouvé' (FCh, 369). The fact is that at the beginning Henri suffers from the opposite fault to Dubreuilh's: he is rather too easily swayed, in one direction or another, by the existence and above all the actual presence of other individuals. We are at first surprised to see him unable to bring himself to deal as honestly with Paule as he ought, but what looks like cowardice stems from a general inability in his private life to turn down personal appeals ('"Je ne sais pas dire non"'; 191), or to do what he originally intended when he is actually faced with the person concerned—an inability of which the story provides numerous examples. It is this characteristic as much as the bewildering political circumstances that leads him astray in the middle of the story (there is a significant personal element in his reactions on the two occasions when he feels betrayed by Dubreuilh). One feels that by the end, with marriage and fatherhood bulking so large for him, he is likely to exercise more consistent control over his personal life and channel his response to the appeals of others in more appropriate directions.

Henri's final decision to stay in France and occupy himself with politics once more can be regarded as arising either out of his realisation that although retreat to Italy would give him more time to write, it would simultaneously deprive him of things to write *about*, or out of his desire to have some influence on events rather than be a passive spectator ('quand un avion pique du nez, il vaut mieux être le pilote qui essaie de le redresser qu'un passager terrorisé'; II, 486), or both. In a more general sense, in any case, it shows that he recognises his need for contact or involvement with others and perceives it more lucidly and realistically than at the beginning of the story. Now, although as Beauvoir claims the general perspective and in particular the ending of Anne's narrative contests the relative optimism of Henri's it is worth pointing out that Anne, too, finally acknowledges that her fate is inextricably bound up with that of others: 'la mort est toujours présente: mais les vivants le sont davantage encore' (II, 499). Just as Henri ultimately rejects escape to Italy, so Anne herself rejects escape through suicide and re-enters the world of the living: 'De nouveau, j'ai sauté à pieds joints dans la vie' (II, 500). There is no enthusiasm for life at all in her decision, but a faint hope is generated by the fact that she is not alone: 'puisqu'ils ont été assez forts pour m'arracher à la mort, peut-être qu'ils sauront m'aider de nouveau à vivre' (II, 501). The theme of the 'appeal' made by others is a familiar one in Beauvoir's fiction—Anne's re-awakening from the dead has obvious parallels with Fosca's regular revivals—and if Henri has had to restrain his tendency to respond almost indiscriminately to all entreaties, in the end neither he nor Anne can remain indifferent to the bidding or even just the very existence of other people. In this sense, there may be less fundamental difference between their general outlooks than at first seems to be the case.

The significance of the dual narrative lies as much in the greater range of places and circumstances that it allows Beauvoir to cover in the novel as in the presentation of different 'truths'.[4] Henri's early visit to Portugal is an obvious example of this flexibility, but the outstanding, and controversial, case is provided by Anne's three long trips to America. Beauvoir admits that this section of the story remains 'marginal', though she makes the valuable point that it gives some substance to the character of Anne, who would otherwise have remained a mere spectator in relation to the main events of the plot, and that it illustrates the way in which the world opened out for French people in the mid-forties (FCh, 365). It is certainly noticeable that whereas Anne initially thinks of America as 'le grand pays libérateur' (109), by the time of her third visit the country has come to mean something quite different to her, as to many of her fellow French intellectuals: 'Maintenant l'Amérique, ça signifiait bombe atomique, menaces de guerre, fascisme naissant' (II, 388). But this in itself is scarcely enough to justify devoting nearly a sixth of the whole book to Anne's 'aventure transatlantique'. And even if the affair with Brogan can be taken to be the crux of the matter, that does not altogether necessitate the fairly detailed descriptions of settings and of the long journey undertaken during Anne's second visit that so much resemble passages from Beauvoir's memoirs. In so far as the centre of gravity of Les Mandarins is what is happening in Paris, one is bound to conclude that the sections taking place in America stand out rather awkwardly and are somewhat out of proportion, in spite of their oblique relevance to more crucial elements of the story.

There is, however, little, if anything else in the work about which this kind of criticism may be made. For the most part, Beauvoir controls the pace and direction of the two narratives with great skill, interweaving them chronologically in such a way that time-gaps are unobtrusive and continuity over the whole period covered is strong. Anne's first-person account consists mostly of retrospective relating of events and her reactions to them (in the past historic tense), but her narrative begins and ends with present-tense monologue (which is also used, more sparingly, at other stages), and this gives greater variety and immediacy to her story than it might otherwise have had. Henri's narrative is more uniform in style, but also much more colourful— and sometimes amusing—because of his extrovert personality and the hectic life he leads. Since Henri and Anne have the same friends and acquaintances, their separate narratives interpenetrate in a very satisfying manner (Paule's story, for instance, is naturally picked up by Anne when Paule is no longer seeing Henri), coming closer together than ever in the end, when Henri marries Nadine. Beauvoir, however, makes less than she claims of the opportunity to modify and 'correct' the story of one character by providing a contrasting version from the point of view of the other. Although there are points at which the presentation of two accounts of the same episode (like the party after the opening of Henri's play) is intriguing and stimulating, on such occasions her purpose is less to set Anne against Henri than to show how one interpretation of events complements the other.

Les Mandarins centres on a tightly-knit group of people, but it would be a serious mistake to regard the novel as lacking in variety or scope. In order to remind us what the main characters have in common and whom they are to be contrasted with, Beauvoir includes in the book a number of sequences where either Henri or Anne comes into contact with people whose values and life-style are entirely repugnant. Thus Anne has to go with Dubreuilh to Trarieux's home (344), and much later to mix with rich Americans (II, 419-24). Both she and Henri have at different times, to survive unspeakable, though from the reader's viewpoint amusing and revealing, occasions laid on by Lucie Belhomme and Claudie Belzunce, which bring together just the kind of pretentious, ambitious people they most despise. And both are horrified at the spectacle of the Parisian theatre-going public at large when Henri's play is first performed. Paris, however, is by no means the exclusive location of the story. Quite apart from Anne's time in America, there is Henri's visit to Portugal and the cycling holiday in central France taken by Anne, Henri and Dubreuilh in the middle of the book. All of these trips give welcome relief from the stifling intensity of the political scene in the capital and include descriptions of the countryside and foreign towns that provide strong points of contrast with the rest of the narrative. Not that the main body of the narrative itself is commonly weighed down by abstractions and rarefied discussions. Dialogue, as was always Beauvoir's ideal, becomes a form of confrontation and action, and it is rarely less than lively. The highly colloquial style that Beauvoir adopts (often for the expression of Henri's thoughts to himself as well as direct speech) is such a positive asset in this respect that it is extremely difficult to agree with the objections raised by purists on this score. Finally, the range of actual events in the plot is much wider than is often appreciated. Since the interaction of the private and public lives of the main figures is an especially important theme, this already enables Beauvoir to portray love-affairs as well as political meetings, personal disasters as well as historical moments. But she also blends into her story crime, suspense and mystery (What escapades have Vincent and Nadine been involved in? How did Lambert's father die? Will Henri's perjury be exposed?), even drugs and murder (through the character of Sézenac). These elements make the book so much more exciting to read than it might easily have been, without in the least detracting from its serious intent.

Les Mandarins is a prodigious work whose many facets call for extensive analysis and commentary, but any general statement of Beauvoir's aims and achievements has to come back to her attempt to conjure up in fictional, therefore structured, form the immediate post-war period in France, without offering any lessons to left-wing intellectuals: 'j'ai décrit certaines manières de vivre l'après-guerre sans proposer de solution aux problèmes qui inquiètent mes héros' (FCh, 369). Her success in this task is beyond dispute. One appreciates her impatience with those who were determined to see as a mere 'roman à clef' what is 'ni une autobiographie, ni un reportage: une évocation' (FCh, 369), and one can only applaud the Prix Goncourt jury for recognising the merits and general significance of a major novel. Beauvoir herself records, however, how much of herself she poured into her book: 'je voulais y mettre tout de moi: mes rapports avec la vie, la mort, le temps, la littérature, l'amour, l'amitié, les voyages' (FCh, 269). It is hardly surprising, therefore, that she should have claimed, in the only interview that she agreed to give after the awarding of the prize: 'Je n'écrirai pas de roman tout de suite. J'ai mis dans *Les Mandarins* une expérience intellectuelle et pratique de plusieurs années, et je me sens un peu "vidée" de matière romanesque'.[5]

Notes

[1] On the political background to *Les Mandarins*, see M.-A. Burnier: *Les Existentialistes et la politique.*

[2] See Maryse Choisy: 'Psychologie, sociologie et syntaxe des *Mandarins*', *Psyché*, 1954.

[3] See my 'Psychiatry in the Post-war Fiction of Simone de Beauvoir', *Literature and Psychology*, 1979.

[4] See Elizabeth Fallaize: 'Narrative structure in *Les Mandarins*' in *Literature and Society. Studies in nineteenth and twentieth century French literature.*

[5] Interview with J.-F. Rolland, *L'Humanité Dimanche*, 1954; reprinted in *Écrits*, pp. 358-62.

10 *Les Belles Images* and *La Femme rompue*

A full twelve years passed after the appearance of *Les Mandarins* before Beauvoir published, in 1966, her next work of fiction, *Les Belles Images*. The shortest of all her novels, it contrasts strongly with the earlier book, although in its very different way it is just as distinctively a product of the nineteen-sixties in France as was *Les Mandarins* of the immediate post-war period. With not a single left-wing intellectual —or, for that matter, any kind of intellectual—in sight, the milieu is that of 'la grosse bourgeoisie technocratique':

> J'ai repris un autre projet: évoquer cette société technocratique dont je me tiens le plus possible à distance mais dans laquelle néanmoins je vis; à travers les journaux, les magazines, la publicité, la radio, elle m'investit. Mon intention n'était pas de décrire l'expérience vécue et singulière de certains de ses membres: je voulais faire entendre ce qu'on appelle aujourd'hui son 'discours'. (TCF, 172)

The plot as such is rather slight and the novel, covering a time-span of only some five months, is constructed around certain interrelated developments in the principal relationships of the central figure Laurence, whose viewpoint is adopted throughout.

At the beginning of the book Laurence is worried about her eldest daughter Catherine, who, at the age of ten and a half, is starting to express concern at the existence of misfortune, unhappiness and suffering in the world. Her husband Jean-Charles has such faith in the future that he thinks it sufficient to explain to Catherine how much better a place the world will be in ten years. Laurence's mother Dominique is far too preoccupied with maintaining her elevated social status to have any interest in the matter, but her father, to whom she is particularly attached, is more helpful. By listening patiently to her daughter and becoming acquainted with her new friend Brigitte, whose knowledge of the world is greater than Catherine's, Laurence comes to understand the problem more clearly. Yet she has diffi-culties of her own: her mother's rich lover Gilbert is about to abandon her for a nineteen-year-old girl; Jean-Charles has become dissatisfied with his job; and her own lover Lucien is expecting more of her than she is willing to give. She makes a clean break with Lucien, but has to devote much more time to her mother, whose reaction to the loss of Gilbert is a violent one. Since Catherine's sensitivity is affecting her school-work, Laurence is eventually persuaded to send her to a psychiatrist while she herself, with undisguised delight, goes off to Greece with her father. However, the trip is far from successful—Laurence does not altogether share his interest in the ancient world and is horrified at the poverty she discovers in Greece—and on her return she becomes ill, when all of her family press her to take the psychiatrist's advice and separate Catherine from her new friend. The news that her father and mother are to begin living together again after their long separation shocks her into acknowledging that she is disillusioned with her father, and at the very end she makes a stand against Jean-Charles, insisting that Catherine must stop seeing the psychiatrist and be allowed to continue her friendship with Brigitte.

The significance of the personal story of Laurence can only be understood by reference to the kind of society and particular social set to which she is shown as belonging. Apart from anything else, *Les Belles Images* conveys better than any other work by Beauvoir the stresses of urban life in industrialised Western countries in the second half of the twentieth century. Some of the disadvantages and problems associated, for instance, with cars, telephones and television are very well illustrated. It is no surprise, therefore, that depressions and breakdowns should bulk quite large in the book—suicide, too, is discussed on more than one occasion—and that there should be frequent allusions to the taking of 'somnifères', 'tranquillisants', 'harmonisateurs', 'décontrariants', and so on. It is not that Beauvoir is opposed to technical advance in itself: 'J'aime les "jets", les beaux appareils, les chaînes de haute fidélité'.[1] *Les Belles Images* takes it for granted, in fact, that, however much of a mixed blessing machines may be, material conditions are slowly being improved for everyone in Western societies. Laurence points out that, thanks to family allowances, nearly all members of the French working classes now have 'une machine à laver, la télé, et même une auto' (73). But attention here is sharply focused on the objectionable attitudes to which this situation gives rise within one class, the bourgeoisie; or, more narrowly, within the upper reaches of the prosperous, professional middle classes.

These attitudes are represented by Dominique, Jean-Charles,

Gilbert and the affluent house-guests with whom Laurence mixes most weekends at her mother's country-house outside Paris (Feuverolles). A not-inconsiderable proportion of the novel—including the brilliant, ironical beginning—is devoted to illustrating in detail how they have so much money (and so little imagination) that they can only waste it on ever-more-unnecessary possessions, ever-more-extravagant entertainments. They are snobs who worship success and who thrive because of the nature of modern capitalist, consumer societies. But perhaps their greatest sin, in Beauvoir's view, is that they contrive to hide—doubtless from themselves as much as from others—the fact that they flourish at the expense of those less fortunate or privileged than themselves. And they hide it behind a whole system of impressive-sounding lies. Above all, there is 'le mythe de l'avenir', whereby they divert attention from the present horrors and injustices in society as a whole— 'Gilbert expliquait qu'en toute société il y a forcément des faux frais' (58)—by arguing that unhappiness and misfortune will be eradicated in a matter of years:

> tout va beaucoup mieux qu'avant, tout ira mieux plus tard. Certains pays sont mal partis: l'Afrique noire, en particulier; la poussée démographique en Chine et dans toute l'Asie est inquiétante; cependant, grâce aux protéines synthétiques, à la contraception, à l'automation, à l'énergie nucléaire, on peut considérer que vers 1990 sera instaurée la civilisation de l'abondance et des loisirs. La terre ne formera plus qu'un seul monde. (72-73)

The press, television and radio (Dominique works for O.R.T.F.), which actually propagate this myth, are said to be instruments which enable us to live 'planétairement' (40). If the novel is full of familiar clichés of this kind, it is because Beauvoir took the trouble to gather them from the appropriate sources: 'j'ai constitué un sottisier aussi consternant que divertissant' (TCF, 172). As she says of the bourgeois characters concerned, 'tels qu'ils se peignent par leurs paroles et leurs actes, on ne peut que les détester. A moins de leur ressembler' (TCF, 174).

What is slightly less obvious, though equally important in the structure of the novel is the point that Laurence's father (unnamed in the book) is himself little better in this respect than Dominique and her friends, whose attitudes he affects to despise. In his scepticism about technical progress—' "nous vivrons dans un monde parfaitement inhumain"'' (40)—he appears to stand out against the trends and justifications described and to represent all of the culture, the humanism, the old values that are being destroyed in the modern world (84). He is an attractive figure in some respects and his views have a certain appeal, to Laurence at least. Yet even she eventually realises that he is ignoring, just as much as the others, the poverty, injustices and inequalities within modern societies. Not only does he fail to show her the 'austère bonheur' that he claimed was to be found in Greece, he also fails to display any more than a token sympathy for the poor and the politically oppressed. However much some of his values may be intrinsically preferable to those of the technocrats, he himself is something of a hypocrite, capable of saying one thing to Laurence on her own and the opposite in public (174). And he is infinitely more inclined to compromise his beliefs than she thought, being happy to participate in a radio debate, for example, in spite of the reservations he has previously expressed about the O.R.T.F. Beauvoir claims that his reconciliation with Dominique at the end of the story 'manifeste la collusion entre la bourgeoisie traditionnelle et la nouvelle: c'est une seule et même classe' (TCF, 174).

Laurence has inherited enough of her father's ostensible values to entertain serious doubts about those of her mother and others like her: 'elle ne peut se contenter du monde factice qu'on lui propose, un monde où tout s'est perdu: le sens de l'amour, du bonheur, de la vérité, de la souffrance'.[2] Yet on the surface she is as much a part of the 'société technocratique' as anyone. Indeed, her work in an advertising agency—which she does very successfully—puts her in the front rank of those who further the cause of a consumer society. Moreover, she is well aware of the illusions or lies that her job involves: 'Je ne vends pas des panneaux de bois: je vends la sécurité, la réussite, et une touche de poésie en supplément' (23). There is very little sign that this troubles her at all, although the 'déformation professionnelle' that causes her to see virtually everything in terms of publicity images prevents her from enjoying many things, so that she is undoubtedly in some measure 'victime des slogans qu'elle a fabriqués' (138). Her general position in relation to the social milieu depicted, then, is characterised by ambiguity. The influence of her father stops her from identifying fully with what her mother or even Jean-Charles stands for, yet she is in many respects a typical product of the society around her:

Personne, dans cet univers auquel je suis hostile, ne pouvait parler en mon nom; cependant pour le donner à voir il me fallait prendre à son égard un certain recul. J'ai choisi comme témoin une jeune femme assez complice de son entourage pour ne pas le juger, assez honnête pour vivre cette connivence dans le malaise. (TCF, 172)

This, however, is to describe Laurence's situation schematically, as if she were static, whereas *Les Belles Images* records a crisis in her life. The moral awakening of her daughter Catherine forces her to face up to a number of fundamental questions and by the end of the book she is far less content with her way of life and in sympathy with the people around her than she was at the beginning. Even so, rather surprisingly, she regards herself—at about thirty-one—as too ensnared in the social web ever to be able to break loose: '"Moi, c'est foutu, j'ai été eue, j'y suis, j'y reste"' (181). (She does not, for instance, consider changing her job, and seems to believe that there is no alternative to staying with Jean-Charles for the rest of her life, whatever her feelings about him may be; 66-67). The fact is that to understand this reaction, as well as the specific nature and outcome of her worries about Catherine, we need to take very careful account of her upbringing, which was entirely dominated by her mother: 'c'est mon père que j'aimais et ma mère qui m'a faite' (33). Her father, in any case, was in a prisoner-of-war camp for four years during her childhood (85), but the crux of the matter is that she was always particularly firmly restrained and constantly made to keep up appearances by Dominique, who was determined that Laurence should not have the kind of childhood that she herself had had:

Elle a toujours été une image. Dominique y a veillé, fascinée dans son enfance par des images si différentes de sa vie, tout entière butée—de toute son intelligence et son énorme énergie—à combler ce fossé. (Tu ne sais pas ce que c'est que d'avoir des souliers déchirés et de sentir à travers sa chaussette qu'on a marché sur un crachat. Tu ne sais pas ce que c'est d'être toisée par des copines aux cheveux bien lavés et qui se poussent du coude. Non, tu ne sortiras pas avec cette tache sur ta jupe, va te changer.) Petite fille impeccable, adolescente accomplie, parfaite jeune fille. Tu étais si nette, si fraîche, si parfaite . . dit Jean-Charles. (21-22)

Dominique not only deprived Laurence of holidays with her father by her concern to be seen in the right places (10), she also ensured that Laurence 'wasted' no time, and prevented her from having girl friends, on the grounds that they were so 'ordinary' (55). Gradually in the course of the book we are brought to realise how serious and extensive have been the consequences of Laurence's upbringing, which show themselves in three intricately interrelated ways: an instability associated with a series of crises in the past that has issued in a strange attitude towards people and the world in general; particular difficulties in her relations with men; and an acute sensitivity about the upbringing of her own daughters.

At the age of eleven Laurence herself, like Catherine, cried about the horrors and suffering in the world (25). Dominique was helpful, but the suggestion is still that Laurence's first crisis was in part due to strained relations between her parents: 'Peut-être n'aurais-je pas tant pleuré sur les enfants juifs assassinés s'il n'y avait pas eu de si lourds silences à la maison' (36). In any case, she was rather ill-prepared for marriage at twenty or so, and for having children so soon. (Chronological factors—Catherine is ten and a half, while Laurence has certainly been married for less than eleven years—together with references to her not having made a decision to marry (119) and to financial difficulties when Catherine was born (66) suggest that it was a shotgun wedding.) She eventually experienced a serious depressive crisis some five years before the events of the book (85), and although going out to work enabled her to pull through, some two years later she almost broke down again (30). On this occasion Jean-Charles helped her greatly, yet it is clear that her subsequent precarious equilibrium has been based upon an avoiding of contact with disquieting material about the world, rather than a real resolution of her problems: 'elle avait désormais évité de lire les journaux' (133).

It is against this background that we have to understand Laurence's general state of mind in the novel. The series of traumas that she has undergone, or at least the constant need to hold herself in check and keep reality at bay, has somehow alienated her from her surroundings and perhaps the world as a whole. There are many references to a kind of distraction or indifference that afflicts her and she is rarely at ease in the company she keeps. Music, literature and history fail to move her any more and in general she seems unwilling to allow herself to experience any strong emotions at all. She has the greatest difficulty in believing in, or maintaining her feelings for, anyone other than her father and her children and this shows itself particularly clearly in her attitude towards Lucien, who has been her lover for eighteen months, but in whom she has now lost interest. It is Lucien, in fact, who categorises this side of her chacter most harshly: '"Tu évites les gros emmerdements en te verrouillant le cœur"' (83). Revealingly, when he accuses her of 'une frigidité du cœur', she does not deny it, but only claims that it is not her fault (112). Yet if Lucien fails to understand what lies behind her defences, Jean-Charles—whom she is deceiving—scarcely knows her better: 'Pour Jean-Charles elle est efficace, loyale, limpide. C'est faux aussi' (108).

The key to her intimate relationships with men—and perhaps to some extent to her relationships with others in general—lies in her feelings for her father. From the first we see her claiming that there is something very special about him (14) and that she loves him more than anyone in the world (33). Given her mother's nature and the circumstances of Laurence's childhood, this is not surprising, but her love and admiration come to seem excessive in themselves as well as misplaced as we learn more about Laurence. It is understandable, for example, that she should have come to life on first meeting Jean-Charles, but a little disturbing that she should have seen him so obviously as a kind of father-substitute, and even more disquieting that she should later have assigned the same role to Lucien:

> pendant des jours et des semaines, je n'ai plus été une image, mais chair et sang, désir, plaisir. Et j'ai retrouvé aussi cette douceur plus secrète que j'avais connue jadis, assise aux pieds de mon père ou tenant sa main dans la mienne . . . De nouveau, il y a dix-huit mois, avec Lucien; le feu dans mes veines, et dans mes os cette exquise déliquescence. (22)

By the time the events of the story take place, neither Jean-Charles nor Lucien excites her in this way any more and she has fallen back on the idea that there is a 'secret' that only her father possesses: 'Ce qu'elle a cru retrouver chez Jean-Charles, chez Lucien, lui seul le possède' (36). One of her reasons for breaking with Lucien is that it will enable her to see more of her father, who is also in some respects more important to her than her husband. Furthermore, Laurence acknowledges that her depression of five years earlier had deeper causes than the obvious ones, though she insists that she has overcome these factors:

les vraies raisons de ma crise, je ne les ignore pas et je les ai dépassées: j'ai explicité le conflit qui oppose mes sentiments à l'égard de Jean-Charles à ceux que j'éprouve pour mon père; il ne me déchire plus. Je suis au net avec moi-même. (44)

Since it is manifestly not the case that Laurence is now entirely stable, one is bound to wonder whether she has not betrayed the true source of all her psychological difficulties at this point. She later dismisses the possibility that her real problem is an unresolved Oedipus complex (179), but in the light of her violent reaction to confirmation that her mother and father are to live together again, her denial is far from convincing.

Be this as it may, the structural strength of *Les Belles Images* consists in the way in which Beauvoir succeeds in drawing all of these various threads together around the issue of Catherine's upbringing. Because Laurence herself has maintained her mental balance only by virtually ignoring the outside world, her first reaction to Catherine's distress is to tell her comforting lies and continue to shield her from reality: 'je devrais l'en protéger' (26). Little by little, however, she realises that she cannot sift everything that Catherine sees and hears. Laurence therefore begins informing herself in order to 'lui faire découvrir la réalité sans l'effrayer' (58). By encouraging Catherine's friendship with Brigitte she sees herself as ensuring that her daughter's sensitivity is being developed and she is prepared to defend her views when opposed by Jean-Charles (131). It becomes more and more apparent, however, that Jean-Charles is totally indifferent to the objects of Catherine's concern—unlike Laurence, whom he accuses of 'sensiblerie' (133)—and that he simply wants his daughter to be as successful and 'impeccable' as he considers Laurence to be. But by this stage Laurence is horrified at the prospect that Catherine may develop the same character as herself. When, after the bitterly disappointing trip to Greece, even her father joins in the chorus of voices advocating that Catherine should be separated from Brigitte, Laurence makes her stand, in order to avoid making the mistakes that her own mother made: 'Je ne permettrai pas qu'on lui fasse ce qu'on m'a fait' (180-81). She considers that her own cause is a lost one, but that if anything at all is worth fighting for, it is the future of her children: 'les enfants auront leur chance. Quelle chance? elle ne le sait même pas' (183).

The density and intensity of the final chapters are rather remarkable when one remembers the tone of the beginning of the book. Towards the end, all of the pressures upon Laurence build up to a kind of crescendo. She has been having increasing difficulty in repressing her feelings—having recourse to deep breathing, glasses of water, exercises and cold showers—and finally her 'côté convulsif' expresses itself through the extreme physical symptoms of anorexia and vomiting. Again she is anxious to deny the kind of explanation of her state that psychiatrists might give (175), but at the beginning of the chapter she appears to be attempting something like self-analysis. She falls asleep exhausted after her crucial recognition that she is disillusioned with her father (179), and when she awakes—the final three pages are narrated in the present tense—she confronts Jean-Charles with her unexpected decision to take sole charge of Catherine's development. The depth and resonance of the final sections of *Les Belles Images* are unmatched anywhere in Beauvoir's fiction and the ending itself confirms that one of the principal themes of the book is that of the complex ramifications of upbringing.

Beauvoir has acknowledged that she is much more concerned than she used to be with the problems of childhood (TCF, 201), although the nature of her interest is a fairly specific one and is perhaps reflected in Lucienne's views at the end of 'La Femme rompue':

> Selon elle, ce qui compte dans une enface, c'est la situation psychanalytique, telle qu'elle existe à l'insu des parents, presque malgré eux. L'éducation, dans ce qu'elle a de conscient, de délibéré, ça serait très secondaire. (FR, 250)

It is not surprising, then, that the novel should once more raise problems rather than offer solutions. Laurence's intentions in relation to Catherine (not to speak of her younger daughter Louise, of whom she admits she is less fond!) remain very vague at the end. And, of course, she believes that there is nothing she can do to counteract the ill-effects of her own upbringing: she is like the mole in her adapted anecdote, opening its eyes underground and finding that there is only darkness (169). But Beauvoir has been anxious to stress that there is far more than darkness in the world and that Laurence is unable to see clearly only because she is conditioned by her class.[3] In short, the examination of the problems of child-rearing in *Les Belles Images* is inseparable from the attack on 'la bourgeoisie technocratique', since Laurence's deep concern over Catherine manifests itself as a revolt against the way in which her own mother forced her into a bourgeois mould. Furthermore, in spite of Beauvoir's reticence about the wider implications of the book, certain fundamental metaphysical questions necessarily come into play, as she recognises in connection with the fiction of others:

> former un individu simplement normal, c'est déjà une tâche ardue. Mérite-t-elle les soins qu'on y apporte? Qu'est-ce qui donne son prix à la vie? et que signifie l'idée de normalité? C'est toute la condition humaine qui se trouve mise en question. (TCF, 224)

The book has its weaknesses as well as its strengths as far as characterisation is concerned. The portrait of Dominique is a frighteningly plausible one and the combination of blithe optimism, 'charm' and egotism in Jean-Charles is especially well registered. On the other hand, the sketches of Mona—Laurence's young militant left-wing colleague—and Laurence's religious younger sister Marthe, while fulfilling obvious thematic purposes in the novel, carry little conviction. The oustanding stylistic feature of the story is undoubtedly the range of techniques that Beauvoir employs for conveying the tentative, somewhat incoherent nature of Laurence's thoughts and her alienation from the people around her. Some of the clichés of the social milieu are incorporated in her own perceptions and comments, but most are recorded in the fatuous and pretentious dialogues that take place during the weekends at Feuverolles. More subtly, Laurence is shown to be holding the prevailing ethos and language at something of a distance by her ironical asides, parenthetical remarks, broken-off sentences and unexpected questions. In the early part of the novel, for instance, the way in which Beauvoir has her reiterate and ring the changes on the refrain, 'Qu'est-ce que les autres ont que je n'ai pas?', is singularly effective. And her strange manner of repeatedly hinting that people are more or less interchangeable ('Juste en ce moment, dans un autre jardin, tout à fait différent, exactement pareil, quelqu'un dit ces mots . . .'; 7) is a biting indicator of the banality that characterises Dominique's social set. Beauvoir also plays on a discrepancy between Laurence's thoughts and her words, which not only reveals her own detachment and hypocrisy, but also constitutes a reminder that nothing is quite what it seems in the conversations that we hear in the book: 'Évidemment elle n'a plus quarante ans. "Tu n'as plus vingt ans, évidemment," dit Laurence' (16). And, of course, the general gap

between appearances and reality in this society is brilliantly evoked by the multifarious uses to which the concept of 'images' or 'belles images' is put: photos in glossy magazines; reflections in the mirror; publicity images; posters; images projected by people; young girls who are 'as pretty as a picture'; and so on.

Les Belles Images is Beauvoir's only full novel narrated exclusively from the point of view of a single character and, given what she wishes to do, she *needs* these small-scale stylistic devices, just as she needs to intermingle past and present, monologue and dialogue in the narrative, since any contrasts necessary to the themes of the book have somehow to be part of Laurence's consciousness of the world. For once the reader's evaluation of the work is directly dependent upon his or her reaction to one main character and the relationship in which she stands to a particular social setting. It is not difficult to understand why some readers should have recognised Laurence's essentially ambiguous, 'trapped' position as their own, or why others should have regarded her picture of bourgeois society as a gross distortion.[4] What is surprising, however, is that some critics should have seen the novel—admittedly, different in so many respects from anything Beauvoir had written previously—as some kind of inferior imitation of the fiction of Françoise Sagan. They can only have completely failed to see the point of the book, in which, as Beauvoir notes, 'il s'agissait de faire parler le silence' (TCF, 172).

She was soon to ask her readers to read between the lines once more, in her collection of stories *La Femme rompue*, which appeared in January 1968. Each of the three stories—'L'Age de discrétion', 'Monologue' and 'La Femme rompue'—is narrated, like *Les Belles Images*, from the viewpoint of one woman character, and each deals with 'la solitude et l'échec': 'J'ai voulu faire entendre ici les voix de trois femmes qui se débattaient avec des mots dans des situations sans issue'.[5]

'L'Age de discrétion' is by far the most direct and explicit of the stories and its central theme is that of ageing, one that Beauvoir had unsuccessfully tried to embody in a novel and would go on to treat in an essay. The main figure is a retired woman teacher of sixty or so, who writes works of literary criticism. (She is unnamed in the text and may be referred to as Madame.) At the beginning she is content with her life: retirement suits her fairly well; relations with her husband André are very good; she is awaiting the arrival of her dearly-beloved son

Philippe; and her latest book seems bound to be a success. It is true that André, a scientist, is beginning to feel his age and doubts whether he will ever again produce original work, but Madame is convinced that this is no more than a passing phase. Her peace of mind is shattered, however, when her son returns from his honeymoon to announce that he is abandoning the academic career that she had planned for him and, having previously opposed the government's cultural policies like his parents, is taking up the offer of a job in the Ministry of Culture. It gradually becomes apparent that this should not have come as such a surprise to Madame, whose past relations with him had been far less smooth than her rather idealised picture at the beginning suggested. More important—Beauvoir admits that 'ce qui m'intéressait c'était le rapport des parents entre eux' (TCF, 176), and Philippe starts to fade out of the story once these last points are established—is the fact that Madame's acrimonious break with her son triggers off a crisis in her relationship with André (40).

This is quite quickly resolved, but the whole sequence of events throws the theme of ageing into greater prominence, firstly because of the very loss of Philippe—'C'est peut-être grâce à lui que je m'accommodais à peu près de mon âge' (27)—and secondly because Madame remains convinced that André's different attitude towards old age is coming between them (47). A number of experiences—not the least of which is the discovery that her latest book is much less original than she had supposed—now force her to acknowledge the reality of ageing and, once certain minor misunderstandings have been cleared up with André, she can at least draw limited consolation from the fact that they will be facing most of the indignities ahead of them together: 'Nous sommes ensemble, c'est notre chance' (84).

Madame's psychology is somewhat less flat and more complex than this summary might suggest. In spite of the fact that the story is presented in the form of a kind of diary that she is keeping, we are given a strong impression of her faults: her faith in intellectual pursuits, for instance, is a rather blind one and yet, paradoxically, her emotional reaction to events is often excessive. Moveover, she is something of a self-deceiver—' "tu te caches la vérité et quand elle te crève enfin les yeux, tu t'effondres ou tu exploses" ' (43)—and an interesting extra dimension is added to the basic tale by the fact that her progression to a more lucid view of her own son, her work, André and the ageing process involves some revision of her ideas about the past.[6] In this respect what we know, for example, about the way in which Philippe was brought up and how he reacted to his parents is made to emerge slowly in the text, appearing much more plausible and important as a result. Madame's self-deception on the matter of ageing, of course, is even more crucial (71), and Beauvoir is as uncompromising as in *La Vieillesse* in her denial that there are gains to make up for all the losses that old age brings. As she suggests, however, the topic is 'trop vaste pour un texte si bref' and her treatment is not an especially telling one.

In fact, the story as a whole is rather too schematic, with the timing of Madame's discoveries about her latest book seeming particularly contrived. The reader has no difficulty in engaging with the two main characters, but the world they inhabit is given little depth: their political commitment is hard to believe in, and most of the references to modern society are too perfunctory and predictable to contribute anything to the story. Even the feminist side of the tale fails to carry any weight, since Beauvoir's categorisation of her other women characters—Martine (19), Irène (23), and Manette (70) constitutes little more than a series of empty formulas. The relationship between Madame and her son, however, is fairly well delineated within the compass of the story, and the course that it takes has important, if obvious, implications: 'C'est le sort commun à toutes les mères: mais qui s'est jamais consolé en se disant que son sort est le sort commun?' (27). This is perhaps the one feature of 'L'Age de discrétion' that one would have liked to see developed further, for in other respects the story is, on the whole, duller and more pedestrian than most of Beauvoir's fiction.

Nothing of the sort could possibly be said of the second story, 'Monologue', which is a brief but startling attempt at self-justification by a lonely and malevolent woman of forty-three, separated from her husband and son. There is no development or plot in the story: the monologue is delivered over a short period of time one New Year's Eve, with Murielle alone in her room, resenting the revelries in the flat above and the street below. The partly unpunctuated stream of prophecies, threats, invective, self-congratulation and self-pity is modulated only by two telephone calls that Murielle makes, first to her mother, then to her second husband Tristan, both of whom are driven to hang up on her. The origin of the story lies in certain letters that Beauvoir had received from women, in which the truth managed to burst through 'des phrases destinées à la dissimuler' (TCF, 176). Murielle's endeavours to prove to herself that she is in the right and the whole of the rest of the world in the wrong—'tout est mesquin en ce monde la nature comme les hommes' (101)—only succeed in convincing the reader that she is shot through with self-deception and has in fact brought all of the reversals and disasters in her life upon herself.

The pivotal incident in her past was the suicide of her daughter Sylvie some five years earlier, since which Tristan and all of her family have obviously had as little contact with her as possible. Despite Murielle's repeated claim that she was a perfect mother, we are given to understand that she was responsible for Sylvie's death. Tackling the question of upbringing from a different angle here and allowing the truth to emerge stage by stage from details that Murielle lets out, Beauvoir contrives to show us that Murielle read her daughter's private diary; was jealous of her good relations with both Tristan and her father, Albert (actually calling in the police on one occasion, when Sylvie fled to him); embarrassed her at school; and tried to foist a friend of her own choosing upon her. When Sylvie eventually killed herself, Murielle tore up the suicide note to Albert and bemoaned her *own* ill luck: 'Sylvie est morte sans m'avoir comprise je ne m'en guérirai pas' (104). She has evidently learned no lesson from what has happened, as her attitude towards her son Francis, who is now living with his father Tristan, reveals. She claims to want them both back because 'un enfant a besoin de sa mère' (88), but her real reason is her own need for the company and security that Tristan would bring. There is no sign that she has much fondness for Francis and we have a clear indication that she is prepared to use him for her own ends (117).

In a number of other respects, too, Murielle's claims about herself and her life are transparently false. For example, she is much more concerned about the advantages that money brings than she pretends to be, and her statement that she has lost all interest in sex and no longer thinks about it, 'pas même en rêve' (105), is belied by her prurience throughout the monologue. Assertions that she is 'trop sentimentale', that 'si on avait su m'aimer j'aurais été la tendresse même' (109), or that 'je ne suis pas de ceux qui croient que tout leur est dû' (110) soon have the remarkable effect of reminding us that the very opposite is the truth. We do, after all, actually witness her conduct towards others when she rings Tristan and rapidly destroys any chance she might have had of redeeming herself during the appointment they have made for the following day. And Beauvoir even takes Murielle's self-delusion to its limits by having her see honesty and integrity as her principal virtues: 'Lucide trop lucide. Ils n'aiment pas qu'on voie clair en eux; moi je suis vraie je ne joue pas le jeu j'arrache les masques' (97). Indeed, Murielle is such an extreme case in many ways that one may talk of mental illness: she had some kind of breakdown after Sylvie's death (113) and Beauvoir sees her as 'poussant jusqu'à la paraphrénie sa distorsion de la réalité' (TCF, 176). In short, in spite of the fact that some of her general attacks on modern society cannot fail to strike home, Murielle's ranting and raving is so self-defeating and self-destructive on the personal level that our reaction to her is bound to be partly one of pity.

The interest of 'Monologue' consists, precisely, in its portrayal of the workings of a sick mind (Beauvoir says that she can see no outcome for Murielle other than madness or suicide; TCF, 177), and some of the odder technical features of the text spring directly from this orientation. Thus the erratic punctuation (like the eighty successive instances of the word 'marre' on page 96) conveys the idea that words are whirling around in Murielle's head and that language itself is being strained to its limits by the intensity of her feelings. And the way in which names come into her monologue without any explanation of who the people concerned are ('Madame Nanard' turns out to be her brother, whom she considers to be a homosexual) helps to create a powerful impression of Murielle's mind as a closed system of references partially cut off from reality. We have to struggle to understand the rather complex web of her relationships, to the extent that the text has something of the fascination of a puzzle. The extent to which Beauvoir has Murielle depend on slang of both the vilest and the least offensive kinds may sometimes make us too conscious of her language as such to sympathise fully with her psychological problems, but mostly we are ready to accept her linguistic excesses as part of the whole pathological pattern. 'Monologue' is a *tour de force*, and one that could be successfully executed only in a story of these dimensions. Having obvious links in its themes and situations with the other two stories in the collection, it achieves rather different goals and provides just the kind of contrasts that are necessary on the artistic level.

Beauvoir records that the final and most substantial story in the collection, 'La Femme rompue', had similar origins to 'Monologue', that is, puzzled letters from women deserted by their husbands:

'D'une autre manière que Laurence elles se débattaient dans l'ignorance et l'idée m'est venue de donner à voir leur nuit' (TCF, 175). The central figure, Monique Lacombe, has been married to Maurice for twenty-two years and the story takes the form of a diary that she keeps for a period of just over six months. It begins not too long after the younger of her two daughters has left home and shortly before Maurice reveals that he is having an affair with Noëllie Guérard, a well-known lawyer who, at thirty-eight, is some six years younger than Monique. The diary traces the stages by which the situation gradually becomes worse for Monique, with Maurice first spending whole nights, then weekends, then holidays with Noëllie, and eventually leaving his wife altogether. It graphically registers Monique's early attempt to be 'compréhensive, conciliante' (140); the manner in which she slips 'de concession en concession'; the traps that prevent her from finding a satisfactory way out of the dilemma and her vain endeavours to gain help from family, friends, even a psychiatrist; and the disastrous disintegration of her image of herself as well as her view of the past: 'Ma vie derrière moi s'est tout entière effondrée, comme dans ces tremblements de terre où le sol se dévore lui-même' (193). There is just enough in the last few pages of the story for us to understand Beauvoir's tentative prediction: 'peut-être . . . aura-t-elle un jour le courage d'affronter la réalité et renouera-t-elle des rapports avec ses semblables' (TCF, 177). But the ending is bleak in the extreme: 'La porte de l'avenir va s'ouvrir . . . J'ai peur. Et je ne peux appeler personne au secours. J'ai peur' (252). Indeed, the author seems perfectly justified in another of her judgements; 'je n'ai jamais rien écrit de plus sombre que cette histoire: toute la seconde partie n'est qu'un cri d'angoisse et l'effritement final de l'héroïne est plus lugubre qu'une mort' (TCF, 178).

When 'La Femme rompue' appeared in instalments in *Elle*, women readers identified with Monique and Beauvoir was 'submergée de lettres émanant de femmes rompues, demi rompues, ou en instance de rupture' (TCF, 177). And yet many of them, as she suggests, must have missed one whole dimension of the story, just as certain critics did, for like Madame and Murielle before her Monique is portrayed as deceiving herself about her life:

Il ne s'agissait pas pour moi de raconter en clair cette banale histoire mais de montrer, à travers son journal intime, comment la victime essayait d'en fuir la vérité. La difficulté était encore plus grande que

> dans *Les Belles Images* car Laurence cherche timidement la lumière
> tandis que tout l'effort de Monique tend à l'oblitérer, par des
> mensonges à soi, des oublis, des erreurs; de page en page le journal
> se conteste: mais à travers de nouvelles fabulations, de nouvelles
> omissions. (TCF, 175)

Beauvoir wanted us to read the story like a detective novel, noticing
clues, checking each detail against the rest of the diary, tracking down
Monique 'comme on dépiste un coupable' (TCF, 176). Because this
story is longer than the previous two put together, such detective work
can be carried out on an extensive scale once we begin trying to
reconstruct Monique's married life.

The ambiguity over whether Maurice willingly gave up his hospital
training to marry Monique or whether she more or less forced him into
marriage is never entirely resolved, but certainly Monique's later
account of the pregnancy that precipitated the event—'j'ai trop fait
confiance au calendrier, mais ce n'est pas de ma faute s'il m'a trahie'
(212)—is rather inconsistent with her earlier claim that they were 'tous
deux responsables' (159). It is obvious, too, that Monique abandoned
her own career as much because the realities of medicine horrified her
(195) as in a spirit of self-sacrifice to her family. Furthermore, we
eventually realise that what she sees as exclusion from Maurice's current
research work at the 'polyclinique', where his patients do not need her,
was precisely what she feared in bitterly resisting his desire for a change
from his job with Simca ten years earlier: 'je le conseillais. Ce lien entre
nous, si important pour moi, il a choisi de le briser' (192). This
involvement clearly acted as a substitute for a career for Monique and the
suggestion is that she has been punishing Maurice for taking it away
from her (178). In fact, this may have been the crucial moment in their
marriage, for we come to see that, largely because of her refusal to
acknowledge that time passes and people change, she has been living
under an illusion about her relationship with Maurice for the last ten
years, systematically suppressing little pieces of evidence and deceiving
herself into thinking that all was well between them (224).

Monique's powers of self-deception are evident in relation to the
present as well as to the past. Her initial reactions to Maurice's affair are
entirely inconsistent: first Noëllie is probably frigid (139), then 'elle sait
certainement comment se conduire au lit' (141); at first the implication
is that her own sex life with Maurice is perfectly satisfactory, then she

talks of his 'tiédeur' (141); and in spite of all the evidence she goes on believing that he still loves her. There is also manifest self-delusion in her resolutions for solving the problem: she gives ground after deciding to adopt a hard line with Maurice, and has outbursts after she decides to be conciliatory. And although she frequently finds reasons for rejecting interpretations and advice that she has sought, she continues to believe that someone like her daughter Lucienne holds the key, only to disregard her views too in the end. Even if some of these phenomena reflect her confusion and anguish more than anything else, there can be no doubt that her diary is a source of constant self-deception. Within the first few pages she gives incompatible accounts of both her state of mind when she left Maurice at Nice airport and her reasons for starting to keep a diary. Towards the end, after a series of hints at the sort of omissions and lies that it involves, she admits that it is one long record of self-delusion: 'Il n'y a pas une ligne de ce journal qui n'appelle une correction ou un démenti . . Je me mentais. Comme je me suis menti' (222-23).

Yet at this point certain qualifications to the picture of Monique that we have taken from Beauvoir's own comments force themselves upon our attention. It is not true, of course, that all of Monique's energy goes into fleeing from the truth. For one thing, the harsh comments about the dishonesty of her diary come, like many of the other insights described, *from Monique herself:* the story would be a very different one indeed if she did not occasionally catch a glimpse of the light. There are moments, if not whole areas of sound thinking recorded in the diary and Monique needs to be seen as a complex mixture of self-deception and lucidity. It is difficult to argue, for example, that there has been any serious self-deception in her relations with her daughters. She has never hidden from herself the fact that her devotion to them was 'une forme d'égoïsme' (143) and in any case Maurice would have to bear his share of reponsibility for any deficiencies in their upbringing. Indeed, we do well to remind ourselves at this point that Maurice is very far from blameless in the whole matter of the breakdown of their marriage. He has, after all, been deceiving Monique for a number of years and her self-deception does nothing to alter the fact or to justify his conduct. Many readers and critics may well have over-simplified 'La Femme rompue' and failed to understand Monique's part in her own tragedy: 'La femme rompue est la victime stupéfaite de la vie qu'elle s'est choisie: une dépendance conjugale qui la laisse dépouillée de tout et de son être même quand l'amour lui est refusé'.[7] But once this is recognised, it is still no reason for exonerating her husband completely. Nor does the point that 'elle tisse elle-même les ténèbres dans lesquelles elle sombre au point de perdre sa propre image' (TCF, 175) in any way diminish the reality or intensity of her suffering. By her own admission, Beauvoir had two aims in writing the story and not just one: to have us 'dépister' Monique and women like her, but also to 'donner à voir leur nuit'.

In fact, there is a general point here that has important application to all of the stories in *La Femme rompue* as well as to *Les Belles Images*. Each of the four tales is written wholly from the point of view of a single woman character. All four women, moreover, are married, with children, and there is little difference between them as far as social class is concerned (their husbands, for instance, are all professional men and they are all sufficiently rich to employ a maid). Hence the links between the situations and topics of the different stories are obvious enough, and the context within which the stories complement one another is a very restricted one (Laurence is about thirty, Murielle and Monique in their forties, Madame in her early sixties; two of the heroines have quite stable marriages, while one has experienced both divorce and separation and the fourth is in the process of being deserted by her husband; one works, two do not, the fourth is retired; and so on). Furthermore, despite some variety in the narrative techniques employed, in each case we have to read between the lines much more carefully than in Beauvoir's earlier fiction. Now, although it is not exactly self-deception that we have to uncover in Laurence's case, as it is in the others, even she is portrayed as being partly responsible for her own difficulties, in that she is 'complice de son entourage'. And yet all four characters suffer to a greater or lesser extent from situations and pressures that have grown up over the years in a male-dominated society.

In other words, although these stories may not carry an overtly feminist message, they do exemplify in a subtle way a thesis at the heart of *Le Deuxième Sexe*, namely that expressed in the Sartrean epigraph to the second volume: 'A moitié victimes, à moitié complices, comme tout le monde'. To make the reader discover this by reading between the lines of stories narrated from a woman's viewpoint was an excellent device on Beauvoir's part, and one admirably in line with her general literary aim of having us participate actively as we engage with the text. Her range in these two books is, admittedly, extremely narrow, so that it might legitimately be asked whether a broader perspective on some of the issues would not have produced a more balanced treatment. After all, we only ever see men and the role they play in events through the eyes of women here, and with so much emphasis falling on the (potentially disastrous) influence of the family situation as a whole upon children, this is perhaps not entirely satisfactory. Nevertheless, *La Femme rompue* provides three powerful images of women for whom we must feel pity, but who can by no means be absolved from responsibility for their situation.[8]*Les Belles Images* provides another such image, but does much else besides.

Notes

[1] Interview with Jacqueline Piatier, *Le Monde*, 1966. This interview, together with other useful material is included in the critical edition of *Les Belles Images* by Blandine Stefanson (Heinemann Educational Books, 1980).

[2] Interview with Piatier.

[3] Ibid.

[4] See P.-H. Simon: '*Les Belles Images* de Simone de Beauvoir', *Le Monde*, 1967 (reprinted in Stefanson pp. 65-69).

[5] Beauvoir's *prière d'insérer*. See *Écrits*, pp. 231-32.

[6] See my 'Simone de Beauvoir's *La Femme rompue:* studies in self-deception', *Essays in French Literature*, 1976.

[7] *Prière d'insérer*, *Écrits*, p.232.

[8] There is detailed analysis of the three stories from a feminist standpoint in Anne Ophir: *Regards féminins*, pp. 13-87.

CONCLUSION

Examination of Simone de Beauvoir's books, however thorough, is bound to leave many aspects of her life, personality, and involvement in the world largely unexplored. The precise nature of her political commitment over the years, the details of her militant feminism since about 1970, her more or less continuous editorial work on *Les Temps modernes* since 1945,[1] the kind of place that she merits in the history of French existentialism—these are some of the significant matters upon which scrutiny of her major published works in itself casts only pale or indirect light. Yet whatever the range of perspectives within which Beauvoir may legitimately be seen, it is clearly appropriate that her repeated claim to be first and foremost a writer—'quelqu'un dont toute l'existence est commandée par l'écriture' (FCh II, 495; cf. TCF, 162)—should be taken seriously and her achievements assessed. In spite of the strong hint in the very first sentence of her latest work (CA, 13), she may yet write other major books, but it is certain, as she herself has been saying for some time, that the bulk of her work is done, the corpus of her writings more or less complete.

Naturally, Beauvoir's attitude towards literature has developed and changed since, as a young girl, she was first captivated by stories and began trying to 'inverser cette magie' by writing them herself. As some of her comments in the recent film about her show, however, there has in fact been great continuity in her views throughout her writing career. She no longer regards herself as having a 'mission', no longer takes literature to be 'sacred', and she now recognises that it is by no means the only way of communicating with others. But her fundamental aim has always been to *speak* to people through her books: 'ce que je voulais essentiellement, c'était parler, comme je le dis dans *Mémoires d'une jeune fille rangée*, parler aux gens, pour ainsi dire, de bouche à oreille'.[2] Difficult as it is to give substance to this formula, it certainly means that she has written only when she had something to say, and never just for the sake of writing; and that she has always written with living readers rather than posterity in mind. It would be wrong to see Beauvoir's innumerable references to preserving or 'saving' features of her life by writing about them as signs of overriding egocentricity. Her central concern has been to communicate and share those aspects of her own life that may be of interest and value to others: 'J'ai cherché vraiment à faire sortir le plus de choses possibles de ma propre expérience, d'en exprimer tout ce qui en était exprimable pour que cela puisse servir à autrui'.[3] There is no doubt that Beauvoir has sought—and found—the justification of her own existence in this process, but she is hardly to be blamed for that and, as she herself has frequently noted, a certain objective vindication of her attempt to convey her own experience is to be found in the hundreds of letters that she receives from her readers, expressing their gratitude. (She clearly regards it as an integral part of her role as a writer to read, digest and answer correspondence from her readers.) Her view that literature provides some compensation for the fact that individuals' different situations in the world radically separate them one from another may be abstract and unfashionable, but it seems, to some extent, to have been borne out in practice in her own career. It also goes some way towards accounting for the frequency with which she treats themes like anguish, solitude and death: 'Nous avons besoin de savoir et d'éprouver que ces expériences sont aussi celles de tous les autres hommes'.[4]

These points constitute a general guide to what we may reasonably expect and not expect from Beauvoir's books, and they help to locate her kind of literature in relation to others. She is strongly opposed to what she sees as the 'ivory tower' attitude adopted, for instance, by the proponents of the New Novel from the nineteen-fifties onwards ('on tourne le dos aux hommes'; FCh II, 459-60). But, equally, she is no literary realist: 'je n'ai pas, non plus, cherché à rendre compte d'une manière réaliste, mais qui est peut-être très riche, du monde tel qu'il est, à la façon d'un Balzac ou d'un Zola'.[5] Her own work is placed somewhere between these two poles, in a realm where there is no question of simply transcribing reality, but where in disclosing the world from her own particular situation, the author attempts to attain the universal. Beauvoir's is a 'committed' literature, certainly, in that she writes—even in *Tous les hommes sont mortels*—about her own times, and from a specific point of view. Yet even if she has not invariably succeeded in doing so, she has always been anxious to avoid didacticism, since for her the role of a work of literature is not to give embodiment to a definite thesis, but to 'manifester des vérités ambiguës, séparées, contradictoires, qu'aucun moment ne totalise ni hors de moi, ni en moi' (FCh, 360).

The deep seriousness of Beauvoir's attitude to writing, then, is one of her distinctive characteristics. Her own major concerns are, in the broadest sense of the term, moral ones and there is very little room indeed, within her perspective, for the idea that literature is an entertainment or has an escapist side. If she is happy to acknowledge that fiction casts a kind of spell over us, this is because the ultimate purpose is to make us see the world from someone else's standpoint. All of this does, however, raise the question of the different literary forms that she has used over the years. From the very first she believed that her own contribution to literature would lie in the sphere of the novel, and from her own account it seems that, in the early forties, she was rather drawn into writing essays, almost against her better judgement. In any case, the underlying implication of 'Littérature et métaphysique' is still that the novel is somehow a richer form and can achieve things that the essay cannot: 'Le lecteur s'interroge, il doute, il prend parti et cette élaboration hésitante de sa pensée lui est un enrichissement qu'aucun enseignement doctrinal ne pourrait remplacer' (ESN, 92). Nevertheless, by the end of the forties Beauvoir's achievements in the two domains could be said to be roughly in equilibrium. Indeed, leaving aside her only play and *L'Amérique au jour le jour*, which is a sort of occasional piece, this is the broadly balanced pattern that her works presented up to the moment when she published the first volume of her memoirs in 1958. Although she has written two further works of fiction and another long essay, it is autobiographical writings that have dominated her work since that time, and the four volumes of memoirs that she has produced, together with *Une Mort très douce* and *La Cérémonie des adieux*, now more than match, quantitatively, her output in either the essay or the novel genre. In relation to the different literary forms, therefore, Beauvoir's range as a writer, though not extensive, is far from negligible. But of course her versatility and craftsmanship within the three genres is a separate matter.

She has argued that the essay-form is just as indispensable to her as the novel, for it is used to express a different order of experience: 'Mes essais reflètent mes options pratiques et mes certitudes intellectuelles; mes romans, l'étonnement où me jette, en gros et dans ses détails, notre condition humaine' (FCh II, 62). Now, as far as Beauvoir's 'options pratiques' are concerned, *La Longue Marche*, designed to correct misapprehensions about Communist China but soon outdated by events in certain respects, has to be considered the least effective of her longer essays. And since there are obvious deficiencies in the two political essays in *Privilèges*, as well as in 'Idéalisme moral et réalisme politique', this all suggests a general weakness in her political writings as such—one doubtless not entirely unconnected with her aversion to day-to-day politics. The same antipathy, in fact, may even come into play when she is writing about social rather than political issues proper. In both *Le Deuxième Sexe* and *La Vieillesse* she takes up and attacks what she sees as far-reaching injustices in society and although there are very strong reasons for supposing that her views on feminism have been far more influential than those on old age, it is of course extremely difficult to measure the practical impact that any book makes. But, in any case, the fact is that neither of Beauvoir's major essays is a particularly militant book in the sense of offering detailed suggestions about courses of action to be taken in order to remedy the social ill concerned. Their main value—and it is just as considerable as any narrowly 'practical' impact that they may have made—has to be seen in relation to the previous stage, when people need to be made aware of a specific problem and have its ramifications traced and described at length. On this level, *Le Deuxième Sexe* and *La Vieillesse*, for all their faults, are extraordinarily informative *and* challenging essays that fully vindicate in themselves Beauvoir's use of this genre.

When her topic is more abstract, however, she never seems entirely at ease with her material. Her early moral essays contain extremely valuable insights into the moral dimension of human existence and they are significant works in the context of the development of French existentialism. Yet they are somewhat hybrid essays, in that Beauvoir fails to sustain a high level of philosophical argument in each case. The best sections are those where she is performing a similar task to that taken up in her novels; that is, looking at situations and dilemmas from the point of view of the moral agent concerned and analysing or exploring the difficulties involved. Her limitations as a philosopher have always been clear to her (FA, 254-55) and they are quite apparent to any reader surveying her essays as a whole. Since the 'certitudes intellectuelles' that they reflect are, for Beauvoir, enshrined in Sartre's major philosophical works, *L'Être et le Néant* and *La Critique de la raison dialectique*, it is perfectly understandable that she should never have attempted to cover the same ground herself in published works. However, not only does this mean that she immediately becomes heir to all of the philosophical difficulties inherent in Sartre's positions, it also means that when such problems arise in her own essays they are doubly puzzling, in so far as it is not always clear why they need to do so. We saw, for instance, that on one major point of disagreement with Sartre, she stifled her own view for a time, but that this resulted in stresses and tensions in her work in relation to the concept of 'situation' (Ch. 5). Even when, from the mid-fifties onwards, Beauvoir, like Sartre, adopts a broadly Marxist perspective on the world (which, notoriously, is not itself easy to reconcile with their early existentialism), there are still many areas in which her assumption that Sartre has definitively settled certain questions leaves the foundations of her own essays looking shaky. In particular, the socio-political theory that lies behind her constant references to the privileged minority in her later essays is unclear. And does not the fact that she continues to write almost exclusively about—and, in a sense, *for*—the privileged few suggest that she has less detailed knowledge of, and acquaintance with, the *un*privileged than she needs to have? There is, in fact, a persistent philosophical vagueness underlying Beauvoir's later works in all three genres. Individuals are still said to be free in a crucial sense, but the precise importance of notions like 'situation' and 'oppression' (like the distinction between being 'conditioned' and 'determined') is never seriously examined. Such theoretical weaknesses, which can clearly be traced back to her earliest philosophical positions, may go some way towards explaining why she tended to adopt a more directly practical and militant stance on certain issues during the seventies, and why she has published only one major essay during the last twenty-five years.

The fact that over a slightly longer period she has written only two much shorter works of fiction is rather a sign of the fact that she sees autobiography as coming much closer to being a substitute for the novel than the essay does ('roman et autobiographie m'absorbent beaucoup plus qu'un essai; ils me donnent aussi plus de joies'; FCh, 374). Both fiction and autobiography deal with 'le sens vécu de l'être-dans-le-monde' rather than conceptual knowledge, but while the novel is concerned with meanings (albeit ambiguities or contradictions), the autobiographical work records the contingency and facticity of our lives. On the whole, Beauvoir's memoirs bear out this view, though *Mémoires d'une jeune fille rangée* has a much greater unity and a firmer shape than the later volumes, so that its form is much more like that of a novel. In any case, the volumes of memoirs do form a coherent whole and we have already had occasion to discuss them as such (Ch. 2). Largely because, as she says, 'le "je" que j'utilise est un "je" qui a une portée générale . . . j'essaie de parler de quelque chose qui déborde infiniment ma singularité',[6] they constitute a very considerable achievement on Beauvoir's part, and even if only the first reaches any artistic heights, they perhaps still make her contribution to the autobiographical form weightier and more significant than her contribution to any other. Of her other autobiographical works, however, if *La Cérémonie des adieux* in particular reminds us that there is truth in her point about the link between contingency or facticity and this genre, *Une Mort très douce* (like *Mémoires d'une jeune fille rangée*) strongly suggests that there is much more to the matter than this. The fact is that Beauvoir has written about her own life and detachable sections of it in a wide variety of ways and with different effects, which are hard to classify. For the most part, this has been an extremely successful side of her work and what most of the books may lack in literary qualities of the purest kind, they more than make up for in a multitude of other virtues.

Perhaps Beauvoir's increasingly frequent claims that her autobiographical works are accurate rather than artistically elegant suggests that she still believes that, of the three genres that she uses, only the novel is literature in the fullest sense. Yet for one who rates fiction so highly, she has achieved surprisingly little range in her stories. She says she has never been interested in being 'une virtuose de l'écriture',[7] and it is certainly true that her general narrative principle of confining herself at any given moment to the subjectivity of one of her characters has almost always resulted in a style based more upon 'le rythme du langage parlé' than anything else (FA, 393-94). Even so, it is somewhat disappointing that she should have failed to make more of the possibility of *conflicting* perspectives in a novel. And although it is no surprise that fifteen of her twenty 'narrators' should be women, the fact that so many of them lose their faith in God during adolescence, need a man to make up for this loss, but at some subsequent stage are obliged to face the world alone in some significant sense argues a certain lack of inventiveness on Beauvoir's part. After what she saw as an early failure to identify sufficiently with her characters, she seems to

have identified with them too much. When she deliberately distanced
herself once more, she produced her most homogeneous and carefully-
wrought work of fiction, *Les Belles Images*. Yet immediately afterwards she fell back on her very earliest techniques, for although
'Monologue' is a technical feat of great skill, in all three stories of *La
Femme rompue* a woman's own thoughts and words are used to reveal
that she is a victim of self-deception in her outlook on the world—
precisely the basis upon which 'Marcelle', and to some extent the other
stories of *Quand prime le spirituel*, was constructed. Nevertheless,
Beauvoir's fiction undoubtedly does add to, modify and qualify the
dogmatism of some of her other writings in exactly the way that she
suggests it should. Our understanding of her early moral essays not
only enhances, but is also enhanced by, a reading of *Le Sang des autres*
and *Tous les hommes sont mortels*. And her portrayal of motherhood,
upbringing and even the ambiguous relationship in which so many of
us stand to the society we live in is incalculably more compassionate
and subtle in, say, *Les Mandarins* and *Les Belles Images* than her
pronouncements in her later essays alone would imply. In fact, limited
and conventional as Beauvoir's fiction is in some respects, its power to
penetrate the mysteries of human relationships *(L'Invitée)*, the direct
and indirect ways in which society and history bear down upon
individuals, even when they may be doing their very best to lead their
own lives properly, and the specific dilemmas of modern women is
highly impressive. And if *Les Belles Images* and 'Monologue' show
that, in relatively short works of fiction, she is capable of the highest
achievements on the artistic level, in *Les Mandarins* she has written a
monumental novel of the greatest political and historical significance.
Whatever the flaws in her books, we can only be grateful for stories
that not only entertain us, but project us so firmly into the mentalities
of imaginary figures that our awareness of people and the real world is
permanently enriched, over however narrow a range.

There has been a tendency, perhaps because of her relationship with
Sartre, to expect too much of Beauvoir's works: detailed moral rules
from her early moral essays; direct pleas for militancy from others;
inspiring, feminist heroines in her novels; and so on. This has con-
spired with other factors to delay the proper kind of evaluation of her
writings. Yet it has to be admitted that qualities in some of the books
themselves rather encourage a dogmatic or hasty response. She *is* often
so emphatic and so sweeping in her assertions in essays that they

immediately set up resistance on the reader's part. A number of her novels *do* have such obvious aesthetic defects that one may be disinclined even to consider whether they are accomplished works of art. And her autobiographical writings mostly leave us *such* strong impressions of contingency or facticity that we are easily drawn into reading them for the information of various kinds that they convey rather than for anything else. There are outstanding exceptions to these generalisations, and quite enough to make Beauvoir a writer of some stature, but a distinctive kind of fragility or vulnerability marks many of her works. Sometimes in the essays and autobiography this vulnerability seems to attach to the writer herself, in so far as it is associated with a certain naïvety: a particular line of argument is *so* implausible or a particular set of examples *so* lop-sided that we can scarcely believe that she means what she says; or within a single text we find admissions that directly cast doubt on the accuracy of other assertions. It may be partly this that has led so many readers to see Beauvoir as such an honest writer, but, in any case, behind the oversimplification there certainly lies an unusually strong awareness of the human being behind the words. Provided that we are willing to listen, to discard prejudices, and sometimes to overlook artistic imperfections, she *does* in the end speak to us 'de bouche à oreille' and make literature fulfil the function that she has always intended:

> Sauvegarder contre les technocraties et contre les bureaucraties ce qu'il y a d'humain dans l'homme, livrer le monde dans sa dimension humaine, c'est-à-dire en tant qu'il se dévoile à des individus à la fois liés entre eux et séparés, je crois que c'est la tâche de la littérature et ce qui la rend irremplaçable.[8]

Notes

[1] All of these topics are covered in, for example, Anne Whitmarsh: *Simone de Beauvoir and the Limits of Commitment.*

[2] *Simone de Beauvoir. Un film de Josée Dayan et Malka Ribowska* (Gallimard, 1979), p.76.

[3] Film, p.77.

[4] Y. Buin (ed.): *Que peut la littérature?*, p.91. Most of the available studies of Beauvoir concentrate on particular themes in her works,

and it has been remarked how many bear subtitles to this effect. No fewer than three treat the theme of death.

5   Film, p.77.

6   'Mon expérience d'écrivain', lecture delivered in Japan in October 1966; in *Écrits*, pp.450-51.

7   Film, p.77.

8   *Que peut la littérature?*, p.92.

APPENDIX English Translations of Indented French Quotations

Chapter 2

31   The year 1929—which was when I ended my studies; became economically independent; left home; was separated from my former friends; and met Sartre—clearly marked the beginning of a new period in my life.

50   The more I go on, the more the world enters into my life, almost causing it to break apart. To relate it I would need a dozen registers and a pedal enabling me to *sustain* the feelings— melancholy, joy, disgust—that have coloured whole periods of it, in spite of their intermittent nature. Each moment contains a reflection of my past, my body, the relationship in which I stand to others, what I have undertaken to do, society, the whole world. At once interlinked and independent, these real factors sometimes reinforce one another and harmonise, some- times fail to come together, clashing or neutralising one another. If the totality is not present all of the time in my descriptions, then what I am saying is inexact. But even if I overcome this difficulty, I stumble up against others. A life is a peculiar thing, translucent and entirely opaque at any given moment, constructed by myself yet imposed upon me. The world gives it its substance but also steals it from me, and though it is pulverised by events, broken up, scattered, scored, it retains its unity.

Chapter 3

60   It was at her bedside that I saw the grinning, mocking figure of Death that appears in the danse macabre; the figure that comes into tales told around the fireside, knocking at doors and carry- ing a scythe; Death which comes from afar as an inhuman stranger. Its face was that of mother showing her gums in a broad smile of unawareness.

60 In spite of appearances, even when I was holding mother's hand I was not with her; I was lying to her. Because she had always been hoodwinked, this supreme act of deception was odious to me. I was in collusion with the destiny that was assaulting her.

Chapter 4

74 Thus began what I might call the 'moral phase' of my literary life, a phase that lasted for a number of years. Since I could no longer take spontaneity as my guide, I was led to question myself about my principles and my goals, and after some hesitation I went so far as to write an essay on the matter.

75 We encounter the same antinomy in the realm of action as on the theoretical level: there is no possibility of bringing anything to a close, because transcendence is the process of forever going beyond what is; yet an unlimited project is an absurdity, since it leads to nothing.

76 Thus it is not *for* other people that we transcend ourselves: books are written and machines are invented which no one called for. Neither is it *for* ourselves, since our 'self' exists only through the very project that launches us into the world. The fact of transcendence precedes all aims, all justifications.

80 Any man who seeks to justify his life must will freedom itself both above all else and absolutely: the demands of freedom involve the universal pursuit of freedom itself, as well as the realisation of concrete aims.

83 In establishing its aims, freedom must put them in parenthesis, constantly measure them against the absolute aim that freedom itself constitutes, and challenge in the name of freedom the means that it adopts in order to achieve freedom.

86 On the whole I took a great deal of trouble over posing in the wrong way a question to which I gave an answer as hollow as Kant's maxims. . . It was absurd to claim to be able to formulate a morality outside any social context.

93 Like Sartre, I had not freed myself enough from the ideologies of my class; even when I was dismissing them, I still used their language. It has become odious to me, for, as I now know, to seek the reasons why we must not trample on someone's face is to accept that his face be trampled on.

Chapter 5

94 The world was a masculine world, my childhood had been nourished by myths forged by men and I had not reacted to them in at all the same way as I would have if I had been a boy.

95 She determines what she is and differentiates herself in relation to man: man does not do so in relation to her. She is the inessential facing the essential. He is the Subject, he is the Absolute: she is the Other.

96 Many men assert, almost in good faith, that women *are* the equals of men and therefore have no demands to make and *at the same time* that women will never be the equals of men and that their demands are futile.

97 It is not the body-object described by scientists that has concrete existence, but the body as lived by the subject . . .It is not nature that defines woman: it is she who defines herself by taking responsibility for nature in her emotional life.

100- All myths presuppose a Subject projecting its hopes and fears
101 towards a transcendent heaven. Since women do not assert themselves as Subjects, they have created no manly myths that reflect their projects; they have no religion or poetry that is exclusively theirs.

101- For each of them the ideal woman is she who embodies most
102 precisely the particular figure of the *Other* that enables him to discover himself. Montherlant, the solar spirit, looks for pure animality in her; Lawrence, the phallicist, expects her to epitomise the female sex in general; Claudel defines her as a kindred soul; Breton cherishes Mélusine, who has her roots in nature; he pins his hopes upon the child-woman; Stendhal wishes his mistress to be intelligent, cultured, free in her thinking and her behaviour: an equal.

102 There is not one of the images of woman that does not immediately give rise to the opposite image.
She represents in a corporeal and living form all the values and anti-values through which life takes on a meaning.
From good to evil she is the physical embodiment of all moral values and their opposites.

103 One is not born a woman: one becomes one. No biological, mental or economic density determines what aspect the human

female takes on within society; it is civilisation as a whole that fashions the product midway between male and eunuch that we call feminine.

109   Each of the sexes is at one and the same time its own victim and the victim of the other . . . each camp is its enemy's accomplice; women pursue their dream of resignation, men their dream of alienation.

109- Women, brought up and formed in exactly the same way as
110   men, would work in the same conditions and for the same wages; moral standards would permit sexual freedom but the sexual act would no longer be considered a 'service' that has to be paid for; women would be *obliged* to have their own way of earning a living; marriage would be based upon a free commitment that the couple could revoke as soon as they wished; maternity would be freely chosen, in that birth-control and abortion would be allowed and that, on the other hand, all mothers and their children would enjoy exactly the same rights, whether within marriage or not; maternity leave would be paid for by the collectivity, which would take charge of the children; this is not to say that children would be *taken away* from their parents, but that they would not be *left entirely* to their parents.

110   I have already said that, on the theoretical level, if I were writing *Le Deuxième Sexe* to-day I would suggest materialist and not idealist foundations for the opposition between Same and Other. I would base the rejection and oppression of the other not upon the antagonism between one consciousness and another, but upon the economic grounds of scarcity.

Chapter 6

124   For the first time I came into contact with the Far East; for the first time I learned the full meaning of the term 'underdeveloped country'; I learned what poverty meant on the scale of 600 million people; for the first time I watched the hard task of constructing socialism being performed.

Chapter 7

141   Perhaps only suffering would gratify her in the end. 'Something

higher than happiness', she murmured . . . For the second time she had the wondrous revelation of her destiny. 'I am a woman of genius', she decided.

149   I adhered to the rule that Sartre and I regarded as fundamental and which he explained a little later in an article on Mauriac and the French novel: in each chapter I coincided with one of my protagonists, forbidding myself to know or think more than he or she.

158   Whereas the philosopher and the essayist provide the reader with an intellectual reconstruction of their experience, it is this experience itself, as it takes place before any process of elucidation, that the novelist claims to reconstitute on an imaginary plane.

158-   'But it *is* concrete', said Françoise. 'The whole meaning of
159   my life is at stake.'

'I'm not denying that', said Pierre, looking at her with curiosity. 'But this ability that you have to live out an idea body and soul is still exceptional.'

'But for me an idea isn't theoretical', said Françoise. 'It's something you experience, or if it remains theoretical, then it doesn't count.'

Chapter 8

161   'I would like my next novel to illustrate our relations with others in their true complexity. To annihilate the other's consciousness is puerile. The plot must be much more bound up with social problems than in my first novel. It would have to culminate in an act that has a social dimension (but is hard to find).'

163   All of time's dimensions were brought together in this death watch: the hero was living it out in the present, while questioning himself through his past about a decision that would commit him in the future.

174   A blade of grass, nothing more than a blade of grass. All individuals considered themselves different from others and preferred themselves to others. And they were all mistaken; she had made the same mistake as the rest.

179   Perhaps there was a way out; she had the feeling of something

passing across her field of awareness, as surreptitiously as the blinking of an eyelid. It was not even a hope and it had already disappeared; she was too tired.

179   If they were infinite, our lives would dissolve into universal indifference. Death challenges our existence but it is what gives our existence its meaning; it brings about definitive separation, but it is also the key to all communication.

Chapter 9

181   The triumph of Good over Evil could no longer be taken for granted: it even seemed to be in serious jeopardy. Along with many others I had fallen from a collective heaven to the dusty earth: the ground was littered with shattered illusions.

185   I have been asserting that beneath my dried-up flesh there survives a young woman as demanding as ever, rejecting all concessions and despising the sad old skin of forty-year-olds; but she no longer exists, she will never be brought back to life, even by Lewis's kisses.

186-   He was much less moved than he would have thought. Going
187   down the stairs, he vaguely thought: 'It's the price that had to be paid.' The price for what? For sleeping with Josette? For wanting to save her? For trying to preserve a private life, whereas taking action requires the whole man? For stubbornly persisting in taking action while he could not devote himself to it wholeheartedly? He didn't know. And even if he had known, it wouldn't have changed anything.

188   'We thought that we had merely to keep up our momentum: whereas there was a radical division between the period of the Occupation and the period following the Liberation.'

190   My attitude towards literature was ambiguous: there was no longer any question of a mandate, of salvation; in the face of the H bomb and human hunger, words seemed to me to be futile; and yet I was working frantically on *Les Mandarins*. Anne was not a writer, but she needed Dubreuilh to go on writing; as for Henri, sometimes he wanted to stop writing, sometimes not. By combining their contradictions I was showing the issue from a variety of angles.

190   I was very familiar with explanations of the type that Mardrus

had used; I used them myself on occasion; I appreciated them for what they were worth. Yes, to liberate Paule it was necessary to destroy her love, even its past. But I couldn't help thinking of those germs that one can kill only by destroying the organism that they are ravaging.

193–
194   I described women as I saw them in general, as I still see them: at variance with themselves. Paule is clinging to the traditionally feminine values: they are not enough for her and she is torn apart, to the point of madness. Nadine can manage neither to accept her femininity nor to go beyond it. Anne is closer than the others to genuine freedom, yet she does not succeed in finding fulfilment in her particular activities. None of them, from a feminist point of view, can be considered as a 'positive heroine.' I accept that, but without self-reproach.

194–
195   'You know what that story proves, don't you?' said Dubreuilh, suddenly becoming animated. 'There is no such thing as private morality. It's another of those things that we believed in and which don't make sense . . . You can't draw a straight line in space that is curved', said Dubreuilh. 'Your life can't be right in a society that isn't right itself. It will always catch up with you, in one way or another'.

Chapter 10

201   I went back to another project: that of evoking the technocratic society that I keep at arm's length as much as I can, but which I live in nonetheless; I am besieged by it, through newspapers, magazines, advertisements and the radio. I did not intend to describe the specific prevailing experience of some of its members: I wanted to record what is now called its tone and terms of reference.

203   Everything is much better than before, everything will be better still in the future. Some countries had a bad start: black Africa in particular. The population growth in China and the whole of Asia is disturbing, but thanks to synthetic proteins, contraception, automation and nuclear energy one can foresee that by about 1990 a civilisation of abundance and leisure will be set up. The planet will then form just a single world.

205   No one in this environment that I am hostile towards could

speak on my behalf; yet to reveal it I needed to step back from it somewhat. I chose as a witness a young woman who is sufficiently in sympathy with her milieu not to judge it, but honest enough to be uneasy about her complicity.

205 She has always been an image. Dominique made sure of that, having been preoccupied in her own childhood with such different images from her life and being stubbornly determined —with all of her intelligence and her enormous energy—to fill the gap. (You don't know what it's like to have holes in your shoes and to feel through your sock that you have stepped on spittle. You don't know what it's like to be scrutinised by girl friends with nicely washed hair, who are nudging one another. No, you can't go out with that stain on your skirt. Go and change.) An impeccable little girl, a refined adolescent, a perfect young woman. You were so flawless, so fresh, so perfect . . . said Jean-Charles.

207 For whole days and weeks I was no longer an image, but flesh and blood, desire, pleasure. And I also rediscovered that more secret tenderness that I had known when sitting at my father's feet or holding his hand in mine . . . Once again with Lucien, eighteen months ago; that fire in my blood, that exquisite melting feeling in my bones.

208 I am not unaware of the real reasons for my crisis and I have overcome them: I have brought the conflict between my feelings for Jean-Charles and my feelings for my father out into the open; it no longer tears me apart. I have come to terms with myself.

209 According to her, what counts in one's childhood is the psychoanalytical situation that exists without the parents' knowledge, almost in spite of them. Education, as a conscious and deliberate process, is quite secondary.

210 Simply to rear a normal child is already an arduous task. Is it worth the pains one takes over it? What is it that makes life worthwhile? And what significance does the idea of normality have? The whole of the human condition is called into question.

217-
218 For me it was not a matter of telling this banal story in a straightforward way, but of showing, through her personal diary, how the victim tried to turn her back on the truth. The difficulty was even greater than in *Les Belles Images*, for

Laurence is timidly trying to see the light, whereas all of Monique's efforts are devoted to shutting it out, through lies that she tells herself, lapses of memory, and errors. From one page to the next the diary calls itself into question: but through new fabrications, new omissions.

Conclusion

229   Protecting what is human in men against technocracies and against bureaucracies, presenting the world in its human dimension, that is as it reveals itself to individuals who are both bound to one another and separate—that, I think, is the task of literature and what makes it irreplaceable.

SELECTED BIBLIOGRAPHY

1. *Beauvoir's Major Works* (See 'Texts, Abbreviations and References').

2. *Minor Works by Beauvoir referred to, including interviews, etc.*
   For a complete list of Beauvoir's writings up to 1977, see Claude
   Francis and Fernande Gontier: *Les Écrits de Simone de Beauvoir*,
   Gallimard, 1979 (*Écrits*).

   (i)   'Simone de Beauvoir, prix Goncourt, nous déclare "Je
          considère que les intellectuels de gauche doivent travailler avec
          les communistes". Interview recueillie par J.-F. Rolland',
          L'Humanité-Dimanche, 19 Dec. 1954. (*Écrits*, pp. 358-62).

   (ii)   *Brigitte Bardot and the Lolita Syndrome, Esquire*, Aug. 1959;
          Deutsch, Weidenfeld & Nicholson, 1960 (French translation
          in *Écrits*, pp. 363-76).

   (iii) 'Entretien avec Madeleine Chapsal' in Madeleine Chapsal (ed.):
          Les Écrivains en personne, Julliard, 1960, pp. 17-37 (*Écrits*,
          pp. 381-96).

   (iv)   *Djamila Boupacha*, témoignage, en collaboration avec Gisèle
          Halimi, Gallimard, 1962.

   (v)   *Que peut la littérature?*, ed. Y. Buin, Union Générale d'Éditions,
          10/18, 1965; Beauvoir's talk, pp. 73-92.

   (vi)   'Entrevue avec Simone de Beauvoir par Madeleine Gobeil', *Cité
          libre* XVI, no. 15, Aug.-Sept. 1964, pp. 30-31.

   (vii) 'Mon expérience d'écrivain', lecture delivered in Japan in
          1966, *Écrits*, pp. 439-57.

   (viii) 'Simone de Beauvoir présente *Les Belles Images*: "J'ai eu
          rarement l'impression de faire une œuvre aussi littéraire"',
          interview with Jacqueline Piatier, *Le Monde*, no. 6826 (23
          Dec. 1966), p. 17 (in B. Stefanson (ed.): *Les Belles Images*,
          Heinemann Educational Books, 1980, pp. 55-61).

   (ix)   'Simone de Beauvoir: *The Second Sex* 25 years later', interview
          with John Gerassi, *Society*, Jan.-Feb. 1976, pp. 79-85 (French
          translation in *Écrits*, pp. 547-65).

(x)   'Ce que je dirais maintenant si je devais récrire mes mémoires', interview with Alice Schwarzer, *Marie Claire*, Jan. 1978.

(xi) *Simone de Beauvoir. Un film de Josée Dayan et Malka Ribowska*, Gallimard, 1979.

(xii) 'Entretien avec Simone de Beauvoir et Jean-Paul Sartre', interview with Michel Sicard, *Obliques*, nos. 18-19, numéro spécial, 1979, pp. 325-29.

3. *Books wholly or partly devoted to Beauvoir*

D. Armogathe	*Le Deuxième Sexe. Simone de Beauvoir*, Hatier, 1977 ('Profil d'une œuvre').
C. Ascher	*Simone de Beauvoir. A Life of Freedom*, Harvester, 1981.
J.-R. Audet	*Simone de Beauvoir face à la mort*, L'Age d'homme, Lausanne, 1979.
H. E. Barnes	*The Literature of Possibility*, Univ. of Nebraska Press, 1959.
C. L. van der Berghe	*Dictionnaire des idées: Simone de Beauvoir*, Paris-The Hague, Mouton, 1967.
K. Bieber	*Simone de Beauvoir*, Twayne, 1979 ('Twayne's world authors').
M.-A. Burnier	*Les Existentialistes et la politique*, Gallimard, 1966 ('Idées').
C. Cayron	*La Nature chez Simone de Beauvoir*, Gallimard, 1973 ('Les essais').
R. D. Cottrell	*Simone de Beauvoir*, Ungar, 1975 ('Modern Literature monographs').
M. Descubes	*Connaître Simone de Beauvoir*, Resma, 1974.
B. T. Fitch	*Le Sentiment d'étrangeté chez Malraux, Sartre, Camus et Simone de Beauvoir*, Minard, 1964.
C. Francis & J. Niepce	*Simone de Beauvoir et le cours du monde*, Klincksieck, 1978.
L. Gagnebin	*Simone de Beauvoir ou le refus de l'indifférence*, Fischbacher, 1968.
G. Gennari	*Simone de Beauvoir*, Ed. Universitaires, 1958.
A. M. Henry	*Simone de Beauvoir ou l'échec d'une chrétienté*, Fayard, 1961.

G. Hourdin	*Simone de Beauvoir et la liberté*, Cerf, 1962.
A.-C. Jaccard	*Simone de Beauvoir*, Juris-Verlag, Zurich, 1968.
F. Jeanson	*Simone de Beauvoir ou l'entreprise de vivre*, Seuil, 1966.
S. Julienne-Caffié	*Simone de Beauvoir*, Gallimard, 1966 ('Bibliothèque Idéale').
A.-M. Lasocki	*Simone de Beauvoir ou l'entreprise d'écrire*, Nijhoff, The Hague, 1971.
J. Leighton	*Simone de Beauvoir on Women*, Associated University Presses, New Jersey, 1975.
S. Lilar	*Le Malentendu du Deuxième Sexe*, P.U.F., 1969.
A. Madsen	*Hearts and Minds*, Morrow, New York, 1977.
E. Marks	*Simone de Beauvoir: encounters with death*, Rutgers, 1973.
M. Merleau-Ponty	*Sens et Non-sens*, Nagel, 1948.
C. Moubachir	*Simone de Beauvoir ou le souci de différence*, Seghers, 1972.
H. Nahas	*La Femme dans la littérature existentielle*, P.U.F., 1957.
A. Ophir	*Regards féminins*, Denoël/Gontier, 1976.
R. D. Reck	*Literature and Responsibility*, Louisiana State Univ. Press, 1969.
C. Z. Romero	*Simone de Beauvoir*, Rowohlt, Hamburg, 1978.
E. Schmalenberg	*Das Todesverständnis bei Simone de Beauvoir*, De Gruyter, Berlin, 1972.
D. Wasmund	*Der 'Skandal' der Simone de Beauvoir*, Max Hüber, Munich, 1963.
A. Whitmarsh	*Simone de Beauvoir and the Limits of Commitment*, C.U.P., 1981.
J. J. Zéphir	*Le Néo-feminisme de Simone de Beauvoir*, Denoël/Gontier, 1982.

4. *Other Books and Articles referred to*

For an extensive bibliography of books and articles on Beauvoir up to 1972, see C. Cayron: *La Nature chez Simone de Beauvoir*.

R. Aron	'Mme de Beauvoir et la pensée de droite', *Le Figaro littéraire*, 21/1/56, p. 5.
M. Choisy	'Psychologie, sociologie et syntaxe des *Mandarins*' *Psyché* 9, no. 95 (Sept. 1954), pp. 521-33.
M. Contat & M. Rybalka	'Les Écrits de Sartre (1973-78)', *Obliques*, nos. 18-19, numéro spécial, 1979, pp. 335-44.
I. Epstein	'Bright light on China', *Mainstream* 11, no. 12 (Dec. 1958), pp. 36-41.
E. Fallaize	'Narrative structure in *Les Mandarins*' in *Literature and Society. Studies in nineteenth and twentieth century French literature*, ed. C. A. Burns, Univ. of Birmingham, 1980.
G. F. Hudson	'Mme de Beauvoir in China', *Encounter* XII, no. 2 (Feb. 1959), pp. 64-67.
R. Jolivet	'La "Morale de l'ambiguïté" de Simone de Beauvoir' *Revue thomiste* XLIX, nos. 1-2, 1949, pp. 278-88.
T. Keefe	'Simone de Beauvoir's *La Femme rompue*: Studies in self-deception', *Essays in French Literature*, no. 13 (Nov. 1976), pp. 77-97.
	'Psychiatry in the post-war fiction of Simone de Beauvoir', *Literature and Psychology* XXIX, no. 3, 1979, pp. 123-33.
	'Simone de Beauvoir and Sartre on *mauvaise foi*', *French Studies* XXXIV, no. 3, (July 1980), pp. 300-14.
J.-P. Sartre	'M. François Mauriac et la liberté', *La Nouvelle Revue Française*, no. 305, (Feb. 1939), pp. 212-32.
	L'Être et le Néant, Gallimard, 1943.
	Réflexions sur la question juive, Gallimard, 1946.

La Critique de la raison dialectique, Gallimard, 1946.

'Sartre talks of Beauvoir', interview by Madeleine Gobeil, *Vogue,* no. 146 (July 1965), pp. 72-73.

'"Autoportrait à soixante-dix ans", entretien avec Michel Contat', *Le Nouvel Observateur*, 23-29 June, 30 June-6 July, 7-13 July, 1975.

'"L'Espoir maintenant" par Jean-Paul Sartre', *Le Nouvel Observateur*, 10-16 Mar., 17-23 Mar., 24-30 Mar. 1980.

P.-H. Simon   *'Les Belles Images* de Simone de Beauvoir', *Le Monde*, 25 Jan, 1967.

B. Stefanson (ed.)   *Les Belles Images*, Heinemann Educational Books, 1980.

INDEX